Management for Professionals

The Springer series *Management for Professionals* comprises high-level business and management books for executives. The authors are experienced business professionals and renowned professors who combine scientific background, best practice, and entrepreneurial vision to provide powerful insights into how to achieve business excellence.

Boris Kaehler

Complementary Management

A Practice-driven Model of People Management and Leadership in Organizations

 Springer

Boris Kaehler
goodHR
Berlin, Germany

ISSN 2192-8096 ISSN 2192-810X (electronic)
Management for Professionals
ISBN 978-3-030-98165-5 ISBN 978-3-030-98163-1 (eBook)
https://doi.org/10.1007/978-3-030-98163-1

Translation from the German language edition: "Komplementäre Führung" by Boris Kaehler, © Springer Fachmedien Wiesbaden GmbH 2020. Published by Springer Fachmedien Wiesbaden GmbH. All Rights Reserved.

This Springer imprint is published by the registered company Springer Nature Switzerland AG
The registered company address is: Gewerbestrasse 11, 6330 Cham, Switzerland

Preface

This book is a contribution to the theory and conceptual practice of organizational people management and leadership. It is aimed at all those interested in theory, but especially at HR professionals and managers who shape management and leadership in their organizations and are looking for convincing theoretical foundations for their work. In other words, it is a book about how organizational people management and leadership can and should be structured.

The mechanisms and concepts presented here are tried and tested. They describe functional people management and leadership as I have come to know it during my many years of work as an HR manager and which I practice today as a university lecturer, HR strategy consultant, and management trainer. The model has already been applied in companies and has undergone substantial further development on the basis of the experience gained. Countless "shop talks" with managers and experts as well as a more than extensive study of the literature have gone into developing the model. As a result, the Complementary Management Model combines elements of a number of established theories of management and leadership, supplements them with essential practical mechanisms of action and integrates them into a new theoretical construct. Empirical studies are underway.

Complementary Management comprises three model elements—hence the name—each with complementary, i.e., mutually supplementary, components. Complementary Management is thus conceived as a service with the two complementary functions of discipline and support. They are concretized in 24 complementary tasks, understood as a canon of performance conditions of human work. These are performed by multiple complementary actors. The role of line managers and HR specialists is to compensate for any self-management deficits of employees. These three elements of the core model can be practically applied through four implementation elements—management routines, management instruments, management unit design, and management resources. Those who find all this overly complicated may compare it to the theoretical complexity of making coffee or driving a car: how many elements would it take to describe these activities? It is commonly expected that a useful theoretical or corporate leadership model can be dealt with in a few sentences, but it is undoubtedly also the reason why many established theoretical models are useless in practice.

Chapter 1 of this book ("Conceptualizing Models of Management and Leadership: Constructs, Differentiations and other Theoretical Considerations") is intended to reveal the theoretical roots of my model and to delineate points of view. Chapter 2 ("The Complementary Management Model") begins by describing the three elements of the core model: the complementary management functions, the complementary management tasks, and the complementary management actors. Then, it presents the implementation elements of Complementary Management: the management routines, the management tools, the management unit design, and the management resources. Furthermore, it describes the conversion of Complementary Management into corporate management models (= guidelines, principles). Chapter 3 ("The Role of Line Managers in Complementary Management") explains the implications of the theory for line managers and for manager development. Finally, Chapter 4 ("The Role of the Specialized HR Function") highlights the role of the HR function as an agent of Complementary Management. The book is preceded by a brief summary of the Complementary Management Model.

The text you are reading is an edited version of the third German edition of "Komplementäre Führung" (Kaehler 2020), which has so far been well received by German-speaking scholars and practitioners. I am very happy to be able to present it to an international audience for the first time and look forward to your feedback. In translating this book, the first challenge was to select an English title; many readers are used to differentiating between management and leadership and I wanted to appeal to those interested in either one of them. The chosen title hopefully does the trick and will draw your attention to Sect. 1.2 where I extensively analyze the matter and, in effect and for good reason, establish both terms as synonyms. However, since we all have a long-accustomed tendency to think of certain connotations when hearing only one of these terms, I often use both in combination to remind the reader as well as myself that they are used interchangeably. A second challenge has been the literature base because, since its first rudimentary publication in 2012, I have not only used English sources, but also a lot of German ones in developing the model. It would not have been fair to the German authors to exclude them from the English edition, so readers from other parts of the world will have to live with a fair amount of German sources in the extensive reference lists. To be honest, I even hope that this might add some value, because while German, Swiss and Austrian authors have certainly contributed a lot to the understanding of management and leadership, only few texts have been translated and seized upon internationally. In any case, they give the Complementary Management Model a distinct European flair that might make it especially thought-provoking for an overseas audience.

Once again, my heartfelt thanks go to my dear family for their support and patience, to my contacts at Springer Nature—Senior Editor Prashanth Mahagaonkar and Project Coordinators Martina Himberger, Ramya Prakash, and Dhivya Savariraj—for their supportive supervision and editing, to Lorri King for her excellent proofreading and wording suggestions, and to Oliver Maas of maasgestaltet for the skillful design of the graphics, as well as to many friends, (former) colleagues, consulting clients, seminar participants, and students with management experience for their valuable suggestions and inspiration.

In Oswald Neuberger's standard scholarly work published in German, he once described management and leadership research as something for masochists or incorrigible optimists—time and again its desolate state is lamented and time and again study resumes with fresh impetus. This book joins the ranks with those of the optimists. May it be of use to them and to you.

Berlin, Germany Boris Kaehler
January 2022

Complementary Management: A Short Overview

The Theoretical Model's Subject and Aspirations (Sect. 2.1)

Subject Matter, Purpose and Development Stage

The subject of the Complementary Management (or Complementary Leadership) Model is people management and leadership in organizations.[1] The term Complementary Management is derived from the three elements of the core model, each of which has complementary components. For instance, the two complementary management functions—the support function and the disciplinary function—make up the totality of the management service. The range of complementary management tasks together generates the totality of the human performance conditions, which consist of enabling and carrying out work in order to achieve organizational goals. And finally, the complementary management actors together make up the totality of the key participants whose joint action shapes the management process.

In its current form, the Complementary Management Model is the result of a theoretical conceptualization process that has developed over many years. It started out as a broad outline and was subsequently further developed, with publications to date reflecting the respective stage of development (see Kaehler 2012, 2013, 2014a, b, 2017, 2020). Like most forms of systematic theorizing, it is based on practical observations, literature studies, and conceptual ideas that are condensed into a consistent web of theoretical assumptions. The individual mechanisms have been tested in practice and reflect functional people management and leadership as it is practiced in many organizations. The overall model has been applied in various companies and substantially refined on the basis of the experience gained. Next, empirical studies should be carried out which accompany its implementation in organizations and examine its effectiveness.

---

[1] For theoretical reasons explained in Sect. 1.2, management and leadership are used synonymously here. Since this will inevitably collide with the common understanding of many readers, I sometimes use "management and leadership" to facilitate reading.

Objective and Benefit

Anyone seeking to understand and shape leadership and management in organizations needs a theoretical framework. The intention of the Complementary Management Model is to illustrate how people management and leadership is to be designed in order to best achieve their purpose of fulfilling the goals of the organization or organizational unit by generating work performance and meeting other requirements. The theory is descriptive in the sense that it describes mechanisms of people management and leadership that are actually used and which function in practice. At the same time, it is normative in the sense that it clearly recommends that—with certain adaptations—leadership and management in organizations should follow this pattern. By no means does the theoretical model need to depict and explain all of the conceivable aspects of leadership and management—only those that can be meaningfully generalized and standardized.

Even though the Complementary Management Model is also intended to be of scientific use and to serve as an orientation for managers, its main purpose is to provide a theoretical basis for corporate models (= principles, guidelines) of management and leadership. These are fundamental stipulations relating to leadership and management in a specific organization in the sense of a constitution of personnel work. They define why, by whom, and how a specific organization or organizational unit (including its personnel) is to be managed and led. Organizations designing such corporate models may use some or all elements of Complementary Management and should progress with the project in five phases (see Sect. 2.6).

Initial Conceptional Considerations (Chap. 1)

Underlying Concept of Management and Leadership

Organizational management, in the sense of *managing people*, is an influence on people in an organization and its units with the aim of achieving the unit's objectives by generating work performance and meeting other requirements. To lead a unit or its members is synonymous with "directing" or "leading" them. The deliverables of people management and leadership consist firstly of the short- and long-term work performance of employees, secondly of short- and long-term personnel costs, and thirdly of the fulfillment of other requirements made by the market, the legal situation, and the stakeholders.

Management and leadership influence can be exercised in two ways: through anticipatory norm-setting or through situational intervention. Both forms can be exercised in hard, externally directed ways or in gentle, non-directive ways. Since hard external influence usually triggers resistance, it is advisable to primarily exert influence in a gentle manner (e.g., in the form of systematic self-direction, instrumental behavioral reinforcement, nudging, collective social norms, or implicit communication).

Management and leadership in organizations, which are highly structured contexts, must be distinguished from political leadership, i.e., being a leader in poorly structured contexts, even though many sources narrow it down to just that. At the same time, people management/leadership, employee management/leadership, and human resource management/leadership are one and the same. Of course, certain aspects of management and leadership are usually assigned to the HR department and others to line managers/leaders. However, these are not separate spheres but rather a division of labor in dealing with a single mandate, namely leadership and management of personnel.

Balance of Regulations and Latitudes

Normative recommendations for leadership are only effective if they contain a meaningful balance of regulations and regulation-free spaces. If corporate people management and leadership is to work well across the whole company, structures and responsibilities must be defined. At the same time, degrees of individual and situational freedom are needed in the right places. Organizations have room for discretion here. Even though certain aspects of management and leadership—including functions, tasks, and actors—need to be regulated, others—e.g., situational and individual modes of application—most definitely should not be. Whether formal leadership rules are actually transformed into informal structures and everyday behavior depends on whether they are a) functional, and b) consistently communicated and called for.

Complexity of Theoretical Management Models

Whether or not Complementary Management is a theory or a theoretical model depends on one's notion of the term and comes down to quibbleism. In fact, most social and economic science theories are limited to simple causality relations between a few variables. The Complementary Management Model is composed of seven model elements, each with various partial elements as well as interrelations, and is therefore quite complex. Those who consider this to be too overblown may prefer to visualize the theoretical complexity of making coffee or driving a car: How many elements could these be broken down into? The expectation of dealing with a useful theoretical or practical leadership model in a few sentences and making it comprehensible at first glance is just as unrealistic as explaining how to drive a car in a few short steps. The lack of practical relevance for many scientific studies may be nothing more than an indicator of the incompleteness of the underlying theories.

People Management and Leadership as a Part of Corporate Management

Organizational people management (in the sense of *managing and leading employees*) is a part of organizational management (in the sense of *managing and leading an organization*). This is defined as a steering influence on market, production, and/or resource operations in an organization and its units that may address both people and non-people issues with the aim of achieving the unit's objectives. This theoretical differentiation between steering and execution only makes sense, of course, if the steering also exists as self-steering, which it indeed does. It can be subdivided into three areas: constitutive management is about the basic setup and positioning of the unit, strategic management is about steering the business within a certain timeframe, and operational management is about the ongoing implementation of the strategic guidelines. All three task fields are required at the overall organization level, but also at the level of each organizational unit. Against this backdrop, the prominent role and relevance of people management and leadership for success becomes clear: It is indeed a specific form of resource administration ("human resource management"), and as such is on par with, for example, the company's administration of financial or material resources. At the same time, however, it encompasses all operational management, since all activities in all areas of the business are carried out by people who are to be managed, i.e., led.

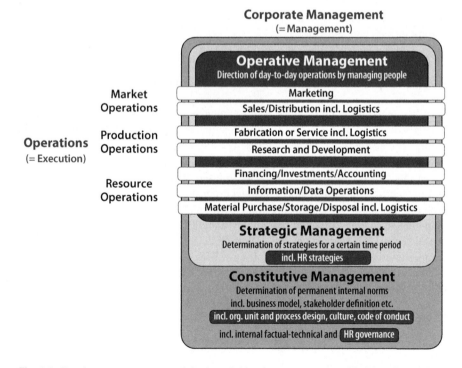

Fig. 1.3 People management parts of the three fields of management (modified from Kaehler and Grundei 2019, S. 33; © Boris Kaehler and Jens Grundei 2019. All rights reserved.)

The Three Elements of the Core Model (Chap. 2)

The core model of Complementary Leadership contains the fundamental aspects and mechanisms of people management and leadership in organizations. It describes them as a bundle of 24 tasks in which two functions take form and which are accomplished by five main actors (see Fig. 2.1).

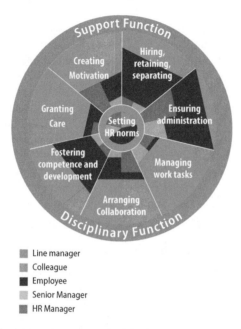

Line manager
Colleague
Employee
Senior Manager
HR Manager

Fig. 2.1 Core complementary management model with a sample distribution of actors per task category (own graphic based on 2014b, p. 460; modified from Kaehler 2017, p. 164; © Boris Kaehler 2017. All rights reserved)

Complementary Management Functions: Leadership as a Service

The first element of the core model consists of the complementary management functions. Organizational people management and leadership is understood to be an internal service. This service has two functions with respect to the personnel in an organizational unit. The support function is to help individual employees perform their jobs. The catchwords "to foster", "appreciation", and "employee orientation" illustrate this. The disciplinary function is to discipline and supervise the performance of individual employees. The catchwords here are "to demand", "added value", and "production orientation". In terms of management and leadership theory, the model element thereby ties in with the approach of "management as a service" and the classic duality of "employee orientation" vs. "production orientation". It has the status of a fundamental principle and is primarily of practical value: The idea of management as a dual service provides orientation for leaders and prevents destructive behavior.

Complementary Management Tasks: Leadership as a Bundle of Tasks

The complementary management tasks form the second model element. People management and leadership consists of 24 tasks that can be grouped into eight categories: "Setting HR norms", "Hiring, retaining, separating", "Ensuring administration", "Managing work tasks", "Arranging collaboration", "Fostering competence and development", "Granting care", and "Crafting motivation". This is based on the premise that precisely these influences are required to generate sustainable human performance. The model is thus in the theoretical tradition of normative task models of leadership and management. However, the management tasks are not understood as activities, but as abstract goals to be realized within the framework of concrete activities ("management routines"). All 24 tasks together complement each other to form the overall task of people management and leadership. In each task, both the disciplinary and the support function are specified.

Table 2.5 The tasks of people management and leadership in organizations according to the Complementary Management Model (modified from Kaehler 2014a, p. 82, 2017, p. 174; © Boris Kaehler 2019. All rights reserved)

Task category	Task	Task content in detail
Setting HR norms	To stipulate HR governance/HR strategies	• The operational leadership and management of the employee follows a coherent and functional internal HR governance consisting of the corporate management model as a metastructure and the HR infrastructure as a set of detailed regulations pertaining to structure, instruments, routines, and resources. • It also follows a coherent and functional HR strategy; all operational areas of HR management (= the other 21 leadership/ management tasks) are backed up in this strategy by strategic goals and demand scenarios for the coming business period.
	To optimize organizational design/ processes	• All work processes, as well as the job and hierarchical integration of each employee, are optimized in terms of time, cost, and quality. • These processes and structures are documented in a comprehensible manner.

(continued)

Table 2.5 (continued)

Task category	Task	Task content in detail
	To shape culture and diversity	• Clear cultural standards—shared values and appearances—applicable to the employee are set at the level of each organizational unit to which he or she belongs. • Clear diversity standards—welcomed differences and rules to protect them—applicable to the employee are set. • General rules of conduct (conduct, handling conflicts of interest, etc.) applicable to the employee are clearly defined.
Hiring, retaining, separating	To recruit and retain	• Applicant target groups with a high profile fit are defined. • All four sourcing areas (external and internal labor market, peripheral or pseudo workforces, and internal flexibility reserves) are considered with the defined target groups in mind. • Appropriate candidates are recruited. • Applicant relationships are systematically maintained. • Top performers are retained.
	To select and put onboard	• The requirement profiles of the positions are accurately recognized. • Personnel selection is carried out in an "end-to-end," process-oriented manner and by means of planned aptitude testing. • Jobs are filled exclusively with suitable and highly capable candidates. • New employees are systematically integrated.
	To dismiss and release	• Possible miscasts are dismissed. • Possible surplus personnel are reduced. • Organizational arrangements are made in the event of unwanted attrition.
Ensuring administration	To handle HR administration	• The administrative work related to the employee is taken care of.
	To collect and analyze data	• The data relevant to the employee and his or her work are collected and evaluated in order to identify optimization potentials.
	To look after employee representatives	• Functional relationships exist with works councils as well as trade unions and other bodies representing staff.
Managing work tasks	To define work tasks and instructions	• The work tasks and work specifications of the employee are sensibly defined and known to him or her. • Development-oriented work task management is practiced, from small-scale leading with instructions to leading with objectives and self-control.

(continued)

Table 2.5 (continued)

Task category	Task	Task content in detail
	To provide working time and resources	• The employee is provided with working time, material resources, and a financial budget in accordance with the tasks at hand.
	To evaluate performance and give feedback	• The work performance of employees is comprehensively appraised, and he or she knows how to properly judge it.
Arranging collaboration	To ensure coordinative communication	• Employee is continuously informed about the issues that are relevant to him or her. • The technical and functional need for coordination with the other group members is determined and the coordinative communication is conducted accordingly. • Wrong decisions and loss of creativity in groups are systematically prevented.
	To maintain relations and solve conflicts	• The employee assumes responsibility for relationships in all directions and maintains internal and external networks. • There is a constructive conflict culture. • Manifest conflicts are resolved quickly.
	To enhance group cohesiveness and identification	• There is an appropriately strong group cohesion. • The team members identify with the collective.
Fostering competence and development	To qualify	• Qualification gaps of the employee are identified and closed.
	To develop	• The employee's development potential is identified and systematically implemented. • Alternatives to a management career are also identified.
	To cultivate knowledge and innovation	• Existing knowledge of the employee is tapped and shared with others as needed. • Divergent and convergent thinking achieves continuous improvement and innovation.
Granting care	To protect health and life balance	• Health hazards are minimized, and disaster, pandemic, and threat scenarios are in place. • The health and work-life balance of the employee are protected, and permanent work overload is prevented. • Resilience and the ability to cope with balance crises are strengthened.
	To create flow conditions	• The employee has a sense of control with respect to his or her work and its conditions. • Work design enables and promotes the phenomenon of flow.

(continued)

Table 2.5 (continued)

Task category	Task	Task content in detail
	To explain and accompany change	• The employee understands the necessity and the context of upcoming changes. • Individual adaptation needs and requirements in connection with changes are taken into account.
Creating motivation	To consider needs and wants	• The permanent motive structures of the employee are recognized and taken into account. • The current motives of the employee are recognized and taken into account.
	To round off the incentive field	• The real existing field of inducements of the managed person is continuously analyzed. • Additional activity inducements, option inducements, social inducements, and monetary inducements are set in order to compensate for misaligned incentives and to generate additional motivation.
	To influence expectations/goals/impulse	• Performance, change, incentives, and justice expectations are consciously shaped. • The work activity is experienced as meaningful. • Goals and behavioral intentions correspond to work requirements. • The employee feels the necessary behavioral impulses to actually take action.

Complementary Management Actors: Leadership as Shared Leadership

The third element of the core model encompasses the complementary management actors. People management and leadership is the responsibility of several key players: the employee, his or her colleagues, the line manager, the senior manager, and the HR advisor. The primary management principle should be self-management, i.e., the employee should ideally take on all management tasks him or herself. Since not all employees always do this, the line manager must intervene in a compensatory manner when necessary. If he or she does not, it is up to the senior manager and the HR advisor acting as "HR co-manager" to intervene in a compensatory manner. These interventions can be corrective, joint, delegative, or substitutive. The complementary actors thus complement each other and collectively perform the 24 management tasks.

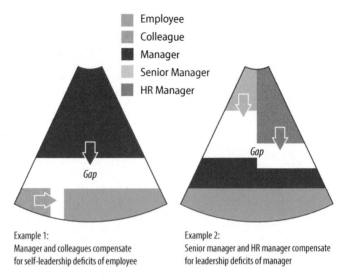

Fig. 2.2 Compensatory situational interaction of the management actors (own graphic based on Kaehler 2014b, p. 460; modified from Kaehler 2017, p. 183; © Boris Kaehler 2017. All rights reserved)

This compensatory mechanism ensures, on the one hand, that all management tasks are actually performed with regard to each individual employee even if the line manager is inactive, thus ensuring that work is performed. On the other hand, this multi-entity system is suitable for preventing an abuse of power by the line manager. In terms of management and leadership theory, the element of complementary management actors takes up the "Shared Leadership" approach, which is combined with the concept of self-management and with a vertical-hierarchical exercise of authority based on the principle of exception.

The core model of Complementary Management thus describes people management and leadership as a bundle of 24 tasks in which two service functions incorporate themselves and which are accomplished by five main actors. With these three core elements, it forms a counter-concept, so to speak, to the widespread idea of leadership and management as a personality-based or systemic relationship phenomenon (= in which there is a lack of clearly defined tasks) brought about by line managers (= in which there is a lack of other actors) which confers on them a reign-like self-image (= in which the idea of service is lacking).

The Four Implementation Elements (Sect. 2.5)

Implementing it requires four further model elements: management unit design, management routines, management instruments, and management resources. The systematic relationship can be summarized as follows: Managers fulfil management tasks (e.g., performance feedback) using management routines (e.g., interviews), apply management instruments (e.g., work schedules), require management resources (e.g., business information), and do all this on the basis of the management unit structure (e.g., the design of their job).

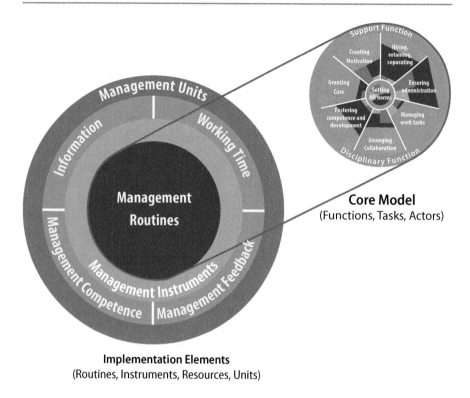

Fig. 2.3 Core model and implementation elements of Complementary Management (modified from Kaehler 2017, p. 317; © Boris Kaehler 2019. All rights reserved)

Management Routines

The management routines, understood as concrete activities, serve as a way to implement the management tasks. For example, performance feedback is initially only an abstract task that must be implemented in regular employee dialogs, among other things. A distinction must be made between annual routines (e.g., annual employee reviews), continuous routines (e.g., weekly work dialogs), and on-demand routines (e.g., crisis interventions or hiring projects). The theoretical basis of this element of the management model is the established construct of organizational routines. Those for whom the term has a negative connotation (in the sense of getting stuck in a rut) may replace it with "management activities". Organizations should clearly define which management routines are to be performed, which actors are involved, and what the frameworks are. The shares each actor has in the routines add up to the totality of their people management activities. This puts management responsibilities into very concrete terms: Has an actor actually carried out the routines incumbent upon him or her and thereby achieved the defined management tasks? If, for example, a line manager does not conduct regular work dialogs, he or she is simply neglecting his or her professional duties.

Management Instruments

Within the framework of management routines, management actors use the management instruments available in their respective organizations. These are formalized tools that support people management and leadership, in particular, rules, systems, programs, and forms. The conceptual differentiation between routines and instruments has significant implications. Leadership and management is not exercised through the instrument (e.g., a salary system or appraisal procedure), but always through its specific application. Good instruments are sometimes devalued by their inadequate use in everyday management. Conversely, dysfunctional and poorly designed HR instruments can be relativized in the course of their application and misguided decisions can be avoided—a question of management quality and certainly also a question of the internal distribution of roles. Above all, however, it becomes clear that HR instruments must be designed in such a way that they effectively support day-to-day people management and leadership.

Management Unit Design

The management unit design encompasses the organizational structures in which the various management actors are integrated. This relates to the structure and hierarchical integration of the organizational units involved in people management and leadership (jobs, groups, departments, divisions, etc.). However, the distribution of tasks among the actors and their respective powers are also connected with it. The general principles of organizational science form the theoretical basis here. The management unit design, like the other elements of the model, does not represent a sub-area of leadership and management but provides a special perspective on it. Thus, it cannot be considered separately from the overall model. Influencing processes certainly take place without permanent management structures, but this has little to do with systematic organizational leadership and management. The Complementary Management Model leaves room for different distributions of tasks among the actors, but its elements provide a rough structural framework. For example, a human resources department that refuses to accept compensatory "HR co-management" would not be compatible with the model. The same applies to management positions without disciplinary authority or with an overstretched management span. Functioning people management and leadership requires a functional management unit design.

Management Resources

In the Complementary Management Model, the implementation element of management resources represents a purely pragmatically reasoned selection of management prerequisites critical to success. In practice, leadership and management often fails because of four essential problematic resources—so much so that it is worth highlighting them prominently by means of a separate element. First: the working time required to perform management routines, which many leaders do not have or do not take. Second, management competencies are required. These consist of action competencies (i.e., skills to successfully perform management routines), which in turn are based on non-managerial elemental competencies (e.g., communication, analysis, assessment, decision-making). Third, management actors need comprehensive directional and situational information. And finally, holistic management feedback is required. All four resources are necessary to enable effective people management and leadership in the first place.

Literature
Kaehler, Boris (2012): Komplementäre Führung – Ein Beitrag zur Theorie und konzeptionellen Praxis der organisationalen Führung; epubli Verlag/ Holtzbrinck 2012.

Kaehler, Boris (2013): Aufgabenorientierte und komplementäre Führung – Grundzüge eines integrativen Modells (Boris Kaehler); Personalführung Juli 2013, pp. 30–37.

Kaehler, Boris (2014a): Komplementäre Führung – Ein praxiserprobtes Modell der organisationalen Führung; 1st edition Springer Gabler 2014.

Kaehler, Boris (2014b): Komplementäre Führung – Ein neues Führungsmodell; Arbeit und Arbeitsrecht 8/2014 (Jahrgang 68); pp. 459–461.

Kaehler, Boris (2017): Komplementäre Führung – Ein praxiserprobtes Modell der Personalführung in Organisationen; 2nd edition Springer Gabler 2017.

Kaehler, Boris (2019): Führen als Beruf; 1st edition Tredition 2019.

Kaehler, Boris (2020): Komplementäre Führung – Ein praxiserprobtes Modell der Personalführung in Organisationen; 3rd edition Springer Gabler 2020.

Kaehler, Boris (2022): www.complementary-management.com (Accessed 01/05, 2022).

Contents

Management and Leadership: Definition, Differentiations, and Other Theoretical Considerations

1.1 Concept of Management and Leadership

The literature contains an almost countless number of definitions of leadership and management. With respect to leadership, some claim to have counted 850 or even 1,500 definitions (Bennis and Nanus 1985, p. 4; Kellerman 2012, p. XXI), which is plausible at best if all variations in formulation and punctuation count as definitions. For management, the situation is no different (Kaehler and Grundei 2019, pp. 5 ff.). This vast number of definitions makes it necessary to clarify one's understanding of these terms before progressing on to the development of theoretical models.

This endeavor is complicated by the fact that many people commonly use the English terms *leadership* and *management* in distinct contexts and that they are often understood to be different concepts. While this book treats them as synonyms (for an in-depth analysis see Sect. 1.2), readers might misunderstand the text if only one of them is used.[1] Thus, the double expression of "management and leadership" in singular is used in this book whenever it appears necessary to facilitate understanding.

1.1.1 Goal-Related Influence as a Core Element

Like any other phenomenon, leadership and management can be described from very different perspectives. Almost all definitions of "leadership" have in common the element of an influence process for facilitating the performance of a collective task (Yukl 2013, p. 36). Leadership can thus be defined in very reduced terms as a goal-related exertion of influence (Rosenstiel 2014, p. 4). As for "management", three definitory elements continue to crop up (Kaehler and Grundei 2019, pp. 5 ff.):

---

[1] In German, the term "Führung" is more general and means both. Thus, a single word can be used to refer to both management and leadership.

© The Author(s), under exclusive license to Springer Nature Switzerland AG 2022
B. Kaehler, *Complementary Management*, Management for Professionals,
https://doi.org/10.1007/978-3-030-98163-1_1

Firstly, Henry Fayol's (1916, p. 5 f.) task catalog of planning, organizing, commanding, coordinating, and controlling (with "commanding" being replaced by "leading" in modern definitions); secondly, the utilization of people or—in a less constrained sense and more often than not—of resources in general; thirdly, the fact that management aims to achieve results or goals.

It should be noted that most literature sources actually only refer to leadership and management in the sense of "people leadership" and "people management". However, just as many definitions of management (and occasionally also of leadership) relate to the sense of corporate management, i.e., managing or leading an organization. Obviously, this is an overlapping construct which, albeit, is not precisely delineated in the literature (Kaehler and Grundei 2019, pp. 5 ff.). On the whole, the conceptual situation remains unsatisfactorily diffuse.

Anyone wanting to precisely describe leadership and management in organizations and to design them effectively will have to be a little more specific and work out their distinctive features. In addition to the fact that influencing is a core element in definitions of *leadership*, the purpose of the act, i.e., the achievement of the goal, as a core element in many *management* definitions, must somehow be included. And since this purpose is by no means arbitrary, and is tied to the organizational framework, the organizational unit, and its business operations should be mentioned as a point of reference. This may sound trivial, but it is an essential insight. Finally, a clear distinction must be made between leading and managing people, and leading and managing organizations—the former obviously being a subset of the latter (more on this in Sect. 1.6.2). All this results in the short definition below (Kaehler and Grundei 2018, p. 206, 2019, pp. 20, 37):

> Organizational *management*, in the sense of managing an organization or its subunits, is a steering influence on market, production and/or resource operations that may address both people and non-people issues with the aim of achieving the unit's objectives. To manage a unit is synonymous with *leading* it.
>
> Organizational *people management*, in the sense of managing the personnel of an organization or its subunits, is an influence on employees with the aim of achieving the unit's objectives by generating work performance and meeting other requirements. To manage a unit's members is synonymous with *leading* them.

1.1.2 Essential Conceptual Extensions

As plausible as these definitions may seem, they are inadequate. This is because they merely summarize generally accepted elements of definitions in a concise manner. They describe the constructs accurately, but only superficially, and evade any real concretization. Like most leadership and management definitions, they thus encourage some prevailing misunderstandings. To avoid these misunderstandings, three essential expansions of the concept are necessary. They will be described in more detail later on in this chapter, but will be included in a comprehensive definition at this point in order to clarify the terms.

The first expansion of the concept concerns the fact that leadership and management always emanates from multiple actors. Certainly, single acts of influence can be attributed to an individual person. As constructs, however, they cannot be meaningfully reduced to the influence of one person. Rather, in the context of an organization, the line manager as a supervisor, the employee as a self-manager, colleagues as lateral managers, and HR advisors as people specialists, among others, all participate in the influence process of the organizational unit and the people working within the unit. Thus, as will be discussed in Sect. 2.4, organizational management and leadership is an influence exercised by multiple actors.

The second expansion of the term concerns the fundamental differentiation between the two possible modes of influence. The influence of leading and managing can be exerted either through anticipatory regulation or through situational intervention in day-to-day operations. These two forms of influence and their implications are explained in more detail in Sect. 1.4. The third addition concerns the distinction between constitutive and strategic norm-setting derived from the St. Gallen Management Model in Sect. 1.5.3. All three points are anything but trivial and certainly not readily clear; they require explanation in the respective sections. At the same time, however, they contribute significantly to a realistic understanding of organizational management and leadership and should therefore definitely be included in a precise definition of terms. This gives rise to the following detailed definitions (Kaehler and Grundei 2018, p. 206, 2019, pp. 20, 37):

> Organizational *management*, in the sense of managing an organization or its subunits, is a steering influence on market, production, and resource operations that may address both people and non-people issues and which is exerted by multiple organizational actors through either anticipatory norm-setting (= constitutive or strategic management) or situational intervention (= operational management) with the aim of achieving the unit's objectives. To manage a unit is synonymous with *leading* it.
>
> Organizational *people management*, in the sense of managing the personnel of an organization or its subunits, is an influence on employees exerted by multiple organizational actors through either anticipatory regulation (= constitutive and strategic people management) or situational intervention (= operational people management) with the aim of achieving the unit's objectives by generating work performance and meeting other requirements. To manage a unit's members is synonymous with *leading* them.

1.1.3   Management and Leadership as a Profession

Leading and managing in an organizational context is a professional activity (Drucker 1954, pp. 6–17, 1998; Malik 2000, pp. 46 ff., 2007, pp. 38, 67; Müller-Stewens 2010; Kaehler 2019; critically Kellerman 2012, pp. 191 f.). All actors practice it professionally as part of their jobs. This also applies to the employee as a self-leader/self-manager who is of course paid not only to perform work but also to self-steer. Human resources specialists are also management and leadership professionals; after all, they deal almost exclusively with influencing personnel day in and day out. Management and leadership as a profession is, of course, also practiced by line managers. Their job, which will be discussed later, has two essential facets: leading and managing the functional-technical business of an organizational unit, as well as leading and managing the unit's personnel. Line managers are therefore professionals in both functional-technical and personnel management/leadership.

The great benefit of the Complementary Leadership Model is that it describes the professional activities of these actors in a very precise and consistent way. It allows organizational leadership and management structures (Sect. 2.6) as well as concepts for manager development (Sect. 3.4) to be designed in a much more targeted manner. Also, understanding their theoretical meaning and context beyond isolated one-off measures is beneficial for the management and leadership work of the individual actors (Chaps. 3 and 4).

The notion of management and leadership as a profession is by no means intended to negate the value and necessity of such influence in leisure time activities and unpaid positions. Even if the word "profession" is not completely appropriate in these areas, the same principles apply in part, and therefore one might speak of semiprofessional activities with regard to hobbies or sports.

1.2   Leadership and Management as a Unified Sphere

Given the many different management and leadership definitions, it is not surprising that many differentiations between related terms are constructed and perpetuated in the literature. There are even entire theoretical models based almost exclusively on postulated differentiations between terms. The main delineation myths will be discussed in more detail below. At this point, however, the result can already be anticipated: Most do not stand up to closer scrutiny and are mere verbiage.

1.2.1   Synonyms and Equations

In principle, there is no reason why different terms should not be used to describe distinct aspects of leadership and management. However, uniform terms have not been developed either in science, in business practice or in everyday language. On the contrary: for every source in which the differences between the two terms are precisely worked out, others can be found which regard this pair of terms as completely synonymous or completely distinct. The matter is further complicated by the fact that the terms "management" and "leadership" are used interchangeably, although one is still used for some matters more than for others (on supposed differences, see Sect. 1.2.3). In the absence of any gains in knowledge for such terminology and due to the many possible misunderstandings that could arise, all relevant terms are regarded here as synonymous. In particular, the line manager's management and the HR department's management are deemed to be equivalent, which goes against the doctrine of many practitioners and academics, but is of

Table 1.1 Terms used synonymously here (© Boris Kaehler 2019. All rights reserved.)

Synonyms for the management and leadership of organizations and their units	Corporate management; also, but less commonly, corporate leadership
	Shortened: management; leadership; direction
Synonyms for the management and leadership of people in organizations	Human resource management; personnel management; workforce management
	Employee management/leadership
	Organizational people management; also, but less commonly, organizational people leadership
	Shortened: management; leadership; direction
	Human relations management
	Human capital management

utmost importance for both the theory and practice of management and leadership (Sect. 1.2.2). Table 1.1 provides an overview of all terms used synonymously here.

1.2.2 The Line Manager's Management and the HR Department's Personnel Management are One and the Same

A classic distinction, but one that should indeed be abolished, is the distinction made between the management or leadership of line managers, on the one hand, and the personnel management of HR specialists on the other. It is still widely assumed that the HR department is responsible for human resource management and line managers are responsible for the leadership/management of employees, and that the two are different, albeit, slightly overlapping spheres. Nothing could be further from the truth.

For decades, HR experts, such as the US-American Dave Ulrich and the German Christian Scholz, have opposed the myth that "HR is HR's job", viewing line managers as primarily responsible for HR work and assigning the HR function a merely supporting and safeguarding role (Scholz 1996, p. 1084; Ulrich 1997, p. 18; Ulrich and Brockbank 2005, p. 72; Prieß 2013, p. 41 f.; see also CIPD 2021b). "Every manager is an HR manager" (Scholz 1996, p. 1081; own translation). After all, line managers play a significant role in what is usually understood to be human resource and personnel management (hiring, developing, compensating personnel, etc.; designing personnel tools). By the same token, every HR manager is a management/leadership actor, because HR managers definitely have a substantial impact on what is usually considered leading employees (work allocation, performance feedback, conflict management, etc.; direct personnel influence). Scholz accurately describes human resources as an integrative process based on the division of labor which distributes responsibility among the HR department, top managers, line managers/leaders and employees (Scholz 2014, p. 4 f.; see also p. 1081).

A frank look at the practice also reveals that neither line managers nor HR departments can manage or lead without the involvement of other actors. While those involved in organizational management/leadership may specialize in certain aspects of it, they still participate—together or in opposition to one another—in the same activity. Placing a theoretical separation between human resource management and employee management/leadership is artificial and hinders a deeper level of understanding as well as the effective design of organizational leadership and management structures. It almost automatically leads to an ineffectiveness of many HR measures and is one of the main causes of the unsatisfactory value contributions of many HR departments (see Chap. 4). They cannot be two distinct spheres, if only because smaller companies generally do not have any HR department at all and because a variety of different solutions can be found in larger ones (Kaehler and Grundei 2019, p. 37). It follows from this that HR management and employee management/leadership are one and the same, with the HR organization being a subsystem of the overall leadership and management structure (as very correctly put by Prieß 2013, p. 41 f.).

1.2.3   Please Don't: Management Versus Leadership

A further distinction is made between "leadership" and "management" that is only plausible on the surface. This differentiation is particularly vexing, not only because it makes little sense, it is also often presented by proponents as if it were a doctrine of salvation: My dear manager, it is time to become a real leader! The differentiation between "manager" and "leader" or "management" and "leadership" in the English language can be traced back to Zaleznik (1977). It was popularized by Bennis and Nanus (1985) and Kotter (1990a, b), and continues to enjoy popularity (see, e.g., Watkins 2012). Here, "management" is said to be the preserving and administering side of steerage, while "leadership" conceptually embodies the visionary, enthusiastic, forward-looking element of followership-based steerage. The two constructs may be understood as complementary or mutually exclusive—both views are supported, though probably most scholars today view leadership as a component of management (Yukl 2013, p. 23).

In fact, the "leadership" construct reflects a political understanding of leadership in the sense of creating and inspiring followership[2] (see Sect. 1.3). It is characterized by the mixture of functional decision-making to provide direction (good leadership can be recognized by bold and wise visions), and man-catching (good leadership enthralls followers and generates allegiance). Ultimately, the term "leadership", which normally is more widely used in English—both scientifically and in general—is reduced to political leadership. "Management" then serves as a catch-all construct for other steering influences. Although, of course, everyone can use language freely—reinterpreting, shortening, and delineating common terms that are actually regarded as synonymous by many—it is highly arbitrary. In addition,

---

[2] Unfortunately, the German term of "Anführrertum", which is most fitting here, has no equivalent in the English language. It means that a person leads a group in a certain direction and implies a certain instability.

the term "leadership", especially in psychology literature, is commonly narrowed down to *leading people* so that it is often primarily associated with this first. But of course, in the English language it also can refer to *leading an organization* or organizational unit (as in "business leader" and "leading a company/business").

A famous thesis of Bennis and Nanus completely misses the mark:

> "The problem with many organizations, and especially the ones that are failing, is that they tend to be overmanaged and underled. [...] Managers are people who do things right and leaders are people who do the right thing. The difference may be summarized as activities of vision and judgment – effectiveness – versus activities of mastering routines – efficiency." (Bennis and Nanus 1985, p. 28 f.)

This semantic maneuver reduces "leadership" to the functional determination of goal and path (in contrast to the optimal mastering of this path by "management"), which is conceivably illogical, because leadership, as a term, is broadly used for the exertion of influence on people, which is not exhausted in the pull effect of a factually correct target vision. Additionally, Bennis and Nanus describe both management and leadership as an activity, and of course every activity must be judged according to its effectiveness and efficiency. To equate one whole activity with effectiveness and another with efficiency contradicts the general meaning of the pair of terms.

The renowned leadership scholar Gary Yukl believes the problem when differentiating between management and leadership lies in the too narrow and fuzzy definition of the descriptions of the corresponding roles (Yukl and Lepsinger 2005, pp. 372–373). He and his coauthor describe three possible solutions. One, conceptualizing leadership as one of many management roles, was already rejected above because it is incompatible with the broader language used in academia and practice. The second, conceptualizing the two constructs more broadly and delineating them more clearly would also be contrary to common language usage, be completely arbitrary, and not be of any discernible use. The third solution he favors is to abandon the differentiation and replace it with a catalog of clearly defined leadership roles. In other words, leadership and management are to be understood as synonyms and differentiated in terms of content, namely—as in the case of Complementary Leadership—by a task model of leadership (Sect. 2.3.1).

The conceptual division of steerage into "leadership" and "management" is therefore artificial and does not contribute in the slightest to understanding how it is actually applied in organizations (Yukl 2013, p. 22 f.; see also Mintzberg 2009, p. 8 f.; Malik 2012). In everyday life, most people are likely to regard the terms as interchangeable anyway (Gulati et al. 2017, p. 8).

1.2.4   Management/Leadership and Direction/Headship as Synonyms

The terms direction and headship are firmly established in literature and practice. Expressions such as "business director" or "team head" are part of everyday language in many organizations. This results in a kind of dichotomy: Whereas "direction/headship" focuses on functional technical aspects, i.e., primarily tasks and work processes, "leadership" encompasses more person-related aspects such as a willingness to perform and motivation (Korff 1971, p. 9; Schulte-Zurhausen 2014, p. 219 f.[3]). However, this differentiation not only contradicts common usage, it is also theoretically untenable. As shown in Sect. 1.6.2, the functional technical aspects and the employee-related aspects of operational management can be analyzed separately, but they cannot be differentiated from each other in terms of content. Even activities which ostensibly focus on only the employee are ultimately aimed at maintaining business operations.

A second variant differentiates between management/leadership and headship based on the criterion of acceptance, whereby both can be exercised together but not automatically (Gibb 1954, p. 882 f.; Weibler 2016, p. 24 f.[4]). However, this differentiation ultimately corresponds to the distinction between management and leadership, making it all the more superfluous (Sect. 1.2.3).

A third distinction between "direction/headship" and "leadership" was proposed by Seidel (1984, p. 463[5]) and has rightly not been accepted. According to this, direction/headship is supposed to be making decisions for others, and management/leadership is supposed to be the enforcement of these external decisions with respect to the employee. This differentiation is deeply rooted in a full Taylorian separation between decision and execution, which, despite the relevance of many other Taylorian ideas, does not fit the context of the organization of modern work. As sensible and common as it is to endow managerial and leadership positions with formal external decision-making, directive, and supervisory authority, it is non-sensical to stylize the exercising of this authority of these competencies as the essential object of managerial activity. Management and leadership as a goal-oriented influence does not primarily consist of making decisions on behalf of others and enforcing them with respect to others, but rather of encouraging employees to make their own decisions alongside various other supporting tasks. Here too, dividing an extremely abbreviated understanding of leadership and management conceptually does not provide any real benefit. If one really wants to establish a meaningful linguistic differentiation, the terms *direction* and *headship* could refer to formal leadership positions (as opposed to leadership influences emanating from other leadership actors, e.g., in the context of self-leadership). However, this view is

---

[3] Both sources refer to the German equivalent "Leitung".

[4] Weibler also refers to the often-used German equivalent "Leitung"; in English, the duality introduced by Gibb is rather uncommon.

[5] Seidel also refers to the German equivalent "Leitung".

hardly encouraged and does not provide any added value either. Thus, the point is made: leadership, management, direction, and headship are synonyms.

1.2.5 Functional-Technical Versus Disciplinary Leadership or Management

In contrast to the conceptual dualities of management/leadership and direction/headship, the differentiation between "functional-technical" and "disciplinary" leadership or management is not just a matter of word fiddling, but is actually lived practice in many companies. In this context, the term "functional-technical" refers to decision-making authority with regard to the execution of work tasks. In contrast, disciplinary leadership or management includes decision-making powers related to other measures, especially formal personnel processes such as performance appraisals, hiring/termination, written warnings, transfers, salary issues, training and development measures, and the approval of vacation, business trips, etc. (depending on the definition, this also includes tasks such as praise/reproach, recording of working hours and attendance/punctuality checks). One widespread model gives the lowest management level of a hierarchy only functional-technical leadership responsibilities and reserves the disciplinary responsibilities for the next higher management level—a principle that can also be continued at higher levels if necessary (Schulte-Zurhausen 2014, p. 173 f.). At Google, for example, disciplinary management powers are largely exercised collectively, i.e., many people at different levels are involved in the relevant decision-making, while leaders and managers at all levels essentially exercise purely functional-technical management (Bock 2015, p. 118 ff.). Another form is that of the matrix organization in which each position is concurrently subordinate to two superior positions, one of which is usually designed as a disciplinary and functional-technical leadership position, and the other as a purely functional-technical one.

At first glance, this differentiation between disciplinary and functional-technical leadership and management appears to correspond to a separation between people and non-people leadership. As will be explained in Sect. 1.6.2, such a separation is not at all possible—neither theoretically nor practically—in the area of operational steerage. And indeed, functional-technical leadership and management also includes people aspects, namely those related to the performance of work. For example, a professional supervisor may motivate, qualify, or care for employees by setting certain work objectives or granting work breaks. On the other hand, disciplinary leadership is not only related to people, but also to work, because disciplinary decisions are, of course, essentially based on aspects of work assignments, working behavior, and work results.

Ultimately, therefore, the differentiation between "functional-technical" and "disciplinary" leadership or management simply means a special allocation of particular management tasks to certain management positions. In principle, these management tasks could also be combined and distributed between the actors in other ways. Moreover, mere functional-technical leadership is by no means found in all organizations. In addition, this duality neglects the existence of yet other leadership actors in the sense that, for instance, written warnings, dismissals, and development decisions are the responsibility of the human resources department in many companies. In this regard, the concept of functional-technical leadership or management must be concretized on a company-specific basis, by asking: "what are the precise tasks, responsibilities and decision-making powers of this particular functional-technical manager in this particular matrix organization?"

Overall, it is striking that the "disciplinary" responsibilities encompass essential power bases of leadership, namely the power to reward and punish. Viewed in this light, the differentiation can be understood as a vote of no confidence in those supervisory levels that are granted only functional-technical instructional power. However, as an organizational structure the model remains schematic. It is impractical insofar as holistic leadership does, as a rule, require such bases of power. Although the control of power is a key issue in the design of leadership and management structures, it can be achieved more elegantly and effectively than by curtailing the lower hierarchy levels (see Sect. 2.4). The distinction between functional-technical and disciplinary leadership or management can therefore be dispensed with, even if the underlying situation does indeed occur in reality and some organizations attach importance to it.

1.3   Distinction Between Organizational and Political Leadership

It has already been mentioned that much of the leadership and management literature does not sufficiently distinguish between political and organizational leadership. In order to establish a clear understanding, both concepts need to be analyzed and a delineation needs to be made.

1.3.1 Political Leadership

Especially in US literature, leadership is primarily understood as building followership:

"... the only definition of a leader is someone who has followers." (Drucker 1988, p. 103)

European authors similarly tend to describe leadership and management as an influence phenomenon in poorly structured situations (see, e.g., Neuberger 2002, p. 47; Blessin and Wick 2014, pp. 41, 228 f.) and/or to link it by definition to an acceptance by those being led (Weibler 2016, p. 22 ff.). These, however, are precisely the salient features of political leadership, regardless of whether it is exercised by professional politicians and diplomats or by leaders of a group of

Table 1.2 Political vs. organizational leadership (modified from Kaehler and Grundei 2019, p. 36; © Boris Kaehler/Jens Grundei 2019. All rights reserved.)

Political leadership	Organizational leadership
Focus on choosing a course of action, acquiring a leadership mandate, and achieving consent	Focus on generating work output using limited resources
Highly unstructured context	Highly structured context, especially through (labor-related) legal requirements, quality standards, and specific organizational unit and process structures; contractually bound employees
Visions and goals as a means of building personnel allegiance	Visions and goals as a tool for managing and breaking down the objectives of the overall organization
The commitment to work and goals essentially results from personnel allegiance	The commitment to work and goals essentially results from objective requirements (employment contract and processes)
Maximum commitment to leader required	Maximum commitment to leader not desirable (e.g., because of possible employee attrition and collective misconduct)

revolutionaries.[6] Indeed, anyone who wants to lead independent individuals in a common direction without a formal mandate and in unstructured contexts needs their allegiance. This, of course, is always a shaky affair. It is not without reason that political leadership in representative democracies is structurally limited to the extent that election winners receive a fixed mandate for a term of government. Political leadership in this sense is limited to the election campaign and to courting deputies (insofar as they act independently). In principle, however, political leadership can also be observed in other contexts where no fixed or permanent social structures have developed. One prototype for this, apart from the election campaigner, is the spontaneously emerging leader of a loose group, e.g., of castaways. In this context, the phenomenon of political leadership or being a leader has two quite different aspects: on the one hand, determining a common goal and choosing the way to achieve it, and on the other hand, attaining a leadership mandate and eliciting actual allegiance. A good political leader chooses the right goals and motivates people to follow him or her.

1.3.2   Differences with Respect to Organizational Leadership

At its core, organizational leadership completely differs from political leadership (Table 1.2; see also Türk 1981, p. 57). First, unlike in the political sphere, the

---

[6] As already mentioned above, a very fitting German term for this with no equivalent in English is "Anführertum", meaning that a person (the "Anführer") leads a group in a certain direction and implies a certain group dynamic and instability.

intention of personnel leadership lies primarily in producing work output effectively and efficiently using limited resources. This requires a different, more comprehensive level of influence than the endeavor of merely obtaining a mandate or approval for a particular course of action. Secondly, organizational leadership takes place in specially created organizational and process structures as well as within the framework of (labor-related) legal requirements. Employees are not just unaffiliated individuals, but have consciously joined an organization and are contractually bound, which gives them rights and obligations. In organizations, there are fixed rules that ensure a certain stability both with regard to the position of the leader/manager and with regard to that of the employees. Generating allegiance is therefore much less relevant here than in the political arena. By delegating work and having it carried out, political leaders go beyond pure allegiance-building and in fact make use of their acquired mandate, i.e., they operate in already solidified, organization-like structures. Third, maximum commitment to leaders is not necessarily desirable in the organizational sphere, at least from an organizational perspective. When leaders and managers really do succeed in getting their employees to personally commit to them, the latter often follow them into ethically problematic areas or to other employers. It may be argued that it is not loyalty to the leader that is desirable, but to the visions and goals he or she has set. However, such "depersonalized" allegiance is clearly not what is meant in the related literature when political leadership mechanisms are transferred to organizational leadership. Rather, it is generally a matter of using visions and goals as a means of building personal allegiance, and personal allegiance as a means of committing to these goals.

Organizational leadership certainly has political elements, but these relate first and foremost to functional-technical constitutive management and strategic management. Like political leaders, leaders in organizations must, of course, choose the right goals, after all nothing is more important for a company than finding a clever business model, correctly determining the relevant regulatory framework, and defining sensible strategies (see Sect. 1.5). All of this determines how the staff is led and managed, however, it is superordinate to it and therefore not part of it. In addition, although leading and managing employees also has political aspects, these are limited to peripheral aspects. This refers in particular to the creation of decisive norms and strategies which, ideally, actually trigger something like a pull effect on employees. It also refers to the communication between senior executives across hierarchies, which has a quasi-political character, e.g., in the case of addressing the masses (see Sect. 3.1.3). Finally, so-called micro-politics should be considered, e.g., strategies for securing power and influencing corporate opinion (see Sect. 3.2).

The bottom line is that personnel management in organizations has very little overlap with political leadership:

> "Organizations are not social groups, a supervisor is not a gang leader. [. . .] Personnel leadership is always institutional leadership [. . .]." (Türk 1981, p. 57; own translation)

When dealing with management and leadership definitions and theories, it is, therefore, advisable to first question the extent to which they take into account the specifics of leadership and management in organizations. Frequently, this is not the case. Those who are content to simply transfer political mechanisms to the organizational context will never achieve good leadership and management. It is, however, quite obvious why political leadership approaches nevertheless play a major role in the theory and practice of organizational leadership and management: the greater the organizational deficiencies, i.e., the more dysfunctional the design of organizational structures, the more unstructured the situation and the greater the need for political leadership. Moreover, more than a few executives—misjudging the structures that support them—enjoy the role of the supposed leader and form a lucrative target group which willing management and leadership authors are only too happy to cater to.

1.4 Forms of Influence

Influence over people and organizations can be exerted in two different ways. From both a practical and theoretical perspective, this is one of the most fundamental and significant aspects of leadership and management.

1.4.1 Norm-Setting Versus Intervention

Despite its importance, this basic duality is described in the literature in such a subordinate, vague, and varied way that hardly anyone is really familiar with the concept at all (see Table 1.3).

None of these established terms seems appropriate or really do justice to the matter at hand. This is probably why the fundamental duality is not given the prominent place it should be given in academic textbooks and practical how-to guides on management and leadership. Experienced practitioners though are well aware of the importance it has on success. It can be defined more precisely by the terms "influence through anticipatory norm-setting" vs. "influence through situational intervention". The former means exerting influence with the help of rules, i.e., behavioral regulations. These behavioral rules can be informal, as is the case of many cultural norms. Usually, however, norms are set down in writing as a guideline for human behavior, for example, in the case of governance or the unit/process organization. Both informal and formal norms are about influencing human behavior through forward-looking regulation. The second form, management and leadership through intervention, refers to an influence through situational actions of a formal or informal nature. A spontaneously pronounced ban falls into this category because it is not a matter of anticipatory but of intervening norm-setting.

Unfortunately, in literature and practice, leadership is often reduced to intervention in poorly structured situations that cannot be solved in a routine manner (see, e.g., Neuberger 2002, p. 47; Blessin and Wick 2014, pp. 41, 228 f.; Weibler 2016, p. 93; see also Sect. 1.3). Following this view, leadership would be regarded as a

Table 1.3 Conventional descriptions of the duality norm-setting/intervention (modified from Kaehler and Grundei 2019, p. 15; © Boris Kaehler/Jens Grundei 2019. All rights reserved.)

Duality	Sources
Personal leadership vs. structural leadership (own translation) (German original: "Personelle Führung" vs. "strukturelle Führung")	Wunderer (2011, pp. 4–14), Armutat (2012, pp. 32, 33), v. Rosenstiel (2014, pp. 3–4)
Interactive leadership vs. structural-systemic management	Wunderer (2001)
Directing activity vs. shaping activity (own translation) (German original: "Lenkungshandeln" vs. "Gestaltungshandeln")	Jung et al. (2008, S. 3–4)
Leadership vs. leadership substitutes	Kerr and Jermier (1978, 1997), Rosenstiel (2011, pp. 359, 360), and Yukl (2013, pp. 21, 171); see also Yukl and Lepsinger (2005, p. 364)
De-personalized management/ leadership vs. un-personal and personal management/leadership (own translation) (German original: "entpersonalisierte Führung vs. unpersönliche/persönliche Führung")	Türk (1995)
Organizing vs. disposing (own translation) (German original: "Organisieren" vs. "disponieren")	Kosiol (1962, p. 28)
Information plane vs. people/action plane	Mintzberg (2009, pp. 49–96)
Systems leadership domain vs. direct leadership domain	Hunt (1991, pp. 27–35)
Direct vs. indirect management/leadership	Lord and Maher (1991, pp. 163–178), Yukl (2013, S. 21), Boddy (2017, pp. 16–27); see also Yukl and Lepsinger (2005, pp. 363–364)
Direct leadership ("face-to-face") vs. contextual (= indirect) leadership (own translation) (German original: "Direkte Führung (face-to-face)" vs. "kontextuelle (= indirekte) Führung")	Weibler (2016, pp. 88 ff.)
Case-specific instruction vs. general rule (own translation) (German original: "fallweise Anordnung" vs. "generelle Regelung")	Gutenberg (1962, pp. 44–45); see also Gutenberg (1979, p. 253)
Leadership behaviors vs. management programs and systems	Yukl and Lepsinger (2005, p. 363)

"gap-filler of organization" (often attributed to Niklas Luhmann; own translation[7]) or a "residual factor" (Türk 1981, p. 65; own translation[8]; see also pp. 67/126). Here, of course, lies a fundamental error in understanding, for the supposedly impersonal structures are by no means independent of the leader/manager and his or her actions,

---

[7] German original: "Lückenbüßer der Organisation".

[8] German original: "Residualfaktor".

but an essential result thereof (see Yukl 2013, p. 21; Blessin and Wick 2014, p. 228). They are even the very key to good and effective leadership and management, which consists precisely of gradually replacing ongoing intervention needs with forward-looking regulations (Kaehler and Grundei 2019, p. 15; see also the substitution principle of organization, Gutenberg 1962, pp. 44, 45):

> "Good management does not permanently get bogged down by daily interventions, but continuously addresses such needs and systematically prevents them." (Kaehler and Grundei 2018, p. 206; own translation)

In order to understand and shape leadership and management, however, both forms of influence must be taken into account. Purely normative influence cannot work because it does not individually adjust to the situation. It, therefore, requires intervention, otherwise there would be no need for the daily actions of line managers in organizations, but only for rules and regulations. This, too, is not a new insight:

> "However, these instances, which are regulated on a case-by-case basis, can never be completely dispensed with. They are like valves that are activated when general regulations of a personal and functional nature cannot withstand the pressure of operational processes requiring individual processing and decision-making." (Gutenberg 1979, S. 253; own translation)

It follows from this that normative theories and operational models of management and leadership cannot and must not rely exclusively on normative influence, but must combine and interlock regulatory and intervening influence mechanisms in a well-calculated way. How this is done in the Complementary Leadership Model is described in Sect. 2.4.

1.4.2 Gentle and Hard Norm-Setting

Of course, there are different approaches to the two forms of influence. As far as norm-setting is concerned, a distinction can be made between hard and gentle norming. It is not at all unusual to work with traditional rules and prohibitions, and there are indeed cases where they can be applied. However, this mostly only involves the rough guardrails of behavior, e.g., issues of legal and regulatory relevance, which are usually addressed by codes of conduct. Regulating large parts of business operations and organizational behavior in this way would be too clumsy though and not very effective overall. But there are also more subtle types of regulation which can be broken down into five aspects (Table 1.4). Naturally, these are by no means mutually exclusive; rather, they intersect and occur in combination. Most gentle norms are gentle in several regards, and the same applies to hard norms. The purpose of this list is therefore not to draw precise boundaries, but rather to highlight the design options.

One form of gentle norm-setting is so-called "nudging" (see the standard work by Thaler and Sunstein 2008, also Bock 2015, pp. 283 ff.; Freibichler et al. 2018), understood to mean the construction of decision architectures. In this process, some

Table 1.4 Gentle and hard norm-setting (© Boris Kaehler 2019. All rights reserved.)

Hard Norm-setting	Gentle Norm-setting
Explicit commands/bans without freedom of choice	Design of decision architectures ("nudging")
Appellative instruction	Behavioral reinforcement through incentive systems ("operant conditioning")
Norms set externally by managers/ leaders	Norms set wholly or partly by employees themselves ("participation")
Postulating norm-setting (naming a demanded behavior)	Functional norm-setting (e.g., through the design of rooms and machines)
Establishment of formal rules	Shaping of cultural group norms of an informal nature
High degree of regulation	Low degree of regulation

of the situation's parameters are designed in advance in such a way that they make it easy for employees to make the desired decision or subliminally suggest this to them. As a result, most employees select this option; however, they could easily select a different one at any time, so they are not restricted in their freedom ("Libertarian Paternalism," Thaler and Sunstein 2008, p. 5). A classic example of this lies in presenting food in a canteen in such a way that, for example, the salads look more appetizing and are thus eaten more than the French fries that are also on offer. Many types of nudging are ultimately based on behavior reinforcement through incentive systems. Because of its importance, however, it is worth highlighting this form of norm-setting separately as a second form of gentle norming. Ultimately, in fact, all aspects of human resource management and leadership—from the compensation system to workplace design and community spirit—can be interpreted as incentives. The design of these structures, which are nothing more than norms, results in incentive systems that underpin desired behavior with rewards and/or negative incentives, thereby reinforcing them. Where such incentives are effective, explicit norms are often not needed. Incentives may be set spontaneously, but their effects always only transpire in the future, which makes them a form of anticipatory norm-setting.

A third form of gentle norm-setting is the participation of the employees in the setting of rules. Work assignments and working conditions do not necessarily have to be externally determined in the sense that work-related behavioral specifications, behavioral consequences, and behavioral conditions are decided and shaped from the top down by managers. Instead, in many organizations today, many of the internal norms are co-created by the employees, whether at the team level or at the level of the organization as a whole. The fourth form of gentle norming is the systematic shaping of corporate culture, i.e., the establishment of collective social norms. Shared collective norms of an informal nature influence the behavior of individual employees without the need for explicit rules. Fifth, it is usually gentler to incorporate norms into the functional work environment (e.g., machines or workspaces) than to enforce them as axioms. With regard to the sixth and final form, even explicit commands/bans need, by no means, regulate all aspects of behavior, but can be made gentler by being limited to certain partial aspects or statements of tendency. Important in all this: Gentle norm-setting does not solve the problem of the meaningfulness of the norms themselves. Dysfunctional procedures have a disruptive and demotivating effect even—or especially—when they are implemented gently.

1.4.3 Gentle and Hard Intervention

Like management influence through anticipatory norm-setting, management influence through situational intervention can also take different forms. Intervention is by no means synonymous with instructing, threatening, shouting, or dominating. There are more subtle ways to exert situational influence that are again more effective than the hard way (Table 1.5).

For example, situational intervention may happen through self-direction (see Sect. 2.4.3). Managers can also take a delegative approach and assign third parties (e.g., sub-/superordinated managers, HR supervisors, and coaches) with the task of influencing. Although this ultimately only shifts the problem of influencing onto this other person, it can help to keep the working relationship positive between the leader and the person being led (e.g., in the case of criticism or punishment). Where the manager makes a personal appearance, he or she does not necessarily have to make an appeal, i.e., explicitly request a certain behavior ("Do this! Don't do that!"). They can also communicate implicitly (= "indirect communication"). Here, the desired behavior is not explicitly addressed, but only suggested by means of implicit messages. These include, for example, metaphors, hints, storytelling, symbols, and role modeling. Of course, not everyone is predisposed to this:

> "We Germans like to fall straight out with our opinions and have not yet made it very far in the indirect." (Johann Wolfgang von Goethe, Conversations with Eckermann)

Discretionary personal decisions also have a hard character. In this case, the leader/manager makes decisions regarding behavioral requirements, consequences,

Table 1.5 Gentle and hard interventions (© Boris Kaehler 2019. All rights reserved.)

Hard intervention	Gentle intervention
External intervention by the manager	Self-determined intervention by the employee (self-control)
Appellative communication	Implicit communication
Ordering	Asking for contribution or help
Harsh and dominative	Friendly and persuasive/soliciting
Personal contact	Contact via third parties
Discretionary personal decisions	Reference to general rules
Intervention without explanation	Explaining the reasons for an intervention
Threat of punishment	Enticing with a reward
Unilateral dominance	Alternating dominance
High degree of intervention	Low degree of intervention

and conditions as he or she sees fit, without the meaning being apparent to the person being led. In contrast to this, the leader/manager can also limit an intervention to reminding people of existing norms and conveying the overriding meaning of the behavioral requirements, consequences, and conditions so that it becomes clear to the person being addressed that these are objectively necessary and there is no arbitrariness. This kind of intervention, of course, presupposes that such norms have been created in advance. Furthermore, leadership and management need not mean that one particular person always influences another person and his or her behavior. Instead of unilateral dominance, alternating dominance is also possible. This can involve a genuine change of roles, or it can happen informally to varying degrees. The prerequisites here are corresponding rules of the game ("Who dominates when?") or a low power distance (equality that allows for alternating dominance in the situation). Finally, different degrees of intervention can be observed depending on the extent to which leaders intervene in the self-leadership of employees (see Sect. 2.4.5).

1.4.4 Effects of Hard and Gentle Norming and Intervention

Gentle management/leadership is generally more effective than hard management/leadership. This applies equally to situational interventions and to anticipatory norm-setting. That is because people generally respond with reactance (psychological defensiveness) and resistance to extensive direct external influence and the accompanying restrictions on their freedom to act. This occurs to an even greater extent if it is one-sided, personal, appealing, or discretionary in nature, and can lead to an employee not doing what is asked of him or her. If this resistance is actively eliminated (e.g., with coercion or compensation), this usually results in a passive attitude on the part of the employee toward the corresponding action and the organization. This usually has a negative impact on the employee's self-esteem, sense of control, and flow experience and, ultimately, on his or her productivity. The employee then does what is required, but no longer identifies with his or her work, does not actively contribute through suggestions/warnings, and performs less over-all. For this reason, leadership and management tends to be more effective and sustainable when leadership influence is exerted through gentle mechanisms. Of course, maximum leadership effectiveness does not lie in providing a maximum amount of gentle leadership. On the contrary, using the gentle approach only is doomed to fail. Organizational management and leadership, for example, always involves a certain degree of external influence, since membership in an organization requires subordination to its respective goals. Appellative communication is not necessarily dysfunctional either, but can elicit the expectation of an incentive and set behavioral impulses that have a positive effect on motivation. Furthermore, hard influence is always necessary whenever gentle influence does not have the required effect. The important thing is the result, and this depends on the circumstances and the characteristics and sensitivities of the leader and of those being managed/led.

These are all, in fact, general principles of communication that apply in many fields. The basic principles of organizational leadership and management influence are naturally the same as, for example, in the field of political leadership (see Sect. 1.3). For this reason, there is no contradiction when management theorists such as Peter F. Drucker see corporate management as committed to the sociopolitical ideal of maximum personal freedom within a set framework (see Drucker 1954, p. 136). Even the analogy to child rearing that is widespread in practice-oriented management literature—in fact, an impertinence from the employee's point of view—can be drawn on here because the basic mechanisms of influence are identical. It should be noted, though, that organizational, political, and educational leadership differ considerably in terms of their objectives and design; they are merely based on the same basic principles of influencing people.

1.5   Managing and Leading Organizations

The term "organizational management" has already been briefly defined above. From this, it should have become clear that the construct as such is anything but trivial. The following section will go into more detail.

1.5.1   Organizational Management as a Steering Influence

The definition of the term organizational management or organizational leadership, as outlined in Sect. 1.1, is admittedly rather complex. Although it is compatible with large parts of the literature, it goes far beyond it and contains various additions and clarifications. While literature on "leadership" hardly ever defines it in the sense of leading an organization and focuses instead on leading people, most literature on "management" does. Unfortunately, the definitions encountered to date can, as surprising as it may sound, be recognized at first glance as unsuitable (see the comprehensive analysis in Kaehler and Grundei 2019, p. 5 ff.). Even the basic characterization of management as a sub-function of business administration that steers an organization's operations, while in line with prevailing opinion and classifications in many textbooks, is rarely clearly stated. This fundamental insight, however—that it is an elevated transverse function in relation to business operations—is of utmost importance in understanding management and leadership in general. In this way, management and leadership is by no means identical with the overall business operation, but only one aspect of it, namely the steering part. For example, serving customers, operating machines, or generating/booking cash flows are purely execution, not management. Deciding which individual work tasks are to be done and then motivating and controlling these activities is management. However, this premise can only be upheld if the construct of management and leadership is also possible with respect to self-control. Anything else would be out of touch with reality because no performance tasks can be totally subjected to an external control (Kaehler and Grundei 2018, p. 206, 2019, p. 3 ff.).

Organizational leadership or management is also called *corporate* leadership or management. Strictly speaking, the term refers to business enterprises, but when more broadly interpreted, it also applies to other organizations such as public authorities, non-profit organizations, and associations (see, e.g., Jung et al. 2008, p. 5; using the German term "Unternehmensführung"). The management and leadership of these institutions essentially follows the same principles, only the concepts of sales, market, and service provision are to be interpreted in the light of their respective characteristics. Thus, the terms "corporate leadership/management", like "organizational leadership/management", will be used here as a proxy for the influencing of a wide variety of institutions.

1.5.2   The Organizational Unit as a Reference Point

Another essential insight applied to the aforementioned definition is that the reference point of influence is not, for example, the manager/leader or those being managed/led, but the abstract organizational unit. In this context, a unit is defined as a bundle of subunits with the smallest unit, the so-called "job", being a bundle of work tasks. Accordingly, the "company" as an overall entity is an organizational unit, but so too are business divisions, departments, working groups and individual positions.

In most organizations, units are superordinated or subordinated to each other by means of reporting lines and are thus nested. This is referred to as a hierarchy. Unfortunately, the term is often used incorrectly and has come to have a rather negative connotation (see Sect. 3.1.4). However, this criticism is usually misguided because the existence of a hierarchy reveals nothing at all about the rigidity of the reporting lines, the flexibility of the structures, or the power of the job holders. In any case, the vast majority of organizations today still have a hierarchy. The way they are nested is reminiscent of the famous Russian matryoshka dolls, except that each doll contains multiple dolls instead of just one (Fig. 1.1). This means that the company as an overarching, superordinate entity contains various subunits, which in turn contain other subunits, down to the "job" as the smallest unit. Classic organizational charts imperfectly represent this relationship as they focus on reporting lines.

Based on this insight, the object of corporate leadership and management can now be described precisely: It is about managing/leading a specific organizational unit. There are few literature sources that even hint at this fundamental insight. Henry Mintzberg does give an indication of this with respect to line managers:

"The manager, by the definition used here, is someone responsible for a whole organization or some identifiable part of it (which, for want of a better term, I shall call a unit)." (Mintzberg 2009, p. 12).

In this respect, the management of a unit always includes the management of its subunits. One of the reasons why many management initiatives (e.g., cost reduction or change campaigns) fail is certainly because they usually only address the overall

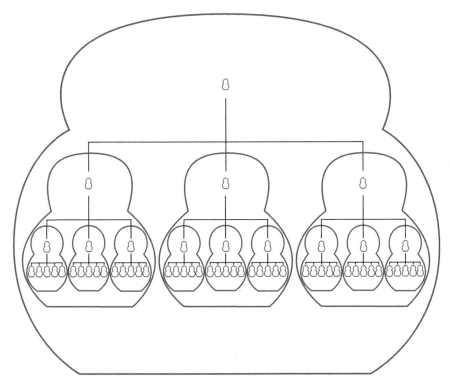

Fig. 1.1 Organizational units as the reference point of leadership and management in organizations (own graphic based on Grundei and Kaehler 2018, p. 590; © Boris Kaehler and Jens Grundei 2019. All rights reserved.)

entity. They are not cascaded down enough to the sub-units, even though the desired results are, after all, primarily achieved at the level of these sub-units. Management must therefore take place at the level of each organizational unit, on down to the individual position/job (Kaehler and Grundei 2018, p. 206, 2019, p. 11 f.).

1.5.3 Constitutive, Strategic and Operational Management and Leadership

In the second German edition of this book, a new management model was proposed that is now available in a revised version (Kaehler 2017, pp. 52 ff.; Kaehler and Grundei 2019, pp. 3–36). It is based on the St. Gallen Management Model with its three task areas: normative, strategic, and operational management (Bleicher 1991, pp. 50–55, 1994, pp. 42–56, 2011, pp. 85–98; Rüegg-Stürm 2003, pp. 70–73; Rüegg-Stürm and Grand 2015, pp. 160–171; see also Ulrich and Krieg 1973, pp. 28–34). Figure 1.2 graphically depicts the three management and leadership fields and their transverse function. The first, more aptly called constitutive

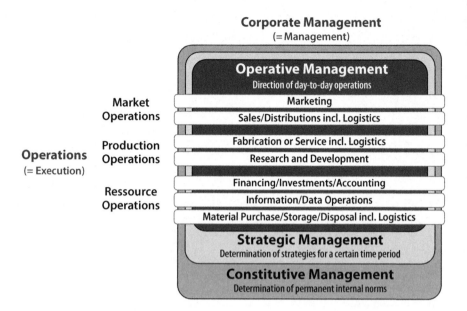

management, involves setting permanent norms, i.e., regulations. These norms are manifold and include, for example, the internal governance of the respective unit, defined as the normative behavior framework for its steerage (see Grundei and Kaehler 2018, p. 589). However, constitutive leadership also includes, for example, the definition of the unit's business model and mission as well as its relevant stakeholders. In addition, it entails the creation of organizational processes and unit structures, the code of conduct as well as informal cultural norms. These do not primarily regulate management and leadership behavior, and thus are not considered governance; they do regulate executing behavior (i.e., conducting/ performing work) in a unit though and thus still fall under the category of constitutive norms.

In contrast to constitutive managment, strategic management is responsible for linking and controlling the operational activities with the constitutive specifications. This is done by defining strategies, which are understood here as normative plans and rules that indicate which long-term goals are to be pursued, how they are to be achieved and how possible obstacles and scenarios are to be dealt with. The reference point here is the medium-term business period of usually one to three years. Finally, the third task field is operational management, which involves translating the constitutive and strategic targets into actual day-to-day business performance and influencing everyday operations. It should be noted that this is influence in the sense of steerage, not execution in the sense of conducting/ performing work. Operational leadership involves monitoring and enforcing the implementation of constitutive and strategic guidelines, but not their potential adjustment (Grundei and Kaehler 2018; Kaehler and Grundei 2019, pp. 15–18).

Bleicher (1991, p. 52, 2011, pp. 87, 88) accurately describes the constitutive (for him "normative") and strategic forms of management, of a shaping nature, on the one hand, and operational forms of management, of an interactive nature, on the other as two sides of the same coin. Indeed, the first two, constitutive and strategic management/leadership, are purely normative in nature since they involve setting constitutive and strategic norms. Operational management/leadership, however, is not normative and involves ongoing interventions. Operational norm-setting (e.g., spontaneously announcing a ban) does exist, but it does not involve genuine regulation in advance, but rather norm-setting as an ad hoc intervention. This closes the loop for the two forms of influence explained in Sect. 1.4, which were also already included in the definition in Sect. 1.1.2. Management and leadership as a steering influence can occur by means of anticipatory norm-setting ($=$ constitutive and strategic management/leadership) or situational intervention ($=$ operational management/leadership).

At the same time, it becomes clear why the organizational unit was highlighted as the point of reference in Sect. 1.5.2. Contrary to what some literature sources assume, the three fields of leadership activity cannot be assigned to organizational levels in so far as constitutive and strategic standards can only be set at the superordinate level of the overall company. Instead, as in the Matryoshka model (Fig. 1.1), all three task areas must be performed for each organizational unit. The overall organization, its business units, departments, teams, and jobs must all be led and managed constitutively and strategically as well as operationally. Only then is it possible to coordinate the nested units. For similar reasons, strategic and constitutive norms are also not just about fundamentally important norms, but about all permanent norms of the respective unit. This is because a demarcation according to importance is simply not tenable: a regulation that is significant for a particular department may be irrelevant for the company as a whole, and vice versa. Admittedly, the term "constitutive" corresponds to that of the "corporate constitution" and may suggest a restriction to the basic rules. However, just as the characteristics of a house do not arise only, or primarily, from its foundations, the organizational unit is not only made up of basic norms. Each permanent norm co-constitutes the unit. Also, the concept of strategy may sound weighty in meaning, but it certainly should not be reserved only for highly important matters. Rather, even minor matters require a strategy in the sense of a plan for achieving goals. The delineation of the three fields is thus only possible through their temporality: constitutive norms are permanent (although they can of course be changed), strategic norms are related to the business period (however long), and operational interventions are situational in nature (Grundei and Kaehler 2018; Kaehler and Grundei 2019, pp. 15–18) (Table 1.6).

Table 1.6 Constitutive, strategic, and operational management on different hierarchical levels (from Kaehler und Grundei 2019, S. 18; © Boris Kaehler and Jens Grundei 2019. All rights reserved.)

Constitutive management (= management through normative regulations)	Of the overall unit (= entire organization)	Determining the framework and management system of the unit (e.g., mission/vision, legal form, business model, stakeholders, possibly tax model; general management model; stipulations with regard to organizational unit structures, processes and fundamental formalized instruments; code of conduct)
	Of any intermediate unit (= team, department, etc.)	
	Of any elementary unit (= job)	
Strategic management (= management through normative regulations)	Of the overall unit (= entire organization)	Determining strategies of the unit for a certain period (i.e., market, production, and resource strategies)
	Of any intermediate unit (= team, department, etc.)	
	Of any elementary unit (= job)	
Operational management (= management through intervention)	Of the overall unit (= entire organization)	Steering (not executing!) day-to-day operations of the unit (incl. control and enforcement of compliance with constitutive/strategic norms)
	Of any intermediate unit (= team, department, etc.)	
	Of any elementary unit (= job)	

1.6 People Management as a Part of Management

As a theoretical construct, leadership and management of an organization cannot be the same as management and leadership of its personnel for the simple reason that there are issues in any organization that have nothing to do with employees. It thus appears logical that the latter is a subset of the former. However, delineating the two is a rather complex endeavor.

1.6.1 The Exceptional Position of Personnel Management

The systematic approach described above implies a special status for personnel management and leadership, which by its very nature is a hybrid of managing corporations and managing a specific resource. The business, i.e., the company as a whole, can only be run with the help of personnel (Ulrich 1968, p. 332 f.). In this respect, people management is elevated to the management of other resources. This is in no way intended to imply that managing and leading personnel is, in and of itself, more important than other organizational tasks. A transportation company without a truck is no better off than one without a driver; a lack of financial liquidity threatens bankruptcy; in many Internet companies, the quality of the algorithms and hardware is more critical to success than the quality of the personnel, etc. When personnel management is compared with sales or production tasks, it is even more difficult to assume any kind of dominance. All market, production, and resource functions are equally indispensable, and the market function (i.e., sales management in sales and marketing) is probably most important for any organization.

Nevertheless, leading and managing people has a special status in the corporate context (Kaehler 2017, pp. 53, 54; Grundei and Kaehler 2018; Kaehler and Grundei 2019, pp. 15–18). As the only of the corporate tasks, it is not only a part of the overall task bundle, but also the medium of all other activities. To build a car, one needs many kinds of resources; however, the process of manufacturing is not implemented by financial resources, construction plans, or materials, but by employees (or by machines operated/programmed by employees). Marketing and financing also requires the help of people. Since management and leadership involves not only the supply of employees, but also the steering of their work performance, it extends beyond the function of other resources. For example, although financing provides the means, e.g., advertising campaigns, the actual campaigns are the responsibility of marketing staff (who have to be led/managed). Therefore, the special significance of people management and leadership does not lie in the undisputed importance of the personnel, but in the fact that this personnel runs the actual business operations. It is only for this reason that personnel management in business administration and management theory is generally attributed to the elevated field of corporate management, i.e., business steerage, and not regarded merely, like the management of other resources, as a functional-technical task, i.e., as part of managed business operations.

In the canon of the three management fields, personnel management also occupies a special position because it represents the entire operational field. As such, it is subordinate to the other two fields—constitutive and strategic management—and involves the implementation of strategies by means of managing and leading people. Organizations achieve business goals only with the help of their employees. Thus, personnel management is to be understood as the very medium of corporate management and leadership. This systematic approach can even be maintained in the case of the solo entrepreneur, because self-leadership is also leadership. At least in the operational field, business is conducted by means of personnel management. Even activities that are ostensibly directed only at the person of the employee are ultimately aimed at maintaining business operations. In daily practice, every management activity fulfills both purposes at the same time (Drucker 1954, p. 16 f.). Personnel work is not an end in and of itself, but serves to operationally implement functional-technical stipulations and strategies (Ulrich 1968, p. 332 f.). There is no such thing as operational management and leadership (situational intervention in day-to-day business) that does not influence personnel.

1.6.2 Differentiation Between Managing People and Managing Functional-Technical Matters

By equating operational management and personnel management, a first step has already been taken in precisely delineating between corporate management, i.e., managing/leading an organization, and personnel management, i.e., managing/leading people. However, this is not the end of the matter because it would be clearly inaccurate to conclude that strategic and constitutive management does not include personnel management. It, therefore, remains to be analyzed which of their parts can be attributed to personnel management. The remainder would then be the functional-technical component of corporate management and leadership. Unfortunately, there is no elegant term for this in English (or German either), which could be one reason why hardly any serious attempts have been made in the literature to draw a distinction between the two. For lack of a better word, the somewhat bumpy term "management/leadership of functional-technical matters" is used here to denote the parts of corporate management/leadership that do not involve influence on personnel (see Kaehler and Grundei 2019, p. 32 ff.).

Established literature acknowledges at best the distinction between management tasks and functional-technical tasks, referring to managing business operations on the one hand, and to conducting these operations on the other (e.g., Gutenberg 1979, p. 243; Malik 2007, pp. 65, 90 ff.; Steinmann et al. 2013, p. 7 ff.). However, the execution of work tasks is not management at all. Advising customers, keeping accounts, and maintaining machines are systematically functional-technical tasks in which operations are conducted, not steered. In addition to their managerial responsibilities, managers also commonly take on some of these executional tasks, whether they assign them to themselves from the outset (e.g., attending to key customers), take them on in the event of a malfunction ("management by exception", see Sect. 2.4.1) or simply do not know how to delegate them ("retained work"). However, management and leadership is concerned with the transverse steerage of such business operations, not with their execution, so that the conventional differentiation misses the actual point.

In order to be able to precisely distinguish between the people and the non-people parts of management/leadership, the model introduced above must be further differentiated (Fig. 1.2). In the area of strategic tasks, for example, there are also recognizable elements of personnel management. Even though the focus here is on market, production and other resource strategies, there is also a need for personnel strategies. In the field of constitutive management, the situation is less clear-cut, but still similar. Here, the first issue is the establishment of corporate governance, defined as the internal and external behavior framework consisting of formalized norms for the direction and control of a corporation and its units (Grundei and Kaehler 2018, p. 589). A distinction must be made between HR governance and functional-technical governance, i.e., the regulations governing the management/leadership of personnel and the regulations governing the management/leadership of functional-technical matters. However, constitutive management also includes setting norms for the pure execution of work (i.e., conducting/performing it). Part of this, in turn, is functional work immanent to management—e.g., determining business areas and relevant stakeholders is not people management. The situation is different when it comes to organizational structures and procedures, codes of conduct, and formal and informal cultural values. These are clearly tools for people management and leadership because they serve to influence employees in the sense of our above-mentioned definition. However, they do not primarily regulate the way in which people are managed in an organizational unit. Instead, they involve norms for the way in which tasks are executed; they are therefore HR management norms, but not HR governance.

Hence, with a little goodwill and theory, it is quite possible to distinguish between the management/leadership of functional-technical matters and the management/ leadership of personnel. This distinction is important in two respects. If, like here, the aim is to explain and shape management and leadership in organizations with the help of theoretical models, it helps to define the subject area and to put its various elements in the right place. From a practical business perspective, it is also important to recognize that personnel work differs from functional-technical work. Leaders who diligently perfect their organizational unit's business model and functional business strategies, and themselves take on the functional tasks of their employees, may have the subjective impression that they are leading well. In reality, however, they neglect personnel management/leadership and thus an essential part of their activity, namely the entire operational management and the personnel-related parts of strategic and constitutive management (Table 1.7).

1.6.3   The Corporate Mission as a Point of Reference and Personnel as an Organizational Resource

The point of reference for all management must be the corporate mission or purpose of the company. This is one of the core messages of Peter F. Drucker, the great management thinker of old, who included this message in almost every one of his writings. It must lie outside the company, in service to the customer. In the case of business enterprises, this function consists of supplying the market with goods or services at prices that the customer is willing to pay (see Drucker 1954, p. 8, 1973, p. 77 ff.). "Customer value and competitiveness are the two . . . orientation variables for corporate management" (Malik 2007, p. 157; own translation). To understand how the corporate purpose and mission determine management and leadership activities, we can refer to the cascade model in Fig. 1.3. According to this model, constitutive management/leadership, which includes the definition of the company's mission and purpose, is translated into strategies through strategic management/ leadership, which in turn must be achieved through operational management/leadership. Only in relation to these three fields of corporate management and leadership, can the success of actor-specific management be defined (specifically for the line manager/leader: see Sect. 3.3).

The objective of management and leadership in organizations lies in the efficient production of work performance and the achievement of the organization's goals.

Table 1.7 Management of functional-technical matters vs. management of personnel (modified from Kaehler and Grundei 2019, p. 34; © Boris Kaehler and Jens Grundei 2019. All rights reserved.)

		Management of functional-technical matters	People management
Constitutive management (= management by normative governance regulations)	Of the overall unit (= entire organization); in part by concretizing superior norms	To stipulate the functional-technical framework of the unit (e.g., mission/vision, business model, stakeholders, tax model; functional-technical general management model; fundamental technical processes and instruments incl. control system) To stipulate the norms that regulate execution of work (i.e., conducting/performing it) (esp. organizational design/processes and codes of conduct)	To stipulate the people management framework of the unit (people management model/system; HR processes and instruments incl. control system; also incl. work processes and organizational units)
	Of any intermediate unit (= team, department, etc.); in part by concretizing superior norms		
	Of any elementary unit (= job); in part by concretizing superior norms		
Strategic management (= management by normative strategy regulations)	Of the overall unit (= entire organization); in part by concretizing superior norms	To stipulate the market strategies, production strategies, and non-human resources strategies (incl. infrastructural technical processes and instruments)	To stipulate the people management strategies
	Of any intermediate unit (= team, department etc.); in part by concretizing superior norms		
	Of any elementary unit (= job) Partly by concretizing superior norms		
Operational management (= management by intervention)	Of the overall unit (= entire organization); in part by concretizing superior norms	To steer (not execute!) day to day business by managing people (incl. control and enforcement of constitutive/strategic norm compliance)	
	Of any intermediate unit (= team, department, etc.); in part by concretizing superior norms		
	Of any elementary unit (= job); in part by concretizing superior norms		

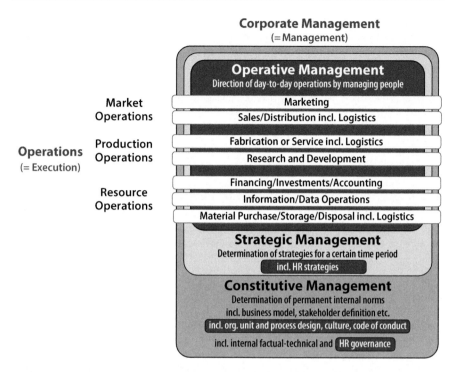

Fig. 1.3 People management parts of the three fields of management (modified from Kaehler and Grundei 2019, S. 33; © Boris Kaehler and Jens Grundei 2019. All rights reserved.)

Apart from a few exceptions, organizations do not maintain a workforce for its own sake, but as a resource to perform work in order to achieve the company's mission and purpose. This idea is expressed in terminology such as "human resource management", "human capital", "human assets", or "human potential". Anyone who wants to generate performance with the help of people—including himself or herself—must necessarily be able to view them soberly from such a resource perspective. This does not mean, of course, that he or she cannot independently value them as human beings from a different perspective. Think of the example of taking a taxi: The fact that the cab driver is perceived by the passenger in his professional capacity does not at all mean that there is contempt for human beings involved here, nor does it deny him his personal qualities as a friend, gamer, poet, or husband.[9]

In any case, the supposed sober view of people as resources is relativized by the dual character of human resources, which of course are not only resources but also human beings. Good management and leadership in organizations therefore necessarily requires both aspects to be considered (see Drucker 1954, p. 14). Just as other

---

[9]In this respect, the choice of the term "human capital" as the German "non-word of the Year 2004" (TU Darmstadt 2004) simply shows a lack of knowledge.

resources have specific characteristics which must be taken into account, people management and leadership cannot be carried out in a meaningful way without taking human needs and characteristics into account. Unfortunately, this self-evident fact is often ignored:

> "The engineer does not blame water for flowing downhill rather than up, nor gases for expanding rather than contracting when heated. However, when people respond to managerial decisions in undesired ways, the normal response is to blame them." (McGregor 1960, p. 12)

1.6.4 Context and Deliverables of People Management and Leadership

In Sect. 1.1.1, organizational people management, in the sense of managing the personnel of an organization or its subunits, was defined as an influence on employees with the aim of achieving the unit's objectives by generating work performance and meeting other requirements. Here, the work performance is undoubtedly in the foreground. It is important to consider both short-term performance in a given business period and long-term structural performance. It is quite easy to make employees work harder and more productively in the short term by putting them under a lot of pressure. In the long term, though, they can then be expected to resign or suffer health problems, which affects the human capital of the organization—defined as the performance, knowledge, and skills of the collective (CIPD 2021a)—and thus the value of the company. Therefore, good personnel management and leadership simultaneously optimizes short- and long-term job performance. Of course, there is no such thing as a free lunch in life. Personnel costs, especially in terms of compensation, training, and workplace equipment, are therefore also among the deliverables of personnel management. If costs were not an issue, it would be possible to buy in any amount of work through additional capacity and high cash incentives. However, the very nature of economics deals with scarce resources. Here too, a distinction must be made between short-term costs in the respective business period and the long-term cost structure. Reducing personnel costs is easy; it is not as easy to do so without demotivating and overworking employees resulting in negative effects on quality. For example, retaining and motivating staff today through the promise of high pensions will incur downstream costs in later years. Thus, good personnel management optimizes both short- and long-term personnel costs. A third deliverable comes from other factors. People management and leadership not only aims at performance and costs. This third point is not about the behavior and compliance of the managers or the satisfaction of the stakeholders with them, because these behavioral parameters are already included in the definition of performance used here (including not only work results, but also work input and work behavior). Rather, it is a question of additional requirements that the legislator and other stakeholders place on organizations. Recently, for example, there has been increasing pressure to raise the quota of women in

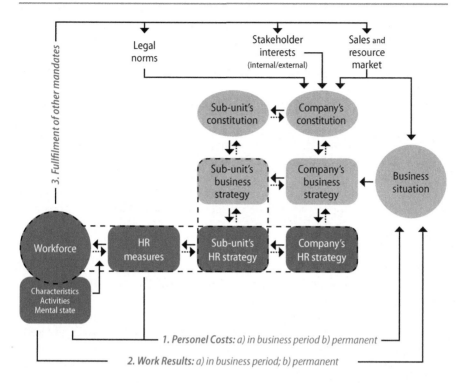

Fig. 1.4 Context and deliverables of HR management (modified from Kaehler 2017, S. 329; © Boris Kaehler 2019. All rights reserved.)

management positions for reasons of gender equality. As a consequence, this is being elevated to a goal of people management and leadership in many organizations, even without the anticipation of significant additional benefits or lower costs. In effect, good people management and leadership also fulfills relevant market, legal, and stakeholder requirements. Hence, its contributions, outcomes, or deliverables consist firstly of employees' short- and long-term work performance, secondly of short- and long-term personnel costs, and thirdly of the fulfillment of other requirements (Kaehler 2017, p. 329; Kaehler and Grundei 2019, pp. 37, 38). Figure 1.4 shows these three contributions toward success in context.

But the figure also shows the context of HR management from yet a different, broader perspective compared with Fig. 1.3 (see Kaehler 2017, p. 329; Kaehler and Grundei 2019, pp. 37, 38). It becomes clear how the market, legal situation, and stakeholders help shape the constitutive norms of the company, how these norms give rise to the strategies at the level of different units, and how these in turn determine the operation-related personnel measures. Also included in this is an essential basic insight into the nature of people management and leadership: The workforce (also: body of personnel, personnel portfolio, personnel factor, human resources) and its work are ultimately nothing more than the result of management and leadership, a "coagulated personnel policy" so to speak (this is the apt description of an unknown colleague). Just as the classic quotation puts it so well:

> "In the long run, every organization has the workforce it deserves." (Attributed to J. Paul Getty or W. Gilbey.)

1.7 Further Conceptual Pre-considerations with Regard to the Construction of Practical Theories

In addition to the definition and delineation of the leadership construct outlined above, a few more aspects have to be considered in order to construct a practical theory.

1.7.1 Process Model Overview of Theoretical Starting Points

Scholars have tried to describe the different aspects of people management and leadership based on numerous theories—Kellerman (2012, p. XXI) counts 40 leadership theories, Dinh et al. (2014, p. 40) distinguish over 60 thematic categories. These approaches are often categorized and systematized in literature (e.g., Yukl 2013; Blessin and Wick 2014; Lang and Rybnikova 2014; Northouse 2022). Occasionally, attempts have been made to integrate different leadership theories and empirical research findings into process models (Comelli and Rosenstiel 2009, p. 86; Antonakis et al. 2012, p. 647; Yukl 2013, p. 27; Rosenstiel 2014, p. 8; see also Blessin and Wick 2014, p. 36). Figure 1.5 ties in with these suggestions and is

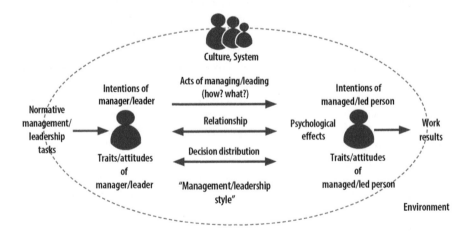

Fig. 1.5 Process model of organizational people management and leadership (modified from Kaehler 2014, p. 25; © Boris Kaehler 2019. All rights reserved.)

intended to provide an overview of the possible theoretical starting points. It is meant to describe the solution space of organizational leadership and management.

The process model presented here can serve as a frame of reference for the categorization of the various theories of leadership and people management described in the literature because almost all established theory models focus on one or a few connecting factors. Admittedly, the classification is sometimes arbitrary because the various aspects can neither be perfectly theoretically delineated from one another nor can all theories be unambiguously assigned. This problem, however, affects every categorization of models, and despite all of its shortcomings, the content-based classification does promise to provide some insights. The fact that the influence process has various aspects that can serve as theoretical starting points does not mean that useful leadership and management theories have to address and describe all these aspects. Depending on the question at hand, different theories always deal with only certain process elements and leave out others.

1.7.2 Too Unspecific: Style and Role

Some of the established theories deal with different leadership and management styles. What "style" exactly means varies completely depending on the model. For example, the classic continuum approach according to Tannenbaum and Schmidt (1958) addresses the freedom of decision-making that the manager gives the employee, with the boss-centered and the subordinated-centered leadership styles at either end of the continuum. Also widely cited in leadership literature is the distinction between the authoritarian style, democratic style, and laissez-faire style. This goes back to Lewin et al. (1939) who studied children and admittedly, like Tannenbaum and Schmidt, did not speak of "styles" at all. The two dual style models of employee orientation vs. task orientation, on the one hand, and transformational leadership vs. transactional leadership, on the other, have been particularly popular, repeatedly emphasized as a major achievement, and undergone empirical study (Steyrer and Meyer 2010). Other approaches to which the term style is applied include charismatic leadership and authentic leadership. Servant leadership and ethical leadership are also referred to by some as leadership styles. In the secondary literature, almost all theoretical approaches are actually occasionally referred to by the word "style."

Many models on leadership and management styles are based on two-dimensional diagrams, where the combination of the two values results in a particular style. Following this pattern, new style models and styles can be created at will (see, e.g., Kanengieter and Rajagopal-Durbin 2012). In any case, as shown above, the term style is understood in completely different ways and is not protected. In a brief survey, the German Association for Personnel Management (DGFP 2012; own translation) uses the following "pairs to define leadership styles": media-supported vs. face-to-face; personal vs. functional; setting pathways vs. setting goals; control-based vs. trust-based; determining vs. involving; rewarding vs. inspiring; company-oriented vs. employee-oriented. Thus, the established styles as well as any new styles are ultimately arbitrary, freely chosen aspects of the influence process and are therefore as reductionist as they are fuzzy. To avoid misunderstandings, theories and concepts of management and leadership had best avoid the term "style" (see Malik 2000, p. 75). It is also unsuitable as a starting point for categorizing existing approaches.

The concept of leadership "roles" is similar. According to the prevailing view, a role is understood to be the totality of expectations directed at a person as the holder of a position. It includes the person's own expectations as well as the expectations of all persons, groups, and institutions within and outside the organization. This is accompanied by different rational and emotional views of the person and the relationship as well as various role conflicts. The concept is borrowed from the world of theater, although the metaphor is misleading in that life roles do not follow a closed and manageable concept. Yet, rather than one ultimate role theory, there are different schools of role theory which can be roughly divided into structuralist, functionalist and symbolic-interactionist approaches (Neuberger 2002, pp. 313 ff; Blessin and Wick 2014, p. 153 ff; see also Stogdill 1950, p. 5; McGregor 1960, pp. 35, 88, 89; Wiswede 2004, p. 1289 ff; Meifert 2010, p. 30; Oelsnitz 2012, p. 54 ff; Nerdinger et al. 2014, p. 572 ff).

All this is very relevant and informative for understanding leadership processes. From a practical perspective, particular attention should be paid to the fact that the behavior of those involved in management and leadership can be effectively shaped by establishing normative institutional role expectations (see, e.g., Pietschmann et al. 1999, p. 506; Weibler 2014, p. 276). However, "role" is a very complex construct and thus it is not surprising that the term is used very differently in the context of different management and leadership theories. For example, Mintzberg's well-known role model (1973, p. 59, 1975; see Sect. 2.3.1) ultimately does not describe roles, but rather tasks in the sense of a goal (the role as a thing to be accomplished). Other approaches use the term "role" in the hierarchical sense of one person in relation to another (the role of the boss, the employee, or the colleague of person X). The term leadership or management "role" is thus hardly suitable for clearly designating certain aspects of the influence process; instead, it provokes misunderstandings. For this reason, it can be used neither to categorize established approaches nor as an element of new theories. Therefore, it will only be used below in the non-specific sense of a sum of positional expectations.

1.7.3 Corporate Models and Structures

Corporate leadership or management models are formalized norms that define why, by whom, and how a particular organization or organizational unit (including its personnel) is led/managed, in the sense of a metastructure or a leadership and management constitution within a concrete organization. Thus, the management/ leadership model is systematically the subject and part of the result of constitutive management. Synonymous terms of "model" are "principles" and "guidelines". Such a leadership/management model is partly HR governance and partly functional-technical governance, or, to put it another way, has people-related and non-people-related aspects. It should codify not only the activities of line managers, but those of all relevant leadership and management actors (see Kaehler and Grundei 2019, pp. 41, 42).

The corporate model of leadership and management model as a metastructure for the conceptualization of formalized regulations is concretized in related detailed regulations, which are referred to here by the term leadership/management infra-structure (in the sense of a substructure; Latin "infra" = under). This includes the organizational structure (i.e., the design of organizational units and their links), as well as all formalized personnel instruments (e.g., process and job descriptions, salary and working time systems, and interview guidelines), as well as regulations relating to the resources of the management/leadership actors and the activities they are expected to perform insofar as these are not already specified in the unit design. The model and the infrastructure together make up the management/leadership structures in the sense of the governance of an organization or organizational unit, i.e. formalized rules for managing and leading the functional business and the personnel. They are to be distinguished from the rules on the way a task is executed, both the formalized ones (especially process organization and codes of conduct) and the potentially informal ones (especially cultural standards). As an alternative to the term "management/leadership structures", the terms "management/leadership archi-tecture" or (in relation to people) "HR architecture" are suitable, but these are used very inconsistently in the literature (see Ulrich et al. 2009, p. 56; Huselid and Becker 2011; Birri and Lebrenz 2013, p. 37 f.; Lebrenz 2017, p. 86). Ideally, organizations should have codified management/leadership structures that consistently bring together all the behavioral prescriptions (and, conversely, behavioral freedoms) that apply to leadership and management. In practice, this is often not the case so that, in effect, the structures consist of a multitude of decentralized fragments.

1.7.4 Theory Building in the Field of Management and Leadership

Anyone who discusses management and leadership in organizations does so on the basis of theoretical assumptions. These assumptions do not have to be explicit; implicit leadership theories also shape thinking and action (see, e.g., Neuberger 2002, p. 394 ff.; Yukl 2013, p. 233; Epitropaki et al. 2013; Junker and van Dick 2014). The protagonists need not even know that they are theorizing when they explain and shape their own actions and those of others through their "theories-in-use" (see Argyris 1982, 1994). These are often premature theories that are discarded as soon as the actors become aware of them. When dealing with questions of organizational leadership and management, it is therefore advisable to keep the theoretical point of reference in view as a vanishing point, so to speak (see Titscher et al. 2010, p. 21). The theoretical-normative assumptions underlying a manage-ment/leadership model should thus be disclosed so that they can be criticized and empirically scrutinized (see Neuberger 2002, p. 394).

Theories can be understood as bundles of causal hypotheses or regularities that explain the relative importance of different variables for a dependent variable. They have the function of describing, explaining, and predicting facts. Their validity depends on how well the theoretically condensed hypotheses prove themselves in reality or on the basis of empirical data. In contrast to scientific theories, many social science theories are rather vaguely formulated; here, too, the aim should be to specify and formalize the statements made. Good theories should a) be logically consistent, i.e., free of contradictions; b) be substantial or informative and thus falsifiable; c) satisfy the principle of parsimony, i.e., explain as many findings as possible with as few assumptions as possible; and d) have proven themselves, i.e., have been successfully tested (Bortz and Döring 2006, pp. 15, 363).

Corporate models of leadership and management therefore always contain theoretical assumptions. This theoretical core can come about in very different ways. For example, Google's leadership model—in the tradition of many US studies—results from an empirical survey and internal generalization of success-relevant behaviors of particularly effective Google executives (Garvin 2013; see also Bock 2015, p. 189 ff.; Harrell and Barbato 2018). Other approaches emphasize the participatory element and have members of an organization use a series of interviews and workshops to determine, each in their own way, what constitutes desirable leadership (see, e.g., Kim and Mauborgne 2014). However, there are methodological weaknesses to such approaches: The entire solution space of optimal models can never be extracted from what exists or what is desired. It, therefore, makes sense to base operational models on scientific theories. However, almost all established leadership and management theories are either unconvincing in terms of content or very limited in their focus (see Kaehler 2020, p. 92 ff., and the exemplary boxes in Chap. 2), which in any case partially devalues the respective empirical findings. Moreover, each of them covers only small areas of the relevant solution space. With this in mind, even proven experts find it difficult to develop well-founded and feasible corporate models from the existing theories.

There is accordingly a definite need for a specific theory model from which corporate leadership and management models can be derived. The actual formation of such theories is preceded by exploration, i.e., a more or less systematic collection of information about the object of investigation. Four approaches are possible: theory-based exploration, method-based exploration, empirical-quantitative exploration, and empirical-qualitative exploration (Bortz and Döring 2006, pp. 354, 358). The path taken here consists of theory-based exploration. In the—quite rare—ideal case, it is possible to integrate the explanatory content of different theories in a conclusive way (Bortz and Döring 2006, pp. 358 ff., 362). However, it is certainly not enough to simply review theoretical and empirical literature and combine existing theoretical approaches in order to develop a holistic and practical model of corporate leadership and management. In view of the incomplete theoretical landscape, it is much more important to draw on practical observations and conceptual ideas and to condense all of this into a consistent network of theoretical assumptions (see Neuberger 2002, p. 393 ff.).

Unfortunately, all too many practitioners have become accustomed to the fact that management and leadership in the literature and at seminars is coated with a theatrical fog of intricacy and myth, but is then actually presented in a less functionally differentiated way than the simplest activities of daily life. This may be the root cause of many of the ills that widely characterize the theory and practice of organizational leadership and management. Consider the theoretical complexity of making coffee or driving a car: how many elements could these activities be broken down into? Expecting to cover a useful theoretical or corporate leadership or management model in a few sentences and for it be instantly comprehensible is as unrealistic as explaining how to drive a car in a similar way. As Albert Einstein (1934) urged us, the primary goal of all theory must be to describe the individual elements as simply and reductively as possible without sacrificing the adequate representation of individual experiential data. In the case of personnel management, this undoubtedly requires details. Therefore, an open commitment to theoretical complexity is called for in the scientific field. In practice, companies should not devalue their corporate models by hastily resorting to simplistic models for the sake of convenience. Provided that they are presented in a well-thought-out, professional manner, models of an appropriate complexity can indeed be communicated. There is neither need nor justification for oversimplification.

1.7.5 On the Normativity of Theoretical Models

Anyone who wants to lead/manage themselves or others must know what it consists of in the first place. Organizations should therefore ensure that all members of the organization have a common understanding of management and leadership (see Malik 2007, p. 243). This is done with the help of corporate models, guidelines, or principles that make normative statements about leadership and management. The principle here is nothing other than the setting of corporate norms, i.e., part of constitutive management. If management and leadership is interpreted as a service, such leadership regulations may also be understood as "production instructions" and "quality promises" with regard to this service (Albach 1977, p. 207). In addition, they provide an orientation framework for the organization's members, specify role expectations, and offer a closed conceptual system that facilitates communication about management and leadership issues (Knebel and Schneider 1994, p. 19 f.; Pietschmann et al. 1999). A statement about Google's leadership model expresses this well:

> "The list of behaviors has served three important functions at Google: giving employees a shared vocabulary for discussing management, offering them straightforward guidelines for improving it, and encapsulating the full range of management responsibilities." (Garvin 2013, S. 77 f.)

By establishing a corporate management and leadership model, companies are ultimately doing nothing other than organizing on a higher normative level, i.e., creating permanent rules and structures for operational processes. On closer examination, it is indeed not at all clear why the same rules and processes should not be required in the area of management and leadership as they are in all other organizational fields. Anyone who foregoes behavioral stipulations in this area accepts—just like everywhere else—that the people involved have to form and negotiate mutual behavioral expectations over and over again. Conversely, those who define clear requirements thus pre-structure the roles of those who lead/manage and those who are led/managed to a certain extent and enable them to refer to them. Malik (2000, p. 46 f.) speaks of "constitutional thought" by which he means, among other things, that leadership in an organization should not depend on the whims and skills of individuals, but should be a function of consciously chosen norms:

> "... managers are not found, managers are made, trained, and molded; and an organizational context – a constitutional framework – is created in which correct action is promoted, rewarded and – if all else fails – enforced. The key question of the constitutional approach is [...] What is correct management?" (Malik 2000, p. 48)

In fact, a general principle of any form of organizing is that one must neither start at the wrong point nor choose the wrong degree of regulation. Also, if management rules are to have a truly normative effect, they must be concrete and comprehensible, on the one hand, and actually implemented on the other. This is how it should look in terms of form and from a labor law perspective: The employer enforces defined management/leadership behavior through clear instructions, supplemented by appropriate behavioral controls. Formulated in such a firm and candid way, it immediately becomes clear that leadership standards can only be sensibly applied to those aspects that (a) should not remain individually and situationally variable, (b) can be meaningfully concretized, and (c) can actually be enforced.

While most companies today already have explicit management/leadership models, guidelines, or principles, it is extremely rare for them to be made of such concrete norms that those involved in management and leadership really know exactly what their jobs are. In this case, it is up to the individual to decide for himself or herself what leadership and management means. These individual ideas give rise to a wide variety of role expectations, which creates friction and usually misses the actual needs by miles. Of course, leadership requirements inevitably come into play in leadership selection, development, and assessment and exist in any organization. Quite often, however, these factual criteria are not an expression of a common understanding in the organization as a whole, but only of the individual ideas of the HR specialists, trainers, and consultants involved. As a result, organizations frequently develop a very inconsistent understanding of leadership and management. This is unsatisfactory because, where several actors interact, they also need a common understanding of this interaction.

While corporate management and leadership models are by definition always normative, scientific leadership theories can have a purely descriptive character and be limited to describing and explaining reality. However, they can also make a normative or prescriptive claim insofar as management and leadership in practice is to be shaped according to the specifications of the theory. The two perspectives are not mutually exclusive (Yukl 2013, p. 35). In practice, there is a great need for well-founded and implementable recommendations and corresponding models. Those who undertake to develop such models should stand by them—Malik (2007, p. 62; own translation) aptly speaks of the "courage for the normative." Although it is argued, particularly in the "systemic" literature, that there are no generally applicable rules for successful management and leadership (see, e.g., Oelsnitz 2012, p. 77), the vast majority of established theories are clearly normative in the sense that they not only explain and describe the influence process, but also provide explicit recommendations for functioning leadership and management. If such normativity makes the claim of being broadly or even generally applicable, the theoretical elements must be generalizable and leave sufficient room for cultural, organizational, personal, and situational differences. Whether or not the claim is justifiably made should be the subject of empirical testing. Ultimately, the decisive question is to what extent the normative recommendations can actually be implemented and contribute to improving the quality of management and leadership in organizations.

1.7.6   Complementarity of Structure and Behavioral Latitude

In casting technology, the term "mold" refers to the negative matrix from which the positive relief to be cast is derived. In precisely this sense, the organizational rules also automatically result in the behavioral latitude. The regulations of the corporate management structures thus determine at which points the actors have to adhere to fixed directives and which aspects are to be handled individually or situationally (a general principle of organizing, see Gutenberg 1962, pp. 44, 45). Of course, only the actual practiced reality is relevant here, in other words, the part of the leadership and management model and infrastructure that is actually implemented by the actors. Like the casting matrix, the leadership model has no raison d'être in and of itself, but only serves to shape the actual object—in this case, the free, individual and situational behavior of the actors in everyday management and leadership—and to steer it in the right direction. Just as a mold that is deformed cannot shape a functionally designed object, a model that regulates the wrong aspects of influencing behavior cannot bring about good leadership and management. And as useless as a completely flat matrix would be, so would be the attempt to regulate all aspects of leadership action, since this can never result in authentic and situationally appropriate behavior. The regulatory freedom provided by a leadership and management model must therefore be considered to the same degree as its regulations.

The goal of responsible norm-setting is not to achieve a maximum degree of regulation; on the contrary, it is to grant maximum room for maneuver and degree of freedom while, at the same time, guaranteeing the system's ability to function. To use another fitting metaphor: Staves and notes are important, but they are not the music. In management, no one has understood and implemented this principle better than Peter F. Drucker. His management technique "management by objectives and self-control," which focuses on work objectives and leaves the path to these objectives up to those who are being managed, is what he himself called "freedom within the law" and "management philosophy" (Drucker 1954, p. 135 f.). Normative requirements, including those of a corporate kind, inevitably interfere with human freedoms, and these interferences weigh all the more heavily the more personal the standardized circumstances are. Individual idiosyncrasies, emotional states, and situational preferences for action should therefore only be regulated if this is essential. That is simply not the case in the area of normal organizational management and leadership work, where there is room for a great diversity of personalities and ways of acting. Only extreme aberrations need to be prevented by systematically selecting personnel and providing clear rules of conduct.

Micro-politics is using other people to pursue one's own interests in organizational zones of uncertainty (Neuberger 2006, p. 18; for alternative definitions, see supplementary material to Blessin and Wick 2014, p. 442). Micro-political maneuvering—arguing, negotiating, persuading, seducing, deceiving, making pacts, threatening, etc.—thus fills a space created by under-organization; the free play of forces replaces formalized rules. This is by no means inherently bad, but rather fulfills an important dynamizing function in organizations (Neuberger 2002, p. 689 ff.; Blessin and Wick 2014, p. 443 ff.), which will be examined in more detail from the perspective of the line manager in Sect. 3.2. Organizational management and leadership on this basis alone, however, is a misguided approach. Where corporate models remain so abstract and general that no concrete rights and duties can be derived from them, micro-politics will run wild. In this case, all actors must and will resort to political power tactics in order to concretize management and leadership in their favor. This must be limited by clear regulations and structures, although there is always a certain amount of room for interpretation and thus a residual need for micro-politics.

The words "regulation", "rules", and "structure" are likely to give some readers the impression of a certain backwardness, as we hear everywhere about the triumph of lean hierarchies, the abolition of organizational rules, and the advantages of agile flexibility. Indeed, it is currently fashionable once again to hold up as role models companies that informalize their management structures in extreme ways (e.g., Netflix, see Hastings 2009; McCord 2014; Netflix 2018 or Spotify, see Ramge 2015) and/or dispense with management positions entirely or to a large extent (e.g., Semco, see Semler 1989, Johnsonville Sausage, see Stayer 1990, or Morning Star, see Hamel 2011; Haas 2015). Underlying this are two fundamental misconceptions. The first is the assumption that, in principle, the abolition of rules increases effectiveness. But this is not the case:

> "Yes, you might be amazed, but hierarchy is structure that enables trust. You can expect a certain behavior and don't have to permanently fight for your position." (Sprenger 2008, p. 91; own translation)

The good old guiding principle of over- and under-organization applies (Kosiol 1962, p. 29 f.): Too few permanent rules are just as inefficient as too many. Supposedly general unbureaucratic clauses like the Netflix maxims "Avoid rules" and "Act in the company's best interest!" (see McCord 2014, p. 56; Netflix 2018) ultimately only mean that downstream entities have to think about each individual case. But this results in less effectiveness and efficiency, not more.

The second misunderstanding lies in the assumption that where no regulations have been made, there are no structures. This is obviously not the case either; rather, norms are also built informally, e.g., through micropolitically negotiated solutions and cultural pattern formation (see already Stogdill 1950, p. 5). In this way, however, the structures simply shift into the realm of the internal shadow economy; they are not eliminated, just ignored. Thus, those who have not defined any hierarchies or responsibilities, who have not laid down any rules of conduct or made any other determinations, leave it to chance or to the free play of forces to form such structures. In the area of leadership and management, such informally emerging structures and organizational cultures are often dysfunctional. Moreover, they generally have large regulatory gaps that run counter to a common understanding and encourage individual misconduct. Furthermore, the supposedly shining examples of lean or flexible management structures almost always originate either from microenterprises (often with a consulting business linked to the organizational forms practiced) or from the US-American legal sphere. European labor law and the local regulatory framework of large companies do not permit many of these lauded concepts—for good reason. Very rightly, Julian Birkinshaw of the London Business School notes:

> "A simple law then applies: above a certain size, structures and rules are needed. [. . .] Structures make life easier, even if some people don't like to hear it." (quoted from Malcher 2015, p. 56 f.; own translation)

It is, therefore, easy to see that the secret of effective and efficient management structures lies not in the complete abolition of rules and regulations, but in the astute determination of the degree of regulation required.

1.7.7   Focus on the Team or on the Employee?

Theories of people management and leadership can be distinguished according to their level of conceptualization. This is based on their point of reference, i.e., the question of whether the influence is described as an intraindividual process, a dyadic process, a group process, or an organizational process. Which level a theory focuses on depends in particular on the respective research interest as well as on what is understood by process outcomes and on which mediating influence processes are targeted (Yukl 2013, p. 30 ff.; see also Dionne et al. 2014). Multilevel theories include constructs at more than one conceptual level. For example, cause and effect relationships between variables on the same level can be examined, but moderator variables on a different level can be included. More complex theories also address cause and effect relationships between multiple levels. By their nature, multilevel theories are less reductionist and have greater explanatory value than single-level theories, but at the same time they are more difficult to test empirically. In leadership research, multilevel theories have risen in importance (Yukl 2013, p. 34; see also Dionne et al. 2014).

Anyone who wants to examine and understand management and leadership scientifically is generally well-advised to include different conceptual levels. After all, it is a matter of supplementary perspectives, each of which addresses important cause and effect relationships. However, multilevel approaches are even more relevant with regard to the practical question of which structures are meaningful and necessary in order to effectively shape management and leadership in organizations. The conceptual levels at which this is done are of fundamental importance. It is too simplistic to define management and leadership only as the exertion of influence on entire organizations and teams and to exclude the individual effects of this influence, as has long been done in leadership research (see Stogdill 1950, pp. 4, 11 ff.). After all, behavior is primarily individual behavior, and to ignore individual phenomena is to exclude the most important conceptual levels, namely the intraindividual (self-leadership) and the dyadic (leader/employee). This is accompanied by an enormous loss of insight and design possibilities.

Another misleading approach is the seemingly pragmatic quadruple tone of "leading/managing organizations," "leading/managing teams," "leading/managing employees," and "leading/managing oneself" contained in many practice-oriented models. This is because it is almost always associated with the claim of defining delimited task bundles at each of these levels. First of all, it does not make sense to conceptually separate out the level of the overall organization. Management takes place at the level of each organizational unit (Sect. 1.5.2), and management models should therefore describe it in such a way that the elements apply simultaneously to the overall organization as well as to each individual organizational unit. Theories and concepts of management and leadership, therefore, do not need to distinguish between different levels of structure ("leading organizations" vs. "leading organizational units") in terms of content. However, the levels do play a role in practical implementation because leading an organizational unit always includes leading all subunits. The quartet "managing companies – managing teams – managing employee positions – managing one's own position" therefore only makes sense insofar as it shows which levels are to be managed simultaneously.

As far as the management and leadership of individuals is concerned, the decisive conceptual level should be the individual because good management and leadership is measured by whether each individual employee is optimally led. Of course, this leadership influence on the individual inevitably has a collective character: Not only the line manager, but also other leadership actors influence the behavior of the individual employees in a goal-oriented manner. A distinction may be made between management activities involving one person (employee dialogs) and those conducted in a group (team meetings), but this is only a superficial categorization and says nothing about the actual tasks. In these tasks—e.g., defining work assignments, solving conflicts, and creating motivation—the levels of the individual and the team overlap. This is because people seldom work alone, and individual work therefore generally also includes aspects of cooperation. In order to capture this in a conceptual and theoretical way, however, structuring based on the four levels of organization/team/employee/self is likewise impractical.

When depicting the collective nature of people management and leadership, it is by no means necessary to focus primarily on the team level. Rather, everything that concerns the cooperation of the team can also be understood as the individual framework of action of the individual employee. Task theories of leadership and management describe this in terms of the leadership tasks to be performed (Sect. 2. 3.1). Here, the task canon can be conceptualized in such a way that the canon of leadership tasks is performed in relation to each individual employee, but also includes tasks that involve aspects of the employee's cooperation with others (e.g., resolving conflicts, coordinating with others, setting social incentives or creating identification with the collective). In this way, the team level is indirectly included even if the actual conceptual reference point of the management and leadership tasks is the individual. On the other hand, these tasks do not have to be understood as tasks of line managers, but can and should be conceived as a collective influence. The management tasks are then performed jointly by different actors, including the employee as a self-leader/self-manager, according to certain distributive mechanisms. This is a cross-hierarchical process that may be traced dyad by dyad, but cannot be assigned to a specific conceptual level. Such a multilevel conception, which integrates an intraindividual, multiple dyadic, group-related, and organization-related focus, is the basis of the Complementary Leadership Model (see Sect. 2.1.2).

1.8 Summary

Any study on management and leadership must begin with a clear definition. *Organizational management*, in the sense of managing an organization or its subunits, can be defined as a steering influence on market, production, and/or resource operations that may address both people and non-people issues with the aim of achieving the unit's objectives. *Organizational people management*, in the sense of managing the personnel of an organization or its subunits, is an influence on employees with the aim of achieving the unit's objectives by generating work performance and meeting other requirements. To manage a unit or its members is synonymous with *leading* them.

Management and leadership influence can be exercised in two ways: through anticipatory norm-setting or through situational intervention. Both forms can be exercised in hard, externally directed ways or in gentle, non-directive ways. Since hard external influence usually triggers resistance, it is advisable to primarily exert influence in a gentle manner (e.g., in the form of systematic self-direction, instrumental behavioral reinforcement, nudging, collective social norms, or implicit communication).

Organizational leadership, i.e., being a leader in highly structured contexts, must be distinguished from political leadership, i.e., being a leader in poorly structured contexts, even though many sources narrow it down to just that. In contrast, people management/leadership, employee management/leadership, and human resource management are one and the same. Of course, certain aspects of management and leadership are usually assigned to the HR department and others to line managers. However, these are not separate spheres, but rather a division of labor in dealing with a single mandate, namely leadership and management of personnel. A number of other conventional demarcations are also discarded here, namely the four dualities of "leadership vs. direction/headship", "functional-technical vs. disciplinary leadership", and "leadership vs. management". The possible theoretical–conceptual starting points have been presented in the form of a process model (Fig. 1.5). The deliverables of people management and leadership consist firstly of the short- and long-term work performance of employees, secondly of short- and long-term personnel costs, and thirdly of the fulfillment of other requirements made by the market, the legal situation, and the stakeholders. Figure 1.4 shows this relationship.

Personnel management is part of management. As a cross-sectional function, the latter is concerned with the steerage of an organization's business operations. The point of reference here is not the manager or the managed, but the organizational unit. In hierarchically structured companies, the units are nested within each other starting with the overall organization down through its divisions/departments/teams, to the job as the smallest organizational unit. Management consists of three task areas to be performed at the level of each individual organizational unit: constitutive, strategic, and operational management/leadership. Operational management/leadership follows the respective strategic and constitutive norms, regardless of whether these are well or poorly chosen and whether they are explicit or implicit in nature. In terms of content, operational management consists of nothing other than people management, because the latter involves the operative implementation of norms and strategies by means of influencing employees. Everything that happens in a company is brought about by people, so business operations can only be exercised through the leadership and management of personnel. To build a car, you need many kinds of resources; however, the process of manufacturing is not carried out by financial resources, blueprints, or materials, but by employees (or machines operated/programmed by employees). Marketing or financing, etc., require the help of people. This results in a special status of people management/leadership within the management construct, because it not only means steering an important corporate resource (the staff), it also represents the medium for all other activities. By its nature, this operational influence is pure situational intervention and pure people management/leadership. In contrast, constitutive and strategic management/leadership are purely anticipatory norm-setting and have functional-technical components as well as personnel-related components. These relationships are illustrated in Fig. 1.3.

In the preliminary stages of constructing a new theory of management and leadership, some further conceptual considerations must also be made. These concern, among other things, the relationship between scientific management/leadership theories and corporate management/leadership models as well as their complexity and normativity. Every corporate management/leadership model—understood as a constitution of management and leadership in a concrete organization—is based on at least implicit theoretical assumptions that should be made transparent. Such corporate models are part of constitutive management/leadership. They serve to establish a uniform understanding of leadership and management within the organization and are by definition always normative. Most scientific theories of leadership and management are also clearly normative in the sense that they not only explain and describe the influence process, but also establish explicit guidelines. Practice-oriented theories should not only consider the manager–employee dyad or the team level, but should encompass several conceptual levels, whereby a traditional-schematic approach does not necessarily have to be chosen.

References

Albach, Horst (1977): Mitarbeiterführung – Text und Fälle; Gabler 1977.

Antonakis, John/Day, David V./Schyns, Birgit (2012): Leadership and individual differences: At the cusp of a renaissance; The Leadership Quarterly 2012 (23); pp. 643–650.

Argyris, Chris (1982): Reasoning, Learning, and Action – Individual and Organizational; Jossey-Bass 1982.

Argyris, Chris (1994): Initiating Change that Perseveres; Journal of Public Administration Research and Theory 3/1994 (4); pp. 343–355.

Armutat, Sascha (2012): Elemente, Zusammenhänge und Formen internationaler HR-Governance-Strukturen; in DGFP Deutsche Gesellschaft für Personalführung e. V. (ed.): Internationales Personalmanagement gestalten – Perspektiven, Strukturen, Erfolgsfaktoren, Praxisbeispiele; DGFP-PraxisEdition Band 103; 2012, pp. 25–50.

Bennis, Warren G./Nanus, Burt (1985): Leaders; 2nd edition HarperCollins 2007.

Birri, Raimund/Lebrenz, Christian (2013): Wege aus der Sackgasse; Personalwirtschaft 2/2013; pp. 36–39.

Bleicher, Knut (1991): Das Konzept Integriertes Management; Campus 1991.

Bleicher, Knut (1994): Normatives Management – Politik, Verfassung und Philosophie des Unternehmens; Campus 1994.

Bleicher, Knut (2011): Normatives Management – Politik, Verfassung und Philosophie des Unternehmens; Campus 2011.

Blessin, Bernd/Wick, Alexander (2014): Führen und Führen lassen; 7th edition UVK/Lucius/UTB 2014.

Bock, Laszlo (2015): Work Rules – Insights from Inside Google That Will Transform How You Live and Lead; John Murray Publishers 2015.

Boddy, David (2017): Management – An Introduction; 7th edition Pearson Education 2017.

Bortz, Jürgen/Döring, Nicola (2006): Forschungsmethoden und Evaluation für Human- und Sozialwissenschaftler; 4th edition Springer 2006.

CIPD Chartered Institute of Personnel and Development (2021a): Strategic human resource management (CIPD-Factsheet); http://www.cipd.co.uk/hr-resources/factsheets/strategic-human-resource-management.aspx (Accessed 01/05, 2022).

CIPD Chartered Institute of Personnel and Development (2021b): Line managers' role in supporting the people profession (CIPD-Factsheet); http://www.cipd.co.uk/hr-resources/factsheets/role-line-managers-hr.aspx (Accessed 1/6/2022).

Comelli, Gerhard/Rosenstiel, Lutz von (2009): Führen durch Motivation, 4th edition Vahlen 2009.

DGFP Deutsche Gesellschaft für Personalführung e. V. (2012): DGFP-Kurzumfrage Führungskräfteentwicklung; https://www.dgfp.de/mediathek/publikationen/ (Accessed 01/05, 2022).

Dinh, Jessica E./Lord, Robert G./Gardner, William L./Meuser, Jeremy D./Liden, Robert C./Hu, Jinyu (2014): Leadership theory and research in the new millennium: Current theoretical trends and changing perspectives; The Leadership Quarterly 2014 (25); pp. 36–62.

Dionne, Shelley D./Gupta, Alka/Sotak, Kristin Lee/Shirreffs, Kristie A./Serban, Andra/Hao, Chanyu/Kim, Dong Ha/Yammarino, Francis J. (2014): A 25-year perspective on levels of analysis in leadership research; The Leadership Quarterly 2014 (25); pp. 6–35.

Drucker, Peter F. (1954): The Practice of Management; new edition Harper Collins 2006 (first edition 1954).

Drucker, Peter F. (1973): Management – Tasks, Responsibilities, Practices; new edition Harper Business 1993 (first edition 1973).

Drucker, Peter F. (1988): Managing for the Future; Butterworth Heinemann 1993 (chapter 15 dated 1988).

Drucker, Peter F. (1998): Peter Drucker on the Profession of Management – A Harvard Business Review Book; Harvard Business Press 1998.

Einstein, Albert (1934): On the Method of Theoretical Physics; Philosophy of Science April 1934 (1); pp. 163–169.

Epitropaki, Olga/Sy, Thomas/Martin, Robin/Tram-Quon, Susanna/Topakas, Anna (2013): Implicit Leadership and Followership Theories in the wild: Taking stock of information-processing approaches to leadership and followership in organizational settings; The Leadership Quarterly 2013 (24); pp. 858–881.

Fayol, H. (1916). General and industrial management (English edition 1949). London: Sir Isaac Pitman & Sons Ltd (first published in French in bulletin de la sociéte de l'industrie minérale 1916).

Freibichler, Wolfgang/Ebert, Philip/Schubert, Tilman (2018): Nudge Management – Wie Führungskräfte kluges Selbstmanagement anstoßen; zfo 2/2017; pp. 84–88.

Garvin, David A. (2013): How Google Sold Its Engineers on Management; Harvard Business Review December 2013; pp. 75–82.

Gibb, Cecil A. (1954): Leadership; in Gardner, Lindzey: Handbook of Social Psychology: Volume II Special Fields and Applications; Addison-Wesley 1954; pp. 877–919.

Grundei, Jens/Kaehler, Boris (2018): Corporate Governance: Zur Notwendigkeit einer Konturschärfung und betriebswirtschaftlichen Erweiterung des Begriffsverständnisses, Der Betrieb 11/2018; pp. 585–592.

Gulati, Ranjay/Mayo, Anthony J./Nohria, Nitin (2017): Management – An Integrated Approach; 2nd edition; Boston: Cengage Learning.

Gutenberg, Erich (1962): Unternehmensführung – Organisation und Entscheidungen; Gabler 1962.

Gutenberg, Erich (1979): Grundlagen der Betriebswirtschaftslehre – Erster Band: Die Produktion; 23rd edition Springer.

Haas, Oliver (2015): Wenn andere Spielregeln gelten (Interview mit Paul Green Jr.); Organisationsentwicklung 1/2015; pp. 30–34.

Hamel, Gary (2011): First, Lets Fire All the Managers; Harvard Business Review December 2011; pp. 48–60.

Harrell, Melissa/Barbato, Lauren (2018): Great managers still matter: the evolution of Google's Project Oxygen; https://rework.withgoogle.com/blog/the-evolution-of-project-oxygen/ (Accessed 01/05, 2022).

Hastings, Reed (2009): Netflix Culture: Freedom & Responsibility (Folienpräsentation); http://de.slideshare.net/reed2001/culture-1798664 (Accessed 1/6/2022).

Hunt, James G. (1991): Leadership – A New Synthesis; Newbury Park: Sage.

Huselid, Mark A./Becker, Brian E. (2011): Bridging Micro and Macro Domains: Workforce Differentiation and Strategic Human Resource Management; Journal of Management 2011 (37); pp. 421–428.

Jung, Rüdiger H./Bruck, Jürgen/Quarg, Sabine (2008): Allgemeine Managementlehre – Lehrbuch für die angewandte Unternehmens- und Personalführung; 3rd edition Erich Schmidt Verlag 2008.

Junker, Nina Mareen/van Dick, Rolf (2014): Implicit theories in organizational settings: A systematic review and research agenda of implicit leadership and followership theories; The Leadership Quarterly 2014 (25); pp. 1154–1173.

Kaehler, Boris (2014): Komplementäre Führung – Ein praxiserprobtes Modell der organisationalen Führung; 1st edition Springer Gabler 2014.

Kaehler, Boris (2017): Komplementäre Führung – Ein praxiserprobtes Modell der Personalführung in Organisationen; 2nd edition Springer Gabler 2017.

Kaehler, Boris (2019): Führen als Beruf – Andere erfolgreich machen; 1st edition Tredition 2019.

Kaehler, Boris (2020): Komplementäre Führung – Ein praxiserprobtes Modell der Personalführung in Organisationen; 3rd edition Springer Gabler 2020.

Kaehler, Boris/Grundei, Jens (2018): HR-Governance im Führungs-Kontext: Der normative Rahmen des Personalmanagements; ZCG Zeitschrift für Corporate Governance 5/2018, pp. 205–210.

Kaehler, Boris/Grundei, Jens (2019): HR Governance – A Theoretical Introduction; Springer 2019.

Kanengieter, John/Rajagopal-Durbin, Aparna (2012): Wilderness Leadership – On the Job; Harvard Business Review April 2012; pp. 127–131.

Kellerman, Barbara (2012): The End of Leadership; HarperCollins 2012.

Kerr, Steven/Jermier, John M. (1978) Substitutes for Leadership – Their Meaning and Measurement; Organizational Behavior and Human Performance 22, pp. 375–403.

Kerr, Steven/Jermier, John M. (1997) Substitutes for Leadership: Their Meaning and Measurement – Contextual Recollections and Current Observations; Leadership Quarterly 2 (8), pp. 95–101.

Kim, Chan/Mauborgne, Renée (2014): Blue Ocean Leadeship; Harvard Business Review 5/2014; pp. 60–72.

Knebel, Heinz/Schneider, Helmut (1994): Führungsgrundsätze – Leitlinien für die Einführung und praktische Umsetzung; 2nd edition Sauer-Verlag 1994.

Korff, Ernst (1971): Leiten und Führen – Profil und Funktionen des leitenden Angestellten; 2nd edition Sauer-Verlag 1971.

Kosiol, Erich (1962): Organisation der Unternehmung; Gabler 1962.

Kotter, John P. (1990a): A Force for Change – How Leadership Differs from Management; The Free Press 1990.

Kotter, John P. (1990b): What Leaders Really Do; Harvard Business Review May/June 1990; pp. 103–111.

Lang, Rainhart/Rybnikova, Irma (2014): Aktuelle Führungstheorien und -konzepte; Springer Gabler 2014.

Lebrenz, Christian (2017): Strategie und Personalmanagement – Konzepte und Instrumente zur Umsetzung im Unternehmen; Springer Gabler 2017.

Lewin, Kurt/Lippitt, Ronald/White, Ralph K. (1939): Patterns of aggressive behavior in experimentally created social climates; The Journal of Social Psychology May 1939 (10); pp. 271–299.

Lord, Robert G./Maher, Karen J. (1991): Leadership and Information Processing – Linking Perceptions and Performance. Volume 1 People and Organizations. Boston: Unwin Hyman.

Malcher, Ingo (2015): Die Dinosaurier leben noch (Interview mit Julain Birkinshaw); Brand Eins 3/2015; pp. 54–57.

Malik, Fredmund (2000). Managing performing living: Effective management for a new era (English edition 2006). Frankfurt am Main: Campus (first published in German 2000).

Malik, Fredmund (2007): Management – das A und O des Handwerks (Band 1 der Serie Management – Komplexität meistern); new edition Campus 2007.

Malik, Fredmund (2012): Leadership im Unternehmen – Trends und Perspektiven; in Bruch, Heike/Krummaker, Stefan/Vogel, Bernd (ed.): Leadership – Best Practices und Trends; 2nd edition Springer Gabler 2012; pp. 307–319.

McCord, Patty (2014): Die Neuerfindung der Personalarbeit; Harvard Business Manager April 2014; pp. 53–61.

McGregor, Douglas (1960): The Human Side of Enterprise; Annotated Edition McGraw-Hill 2006 (first published 1960).

Meifert, Matthias (2010) (ed.): Führen – Die erfolgreichsten Instrumente und Techniken; Haufe 2010.

Mintzberg, Henry (1973): The Nature of Managerial Work; Harper & Row 1973.

Mintzberg, Henry (1975): The manager's job – folklore and fact; Harvard Business Review July/August 1975; pp. 49–61.

Mintzberg, Henry (2009): Managing; Berret-Koehler Publishers 2009.

Müller-Stewens, Günter (2010): Management und Strategie als Beruf – Ein Plädoyer für eine Professionalisierungsinitiative; in Kunisch, Sven/Welling, Christian/Schmitt, Ramona: Strategische Führung auf dem Prüfstand – Chancen und Herausforderungen in Zeiten des Wandels; Springer 2010.

Nerdinger, Friedemann W./Blickle, Gerhard/Schaper, Niclas (2014): Arbeits- und Organisationspsychologie; 3rd edition Springer 2014.

Netflix (2018): Netflix Culture (Website); https://jobs.netflix.com/culture (Accessed 01/05, 2022).

Neuberger, Oswald (2002): Führen und führen lassen; 6th edition UTB Lucius & Lucius 2002.

Neuberger, Oswald (2006): Mikropolitik und Moral in Organisationen; 2nd edition UTB Lucius & Lucius 2006.

Northouse, Peter G. (2022): Leadership: Theory and Practice; Sage 2022.

Oelsnitz, Dietrich von der (2012): Einführung in die systemische Personalführung; Carl Auer Verlag 2012.

Pietschmann, Bernd P./Huppertz, Silke/Ruhtz, Vanessa (1999): Was macht Führungsgrundsätze erfolgreich?; Personal 10/1999; pp. 506–510.

Prieß, Arne (2013): Kompetenz sorgt für Akzeptanz; Personalmagazin 11/2013; pp. 41–43.

Ramge, Thomas (2015): Nicht fragen. Machen.; Brand Eins 3/2015; p. 88–93.

Rosenstiel, Lutz von (2011): Employee Behavior in Organizations – On the Current State of Research. Management Revue 22 (4), pp. 344–366.

Rosenstiel, Lutz von (2014): Grundlagen der Führung; in von Rosenstiel, Lutz/Regnet, Erika/Domsch, Michel E. (ed.): Führung von Mitarbeitern – Handbuch für erfolgreiches Personalmanagement; Schäffer-Poeschel 2014; pp. 3–28.

Rüegg-Stürm, Johannes (2003): Das neue St. Galler Management-Modell: Grundkategorien einer integrierten Managementlehre – Der HSG-Ansatz; 2nd edition Paul Haupt Verlag 2003.

Rüegg-Stürm, Johannes/Grand, Simon (2015): Das St. Galler Management-Modell; 2nd edition Haupt Verlag 2015.

Scholz, Christian (1996): Die virtuelle Personalabteilung – Ein Jahr später; Personalführung 12/1996; pp. 1080–1086.

Scholz, Christian (2014): Personalmanagement – Informationsorientierte und verhaltenstheoretische Grundlagen; 6th edition Vahlen 2014.

Schulte-Zurhausen, Manfred (2014): Organisation; 6th edition Vahlen 2014.

Seidel, Eberhard (1984): Die Unterscheidung von Führungs- und Leitungsanteilen an der Vorgesetztentätigkeit; BFuP Betriebswirtschaftliche Forschung und Praxis 5/1984; pp. 460–469.

Semler, Ricardo (1989): Managing without Managers; Harvard Business Review September/October 1989; pp. 76–84.

Sprenger, Reinhard K. (2008): Gut aufgestellt – Fußballstrategien für Manager, Campus 2008.

Stayer, Ralph (1990): How I Learned to Let My Workers Lead; Harvard Business Review November-December 1990; pp. 66–83.

Steinmann, Horst/Schreyögg, Georg/Koch, Jochen (2013): Management – Grundlagen der Unternehmensführung; 7th edition Springer Gabler 2013.

Steyrer, Johannes/Meyer, Michael (2010): Welcher Führungsstil führt zum Erfolg? 60 Jahre Führungsstilforschung – Einsichten und Aussichten; zfo 3/2010; pp. 148–155.

Stogdill, Ralph M. (1950): Leadership, Membership and Organization; Psychological Bulletin 1/1950 (47); pp. 1–14.

Tannenbaum, Robert/Schmidt, Warren H. (1958): How to Choose a Leadership Patter; Harvard Business Review March/April 1958; pp. 95–101.

Thaler, Richard H./Sunstein, Cass R. (2008): Nudge – Improving Decisions About Health, Wealth and Happiness; Yale University Press 2008.

Titscher, Stefan/Mayrhofer, Wolfgang/Meyer, Michael (2010): Zur Praxis der Organisationsforschung; in Mayrhofer, Wolfgang/Meyer, Michael/Titscher, Stefan: Praxis der Organisationsanalyse – Anwendungsfelder und Methoden; Facultas/UTB 2010; pp. 17–44.

TU Darmstadt (2004): Die Unwörter von 2000 bis 2009 (Website); http://www.unwortdesjahres.net/index.php?id=34 (Accessed 1/6/2022).

Türk, Klaus (1981): Personalführung und soziale Kontrolle; Ferdinand Enke Verlag 1981.

Türk, Klaus (1995): Entpersonalisierte Führung; in Kieser, Alfred/Reber, Gerhard/Wunderer, Rolf (ed.): Handwörterbuch der Führung; 2nd edition Schäffer-Poeschel 1995. p. 327–339.

Ulrich, Hans (1968): Die Unternehmung als produktives soziales System – Grundlagen der allgemeinen Unternehmenslehre; Verlag Paul Haupt 1968.

Ulrich, Hans/Krieg, Walter (1973): Das St. Galler Management-Modell; 2nd edition Paul Haupt Verlag 1973.

Ulrich, Dave (1997): Human Resource Champions – The next agenda for adding Value and Delivering Results; Harvard Business School Press 1997.

Ulrich, Dave/Brockbank, Wayne (2005): The HR Value Proposition; Harvard Business School Press 2005.

Ulrich, Dave/Alen, Justin/Brockbank, Wayne/Younger, Jon/Nyman, Mark (2009): HR Transformation – Building Human Resources from the Outside in; McGraw-Hill 2009.

Watkins, Michael D. (2012): How Managers Become Leaders; Harvard Business Review June 2012; pp. 64–72.

Weibler, Jürgen (2014): Führung der Mitarbeiter durch den nächsthöheren Vorgesetzten; in von Rosenstiel, Lutz/Regnet, Erika/Domsch, Michel E.: Führung von Mitarbeitern – Handbuch für erfolgreiches Personalmanagement; 7th edition Schäffer-Poeschel 2014; pp. 271–283

Weibler, Jürgen (2016): Personalführung; 3rd edition Vahlen 2016.

Wiswede, Günter (2004): Rollentheorie; in Schreyögg, Georg/von Werder, Axel (2004): Handwörterbuch Unternehmensführung und Organisation; 4th edition Schäffer-Poeschel 2004.

Wunderer, Rolf (2001): Employees as co-intrapreneurs – a transformation concept. Leadership & Organization Development Journal 22 (5), pp. 193–211.

Wunderer, Rolf (2011): Führung und Zusammenarbeit – Eine unternehmerische Führungslehre; 9th edition Luchterhand.

Yukl, Gary/Lepsinger, Richard (2005): Why Integrating the Leading and Managing Roles Is Essential for Organizational Effectiveness; Organizational Dynamics 4/2005; pp. 361–375.

Yukl, Gary (2013): Leadership in Organizations; 8th edition Pearson 2013.

Zaleznik, Abraham (1977): Managers and leaders – Are they different?; Harvard Business Review May/June 1977; pp. 67–78.

The Complementary Management Model

2

2.1 Disambiguation, Theoretical Demarcation, and Overview

The first chapter of this book contains the theoretical foundations and preliminary considerations for conceptualizing models of leadership and management. Building upon this, a new theoretical model of leadership and management is introduced here, which draws on the previous insights.

2.1.1 State of Development and Theoretical Premises of the Model

In its current form, the Complementary Management Model is the result of a theoretical conceptualization process that has developed over many years. It started out as a broad outline and was subsequently further developed, with publications to date reflecting the respective stage of development (see Kaehler 2012, 2013, 2014a, b, 2017, 2020).

Like most forms of systematic theorizing, it is based on practical observations, literature studies, and conceptual ideas that are condensed into a consistent web of theoretical assumptions (see, e.g., Neuberger 2002, p. 393 ff.). The individual mechanisms have been tested in practice and reflect functional people management and leadership as it is practiced in many organizations. The overall model has been applied in various companies and substantially refined on the basis of the experience gained. Next, empirical studies should be carried out which accompany its implementation in organizations and examine its effectiveness. Due to its clear structure and transparent theoretical derivation, the theory model can easily undergo critical analysis by theorists and researchers alike. The development process thus corresponds to the usual and methodologically desirable oscillation between theory building, fieldwork, and empirical testing (see Titscher et al. 2010, p. 26).

The Complementary Management Model encompasses people management in organizations. This is understood here as an influence on people in an organization and its units with the aim of achieving the unit's objectives by generating work

B. Kaehler, *Complementary Management*, Management for Professionals,
https://doi.org/10.1007/978-3-030-98163-1_2

performance and meeting other requirements. Managing a unit's members is synonymous with "leading" or "directing" them. This organizational form of management and leadership can be distinguished from political leadership and from management of functional-technical activities. People management is a collective phenomenon that involves multiple actors, including employees, line managers, and HR advisors. This implies that the employee leadership by line managers and the human resource management by HR departments are one and the same, i.e., people management. Of course, certain aspects are usually assigned to the HR department and others to line managers. However, these are not separate spheres, but rather a division of labor for handling a single mandate, namely the leadership and management of personnel. Management influence can be exercised in two different ways, either through anticipatory norm-setting (constitutive and strategic leadership/management) or through situational intervention (operational leadership/management). All of these aspects were discussed in detail in Chap. 1.

Anyone seeking to understand and shape leadership and management in organizations needs a theoretical framework. The intention of the Complementary Management Model is to illustrate how people management and leadership is to be designed in order to best achieve their purpose of fulfilling the goals of the organizational unit by generating work performance and meeting other requirements. The model is descriptive in the sense that it describes mechanisms that are actually used and which function in practice. At the same time, it is normative in the sense that it clearly recommends that—with certain adaptations—leadership and management in organizations should precisely follow this pattern. By no means does the theoretical model need to depict and explain all of the conceivable aspects of leadership and management—only those that can be meaningfully generalized and standardized. Even though the Complementary Management Model is also intended to be of scientific use and to serve as an orientation for leaders, its main purpose is to provide a theoretical basis for corporate models of management and leadership (see Sect. 2.6).

2.1.2 Level of Complexity

The Complementary Management Model consists of three core elements and four implementation elements. Since all seven elements are made up of a range of sub-elements, the model has a significantly higher degree of complexity overall than other theories of management and leadership, no matter how generally comprehensible the individual elements may be. This is necessary and intentional. As Albert Einstein (1934) suggested, the primary goal of all theories should be to describe the individual elements as simply and reductively as possible without sacrificing the adequate representation of individual experiential data. In the case of people management and leadership, this requires a degree of complexity. The variant chosen here already represents a considerable reduction in complexity. Anyone attempting to similarly systematize everyday processes, such as driving a car, will find they will need to consider just as many aspects.

The Complementary Management Model is based on the assumption that precisely these seven elements are required to holistically map organizational people management and leadership. Since all seven elements harbor special opportunities as well as risks, and are closely interwoven, none of them should be ignored without good reason. It may make sense for some organizations to initially implement rudimentary solutions in the course of developing their own corporate management models (Sect. 2.6). Before such considerations are made, however, a conceptual examination of the entire solution space is called for. This book is aimed at those interested in management and leadership concepts and it intends to describe all facets of the model; hence its explanations are correspondingly detailed. However, assuming the Complementary Management Model is presented in a well-thought-out and simplified manner, it can certainly be communicated in its entirety to its "end users" in organizations as well, i.e., the line managers and employees. Here the book "Führen als Beruf" (Kaehler 2019) is recommended reading, an English edition of which is planned for 2023.

Section 1.7.7 discusses how theories can be differentiated based on their "level of conceptualization". This refers to the reference point of the theories, i.e., the question of whether leadership and management is described as an intraindividual process, a dyadic process, a group process, or a process at the level of the organization as a whole. The conceptual starting point of the Complementary Management Model consists of the management tasks, which are to be fulfilled in relation to each individual employee. On the one hand, these individualized management tasks include aspects of the employee's cooperation with others (e.g., resolving conflicts). Since people rarely work alone, the leadership and management of individual employees cannot ignore these issues. Thus, the team level is indirectly included in the model, even when the actual conceptual reference point of the management tasks is the individual. On the other hand, management tasks are not only performed by line managers, they are fulfilled jointly by different management actors according to a certain distribution mechanism. This cross-hierarchical process can be traced dyad by dyad, but cannot be assigned to a specific conceptual level. Complementary Management thus describes organizational leadership at both the level of different dyads and at the group and organizational level, thus making it a multilevel theory.

2.1.3   Normative Presets and Deliberate Free Spaces

Sections 1.7.5 and 1.7.6 covered the normativity of theoretical models as well as the complementarity of norms and regulatory freedom. The bottom line is that the structures and the regulatory freedom of normative models are mutually dependent. Leadership and management models must therefore regulate the right aspects of organizational behavior in order to be effective. At the same time, however, they must leave out certain aspects, namely those that cannot be meaningfully generalized. Accordingly, in the Complementary Management Model, the final definition of the seven generalized elements automatically shapes the model spaces. Thus, the model implicitly also defines all those aspects that should not be regulated because they are postulated as organization-specific or individually/situationally varying. Table 2.1 presents an overview of the deliberate normative omissions of the Complementary Management Theory.

2.1.4 Explanation of the Term Complementary Management and Other Terms

Complementarity is when various elements supplement one another to form a whole. The term Complementary Management is derived from the three elements of the core model, each of which has complementary components. For instance, the two complementary management functions—the support function and the disciplinary function—make up the totality of the management service. The range of complementary management tasks together generates the totality of the human performance conditions, which consist of enabling and carrying out work in order to achieve organizational goals. And finally, the complementary management actors together make up the totality of the key participants whose joint action shapes the management process.

In principle, complementarity does also exist at the overall model level. Based on the premise of the model, the three core elements and the four implementation elements together make up the totality of the management norms that are required to effectively shape people management and leadership in organizations. Fundamentally, the regulations and regulatory freedom defined by the model are also complementary; however, this is not a specific feature of Complementary Management, but in a certain sense the basic principle of organizing and managing as a whole.

Conceptual creations, such as those of Complementary Management, have characterized leadership and management science since its inception. The names of many of the theoretical approaches in the field of leadership are formed by combining an adjective with the word "leadership" or "management"—from "authoritarian leadership" to "situational leadership" to "agile management". Very rightly, this has been called "adjectivist" and the monothematic focus of these approaches has been criticized (Blessin and Wick 2017, p. 6). Complementary Management has several such aspects, though, and can thus hardly be deemed monothematic. As a concession to the conventions of the subject area, and in order to concisely characterize the substantive features of the model, the name "Complementary Management" seems well chosen. Of course, since the terms "leadership" and "management" are used synonymous here (see Sect. 1.2), the model could just as well be called Complementary Leadership, and sometimes is. Given that in the past, scientific modeling in fact almost exclusively made use of the term leadership, the latter choice of name would also have fit into this tradition. However, in contrast to the more general influence phenomena that most of these models describe, the majority of researchers and practitioners still associate the term "leadership" with the idea of a political leader (Sect. 1.3), making it very difficult to avoid misunderstandings in a longer text. As a result, the choice was made to name the model "Complementary Management".

Table 2.1 Deliberate free spaces of the complementary management model (modified from Kaehler 2017, p. 165; © Boris Kaehler 2019. All rights reserved)

Concrete distribution of tasks among the management actors	The model emphasizes the necessity of performing all management tasks/routines and shows possible ways of distributing tasks, but does not standardize any specific static or dynamic actor distributions. These are to be determined in the course of introducing the organization-specific corporate model (see Sect. 2.6) or they result situationally from the compensatory interaction of the actors (see Sect. 2.4.5).
Situational variables	The model deliberately refrains from decisively enumerating situational variables in the style of conventional contingency theories. Instead, the compensatory bodies are assigned the responsibility of determining the situational degree of fulfillment of the management tasks and reacting appropriately to the situation so that they are fulfilled (see Sect. 2.4.5).
Personal and communication requirements	The model does not define requirements for the personality, preferences, or moods of the actors, nor does it define specific communication styles. Leaders and managers must be able to handle management tasks (e.g., "define work assignments") within the framework of management routines (e.g., work meetings) and have the elementary competencies required for this (e.g., communication competence). The range of people and forms of communication suitable for leadership and management is enormous, and standardizing ideal types is not expedient. However, rules of conduct are required that lay down minimum standards of respectful and professional communication. In addition, like all people, leaders and managers must of course adapt their (individual!) communication behavior to the situation of the communication partners and need feedback for this (see Sect. 2.5.5).
Application conflicts and dilemmas	The model describes a normative framework that determines the direction and structure of people management and leadership and eliminates many of those organizational deficits and conceptual contradictions that too often make it impossible from the outset. That is all that theoretical models can do. Naturally, the implementation of these guidelines in everyday management brings with it many individual problems and challenges. Application conflicts and dilemmas arise, and a wide variety of contextual variables require situational action (see Sect. 3.2). Actually performing leadership and management—i.e., perceiving routines and all the associated situational considerations—is not the subject of the theoretical model. However, practical recommendations can be developed for the individual routines, which can serve as guidelines for leaders and facilitate their application. This is usually done in the context of introducing corporate leadership models (see Sect. 2.6).

The term "complementarity" describes a commonplace fact and is therefore naturally also used in the management literature in a wide variety of contexts. Steinmann et al. (2013, p. 8) describe a "complementary relationship" between management functions and factual functions of corporate management. The term "complementary consulting" has been proposed for a mixture of expert consulting and systemic consulting (Pichler 2006; Königswieser et al. 2009). Gebert and Kearney (2011, p. 81) postulate four complementary leadership dimensions, in each of which contrasting leadership styles can be practiced: decision-making authority (delegative/directive), time constraints (time-limited/time-granting), knowledge use (existing/new knowledge), communication (consensus/dissensus-oriented). Piccolo et al. (2012) aim to integrate the concepts of Transformational Leadership and employee orientation and, thus, use the term "complementary leader behaviors". Von der Oelsnitz (2012, p. 19) speaks of a complementary coexistence of set and emergent order in the context of leadership and management. Some authors use the word combination "complementary" to describe a postulated duality of leadership vs. management, both of which are necessary (e.g., Scheiring and Mattheis 2008; Hinsen 2012; see the critical comments in Sect. 1.2.3). O'Toole et al. (2002), Bradt (2012), Miles and Watkins (2007), and Zimmermann and Welling (2010) relate it to complementary competencies, expertise, and/or styles within a leadership/management team and the resulting opportunities for strengths-based staffing. Similarly, Etzioni (1965, p. 689, 1969, p. 388 f.) and Alvarez et al. (2007) use the word complementarity to refer to complementary leadership skills or roles in leadership duos (see also Bales and Slater 1969, p. 274). Blessin and Wick (2017, p. 78) speak of the complementarity of those being led with their leaders in the context of the construction of charisma. The pair of words "complementary actors" is often used with respect to social and strategic networks (see, e.g., Ferrary 2001; Mazzarol and Reboud 2008). Reiß (2011a, b) transfers it to internal and external leadership/management actors and thus describes phenomena of shared leadership, as Schall et al. (2004, p. 29) already did to some extent. Crevani et al. (2007) discuss "complementary roles" in the context of Shared Leadership. Allport (1962, p. 17) has described "complementary acts" within collective social structures. Streich (2013, p. 73 ff.) uses "complementary management" to describe both a complementary interaction of two or more actors and the complementarity of professional and private roles and values of an individual. An independent theoretical approach called "Complementary Management" or "Complementary Leadership"[1] was first established by the model described here (Kaehler 2012, 2013, 2014a, b, 2017, 2020).

Complementary Management is a theoretical leadership and management model; it can also be referred to as a theory, concept, or approach. The model can be translated into corporate models of leadership and management, which are linguistically equated here with principles, policies, and guidelines. They are formalized norms that define why, by whom, and how a particular organization or

---

[1] German original: "Komplementäre Führung"

organizational unit (including its personnel) is led/managed, in the sense of a constitution of personnel work that is authoritative for all management/leadership actors. Such models are partly HR governance and partly governance of functional-technical matters, or, in other words, they have people-related and non-people-related aspects (Kaehler and Grundei 2018, p. 208, 2019, p. 41). Although the Complementary Management Model is about *people* management and leadership, it establishes their place in the structure of corporate governance so clearly that it already pre-structures the management of functional-technical matters to a good extent.

Ideally, organizations should be equipped with an integrated HR governance (in the sense of codified regulations) that encompasses the corporate management/leadership model as well as the HR management infrastructure (including all HR instruments), and consistently brings together all the specifications—and, conversely, latitudes—that are applicable to the steerage of an organization and its personnel. It is the subject and result of the constitutive task of "stipulating HR governance". This is often not the case in practice, with the result that the HR governance structures consist of a large number of decentralized fragments.

2.1.5 Overview of the Setup of the Core Model

The Complementary Management Model describes people management and leadership as a bundle of specific tasks in which certain functions are concretized and which are assumed by certain actors. The model consists of eight categories of three tasks each. In each task, both the disciplinary and the support functions are specified. Several management actors—line managers, employees, colleagues, senior managers, and HR advisors—each take on parts of all tasks. With these three elements of the core model, Complementary Management ties in with, among other things, the theoretical approaches of Shared Leadership and Leadership as a Service as well as with task models of leadership and management. In this way, it forms a counter-concept, so to speak, to the widespread idea of leadership and management as a personality-based or systemic relationship phenomenon (= in which there is a lack of clearly defined tasks) brought about by line managers (= in which there is a lack of other actors) which confers on them a reign-like self-image (= in which the idea of service is lacking).

In Fig. 2.1, the management functions (support/discipline) are shown in the outer circle and the management tasks (summarized in eight categories) in the inner area. It illustrates how all tasks serve to achieve both functions simultaneously. In each category of task, an example is given of a situational division of the management actors. This exemplifies the task-related nature of the work division between the management actors, which varies from management task to management task (the corresponding mechanism is explained in more detail below in Sect. 2.4.5). Each management task category contains several individual tasks which are not depicted in the figure for reasons of clarity (a detailed list is provided in the following section). The task category "Setting HR norms" is placed in the middle and thus occupies a

Fig. 2.1 Core complementary management model with a sample distribution of actors per task category (own graphic based on 2014b, p. 460; modified from Kaehler 2017, p. 164; © Boris Kaehler 2017. All rights reserved)

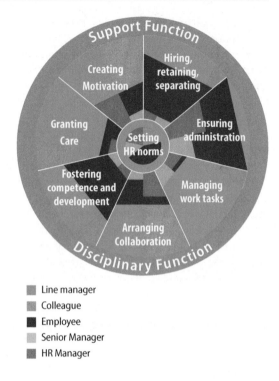

special position. This graphic representation highlights the fact that this particular category pre-structures and significantly shapes the other categories (which are of an operational nature) through constitutive and strategic regulations. Naturally, there are also various interrelationships between the individual task categories beyond this; however, the diagram does not show this complexity and never would be able.

This core Complementary Management Model describes the three essential elements of people management and leadership as well as the way they interact. Further model elements are required before it can be put into practice in organizations. These implementation elements consist of the management routines (= activities), the management instruments (= formalized tools), the management resources (= prerequisites), and the management unit design (= positions and units). They are presented and explained in Sect. 2.5. All seven elements are needed to make organizational leadership and management effective.

2.2 Complementary Management Functions: Leadership as a Service

The first core element of the Complementary Management Model contains the complementary management functions. Unfortunately, although the term "function" is very common in the context of management, it also has multiple connotations and is therefore misleading. It is used in at least three ways: first, in the sense of a specific task area ("what is to be done?" e.g., marketing tasks), second, in the sense of a specific organizational unit ("who focuses on something?" e.g., the marketing department) and third, in the sense of an actual objective ("what is to be achieved" e.g., understanding the market or market development). In terms of the complementary management functions, the latter idea is assumed, i.e., it is a question of which objectives people management and leadership fulfill with regard to those being managed/led. Admittedly, this book sometimes refers to the human resources department as the "HR function", since this corresponds to general usage and there is a lack of suitable synonyms. The model element "management functions," however, refers to the two objectives of the influence of personnel management.

2.2.1 Theoretical Derivation: Leadership as a Service and Employee Versus Production Orientation

The theoretical basis of the complementary management functions is the Leadership as a Service concept (see excursus box). This approach, which is also alluded to in older sources, was redeveloped in the 1990s in the marketing and quality management literature published in the German-speaking world. It involves the transfer of the idea of "internal service" to the dyad of manager and employee. It may be considered a secularized form of Servant Leadership, a related and internationally established theoretical approach (Krost and Kaehler 2010). Reinhard K. Sprenger expresses the basic idea well:

> "... Management could see itself ... as a supplier: as a supplier of opportunities, freedom, support. ... And the motto of management would be: 'I am there so that the others can do their job.'" (Sprenger 2012, p. 124 f.; own translation)

The Complementary Management Model expands on the Leadership as a Service approach in three respects. One aspect is the weighting of the disciplinary function, which is given equal standing alongside the support function. The two thrusts of leadership—employee and company—are indeed recognized in parts of the related literature, but are not conceived of as equivalent functions of "support" and "discipline" (see Bühner and Horn 1995, p. 664 f.; Bühner 1998, p. 739; Reiß 2011a, p. 26). Second, the Complementary Management Model removes the conventional assignment of management/leadership tasks to one of the two functions. In fact, supporting performance and maintaining discipline are not distinct functions, but rather a relationship of tension that characterizes all people management and leadership tasks. Third, service is not only defined through examples of single tasks (Bühner and Horn 1995, p. 664 f.; Krost and Kaehler 2010, p. 56; Reiß 2011a, p. 26, 2011b, p. 10), but across the full breadth of all tasks.

Excursus: Servant Leadership and Leadership as a Service

The Servant Leadership Model, devised by Robert Greenleaf (Greenleaf 1970), flips the perspective from the employee as a servant of the manager, to leadership as a service to the employee. Servant Leadership is highly established as a leadership theory in international leadership research (see, among others, Dierendonck 2011; Sun 2013; Hunter et al. 2013; Pircher Verdorfer and Peus 2014, 2015; Rivkin et al. 2014; van Dierendonck et al. 2014; Liden et al. 2014). Despite the fact that popular leadership bestsellers also draw on the approach (e.g., Tenney 2014), Servant Leadership is still widely unknown outside research circles. The underlying idea is universal though, and so other sources contain examples of leaders who want people management to be regarded as a modest effort to help those being led. Hans L. Merkle, former chairman of the board of management and supervisory board of the German multinational engineering and technology company Bosch, regarded serving and leading "as aspects of a basic fact, as a manifestation of a phenomenon" and held the view that "leadership aptitude arises from the willingness to serve, that leading is a special category of serving" (Merkle 1979, p. 162; own translation). In the USA, Frederick W. Taylor noted as early as 1912 that "managers [are] more the servants of teams than teams are the servants of managers" (Taylor 1912, p. 34; own translation). According to his own statements, Greenleaf himself was inspired by the idea of Hermann Hesse's novel "Morgenlandfahrt," (perhaps he thought a reference to Taylor seemed a little too unromantic) at the end of which the supporting role of a supposed servant is revealed (Greenleaf 1970, p. 1).

Respectable as the concept may be, it seems problematic as a basis for shaping leadership and management in organizations. The Servant Leadership approach is deeply rooted in Christian values and seeks not only to change the perspective of leadership and management, but to align it with the principle of altruism:

> "A servant-leader loves people and wants to help them. The mission of a servant-leader is, therefore, to identify the needs of others and try to satisfy those needs" (Kent Keith, Former CEO of the Greenleaf Center for Servant Leadership, cited from Trompenaars and Voerman 2009; p. 8)

This seems a bit excessive, at least by European standards (Krost and Kaehler 2010; very similarly the Heidelberger Institut 2017; see also Grün 1998, pp. 50–52). Moreover, it will hardly be possible to make such a demanding approach mandatory for all leaders in an ideologically neutral

(continued)

organization with a diverse workforce. In order to dissuade managers from acting like kings, we do not have to turn them into servants or saints; consistently orientating them toward the service and task principle is completely sufficient (Krost and Kaehler 2010).

The alternative approach of Leadership as Service may be considered a secularized form of Servant Leadership (see Krost and Kaehler 2010). Indeed, when there is explicit mention of "serving" and "servants" in the literature, this often does not mean self-sacrificing service, but a clearly defined and professionalized service:

> "The ruler is the premier servant of the state. He is well paid so as to retain the dignity of his position. But he is required to work diligently for the good of the state and . . . to conduct the main affairs with care." (Frederick II, King of Prussia, 1752, p. 53 f.; own translation; in the French original it reads "Le souverain est le premier serviteur de l'état.")

Frederick W. Taylor used the word "servant" in this sense. Within the framework of his Scientific Management approach, he defined clear responsibilities of the leaders and proclaimed an increased sense of duty and demands: "They have to do their share and be always ready" (Taylor 1912, p. 34 f.). Peter F. Drucker strikes the same chord:

> "The manager is a servant. His master is the institution he manages and his first responsibility must therefore be to it." (1973, p. 343)

Albach (1977, p. 207) advocates a "marketing thesis" according to which employees are to be regarded as buyers, line managers as industrial suppliers, and leadership principles as "production instructions" and "quality promises". In the 1990s, the concept was redeveloped in the marketing and quality management literature of the German-speaking world, and the catchphrase Leadership as Service ("Führen als Dienstleistung") was established (Jacobi 1990, pp. 172, 178, 1991, p. 503, 1993, p. 449; without author 1992; Laszlo and Leonhardt 1994, p. 36; Bühner and Horn 1995, p. 674; Nerdinger and Rosenstiel 1996, pp. 301 f., 312; Holch 1997; Bühner 1998, p. 739; critically Krell 2001, p. 14). Here, the idea of an "internal service," which was highly popular at the time, was simply transferred to the line manager/employee dyad:

> "The marketing idea of offering the customer a benefit and making a profit in the process can, in principle, also be transferred to the relationship between the supervisor and the supervised in the form of a customer-supplier relationship, which opens up new dimensions in dealing with each other. . . . Then the supervisor must react to customer requirements and help employees meet the quality demands." (Jacobi 1993, p. 450; own translation)

(continued)

The service is predominantly seen as providing support for those being managed and consists of specific services that a manager has to provide employees, e.g., establishing work goals, passing on information, outward representation, and developing people (Jacobi 1991, p. 503; Bühner and Horn 1995, p. 664 f.; Nerdinger and Rosenstiel 1996, pp. 301 f., 312; Fuchs and Stolarz 2001, p. 150; Reiß 2011b, p. 10). Some authors do emphasize that, in addition to the employee, the company should also be regarded as an "internal customer" and thus services are to be provided to it at the same time (e.g., initiating quality concepts, coordinating, and making decisions). However, the concept of service is generally reserved for employee-related support services (see Bühner and Horn 1995, p. 664 f.; Bühner 1998, p. 739). Other sources also regard the leadership services provided to the overall organization as a service, but, in terms of content, reduce these to the indirect provision of work output by employees (Reiß 2011a, p. 26). The idea of leadership and management as a service is still common today in the practice-oriented leadership literature and in individual companies, although it is rarely considered more than just a mere buzzword (Fournier 2006; Sprenger 2007b, p. 120; Dreyer and Schlippe 2008, p. 328; Krusche 2012; ESG 2014; Jäger 2014).

The theory of Leadership as a Service generated a lot of resistance among practitioners for a long time, mainly because the concept was insufficiently understood. For one thing, it does not automatically mean a market-based, i.e., sales-oriented organization of leadership and management (even if this is advocated in isolated cases, e.g., by Kim and Mauborgne 2014, p. 62). Rather, it is an analogy in the general sense of a customer-oriented attitude toward internal service recipients. Moreover, leading as a service does not mean serving unconditionally; instead, it refers to performing work that is clearly defined by specific tasks and is thus also limited. And finally, it has a dual thrust, because part of the service is provided to the employee and another part to the organization (Krost and Kaehler 2010; see also Bühner and Horn 1995, p. 664 f.; Bühner 1998, p. 739; Reiß 2011a, p. 26). In this respect, leaders in organizations are no different from other service providers—like waiters, sales representatives, teachers, and police officers—because they, too, have to fulfill the dual function of providing support to the "customer" and preserving the order of the collective. The mix of these functions, of course, varies from profession to profession. Even the waiter, however, will not fulfill every abstruse wish of the customer and call them out if they violate the rules of the game (e.g., get rowdy or do not pay). People management and leadership can thus very well be conceived of as a service with a dual focus, which certainly makes the responsibilities complex and challenging, but not impossible or extraordinary. Besides, management is only one

Table 2.2 Ohio State Studies—questionnaire items with high factor loading (verbatim quotes[a] from Halpin and Winer 1957, p. 42; tabular compilation: © Boris Kaehler 2019. All rights reserved.)

Factor "initiating structure"	Factor "consideration"
Asks that crew follows S.O.P.	Does personal favors for crew members
Maintains definite standards of performance	Looks out for personal welfare of crew members
Makes sure his part in the crew is understood	Refuses to explain his actions
Tries out his new ideas on the crew	Treats all crew members as his equal
Makes his attitude clear to the crew	Is friendly and approachable
Assigns crew members to particular tasks	Finds time to listen to crew members

[a]Without quotation marks in the interest of readability; own translation

of many internal services in the company and its service provider is, thus, often a customer or client elsewhere (Reiß 2011a, p. 25, speaks of "double agents").

Another theoretical basis of the two complementary management functions are the Ohio and Michigan studies with their classical distinction between employee- and production-oriented leadership. This approach is the most established, and, while actually not tenable in terms of content, is still considered relevant in theory and useful in practice (see excursus box). Therefore, the concept is adopted and further developed here. In doing so, the duality is firstly joined up with the principle of Leadership as a Service, which, after all, also has two directions of thrust, namely the employees and the corporation. Second, the unspecific "orientation" is understood here as a goal functionality that is specified in the leadership/management tasks. Thirdly, employee orientation is not conceived of in terms of unspecific caring, but in terms of support in the performance process. Furthermore, production orientation extends to aspects of maintaining discipline and order.

> **Excursus: Ohio and Michigan Studies**
>
> The classic distinction between employee- and production-oriented leadership goes back to the so-called Ohio and Michigan studies. The "leader behavior description questionnaire" was developed in the course of empirical studies at Ohio State University which surveyed employees about the leadership behavior of their superiors (Hemphill and Coons 1957). A factor analysis of the results revealed two major factors that best summarized statistically the demonstrated variances, namely "initiating structure" and "consideration" (Halpin and Winer 1957, p. 41 f.). These contain completely different aspects of leadership behavior, which is justified within the context of the factor analysis, but in itself hardly seems plausible (Table 2.2). At about the same time, two very similar main types of leadership behavior were identified at the University of Michigan: employee-oriented and production-oriented. They were initially postulated as being opposing factors, but were later regarded as being complementary and analogous to the two factors in the Ohio studies

(continued)

(Stippler et al. 2011, p. 20). The high plausibility of these two factors led to the mostly uncritical adoption of the approach in the leadership literature of the following decades. It is still considered one of the most important leadership theories today (Judge et al. 2004; Steyrer and Meyer 2010).

However, the duality of employee and production orientation is actually untenable in terms of content. This is because people management/leadership, as an operative part of corporate management/leadership, is about achieving an organization's objectives by generating work performance (see Sect. 1.1). The two aspects are therefore inextricably linked. Promoting employees personally and protecting them in a caring manner may superficially appear to be employee orientation, but it ultimately serves production purposes (based on the realization that human performers also require human treatment in order to perform sustainably). Conversely, assigning work tasks to employees and demanding or monitoring their fulfillment may superficially appear to be production orientation. In reality, however, the right amount of work pressure promotes motivation and "flow"; the manager's interest in the work results is regularly perceived as interest in the working person and thus as appreciation. By definition, those who lead and manage personnel exert influence on people to achieve work performance. Accordingly, the performance and the performer are not opposites or independent dimensions, but rather mutually dependent aspects of the work process. All leadership/management tasks—from assigning jobs based on qualifications to conflict resolution—are equally determined by both orientations. Nevertheless, the distinction has become established over the years, and not without reason: it is useful. As obvious as the theoretical inseparability of the two aspects is, it is easy for one side to become dominant in everyday leadership and management. Leaders are more likely to do justice to their job if they are told that it takes place in the field of tension of such a duality and that neither productivity nor employees should be neglected. In light of this, the model continues to be relevant and practical.

2.2.2   Integration into the Overall Context of People Management and Leadership

In order to place the two complementary functions within the context of corporate management, several issues have to be discussed. First of all, the function of people management and leadership with regard to the organizational unit and its steerage. After all, people management in organizations is not an end in and of itself, but an essential part of corporate management as a whole. The latter was defined in Sect. 1.6 as a steering influence on market, production, and resource-related business operations in an organization and its units that may address both people and non-people issues with the aim of achieving the unit's objectives. People management, defined as an influence on people (and equated with leading people), is a part of this and serves to achieve the unit's goals by generating work performance and fulfilling other requirements. If managers lose sight of this connection, people management and leadership degenerates into bureaucratic busywork and/or uneconomic charity. Concepts of personnel management must therefore relate to all facets of organizational goals. It cannot be stated often enough that people management and leadership, even in everyday life, serve to enable and promote the actual business of the organization. While this certainly can also be described as its "function", it is not the same as the narrower concept expressed by "complementary functions".

What is really meant by complementary functions is the effects that people management and leadership have on those being led/managed and their work. Complementary Management is a theoretical model of people management and leadership. If management functions is one element of the model, it is systematically not about the function of people management in relation to the organizational unit and its steerage, as just explained, but about the functions in relation to the unit's people. After all, people management is about influencing those people who maintain the unit's operations. Accordingly, the question arises as to what functions this act of influence has in relation to the unit's personnel and their work if the overall goal of generating work performance and meeting other requirements is to be achieved. According to the model, these are the two service functions of support and discipline.

This brings us to the systematic connection between the two service functions and the tasks as well as the actors of people management and leadership. These complementary functions, which will be defined in more detail below, are in themselves already suitable for providing leaders and managers with a constructive self-image. However, they in turn must be specified, and this takes place through the complementary management tasks. The special feature here is that each task serves both functions. For example, anyone who defines work, sets incentives, or resolves conflicts must not only optimize the performance-enhancing effect on the people concerned (support function), but also take into account the requirements, norms, costs, and social structures of the organization (disciplinary function). However, the paradigm of the dual service function applies not only to all management tasks, but also to all management actors. Whether line manager, colleague, or HR advisor, those who perform management tasks simultaneously fulfill a support function and a disciplinary function. This system even applies when employees lead themselves, even if the terminology may seem unusual. If someone paints his/her own apartment or cuts his/her own hair, he/she is in fact performing a service to himself/herself. In doing so, he/she has to take into account not only the desired progress of the work but also the social requirements (e.g., the aesthetic ideas of his family or the sensitivities of the neighbors, who want neither paint nor hair on their doorstep). The situation is no different in the case of organizational self-management, which—if successful—involves the employee fostering his or her own performance, but also auto-disciplining in his or her overall best interest.

2.2.3   The Two Service Functions

People management and leadership, defined as an influence on people in an organization and its units with the aim of achieving the unit's objectives by generating work performance and meeting other requirements, has two essential functions: the disciplinary function and support function. The two functions are specified in Table 2.3. Both are recognizably different in their thrust. However, it is important to remember that they are conceptual creations, language constructs. The two aspects cannot be perfectly delineated from one another. Thus, the disciplinary function undoubtedly also shows traces of promoting performance and the support function shows traces of regimentation. Nevertheless, the distinction is essential and of high practical value in clarifying the dual service nature of management and leadership. Since the functions are specified in leadership/management tasks anyway, and each task always achieves both functions, the two functions do not need to be clearly delineated.

Thus, people management and leadership should support employees in performing their work, i.e., enable them to work as productively as possible. At the same time, it should maintain the discipline of the overall organization, i.e., enforce its rules, meet cost targets and fulfill performance requirements. No support may result in no work performance; if discipline is missing, the work performance may not fit into the framework of the organization. It is easy to enforce an organization's principles of order on employees without supporting them in the performance of their work—this was the weakness of traditional, strongly authoritarian leadership and management. It is equally easy to promote employees' performance and well-being without taking into account the regulatory framework of the organization—norms, requirements, costs, and social structures. This may be seen as the weakness of modern concepts of people management and leadership, which often substitute ideal concepts for reality and disregard aspects such as structure, provision, and control. Regarding people management and leadership as a service with a dual thrust is a suitable way of preventing self-referential headship in the

Table 2.3 Specifications of the complementary management functions (modified from Kaehler 2017, p. 170; © Boris Kaehler 2019. All rights reserved)

Support function	Disciplinary function
The management influence helps the employee to perform his or her work.	The management influence disciplines and supervises the employee in the delivery of services.
The management influence generates the supply of the needed employee capacities and the activation of this performance potential.	The management influence produces an alignment of performance contributions and performance costs with organizational goals and the organization's regulatory framework.
The main "customer" here is the individual employee as the performer of the work.	The main "customer" here is the organization as a collective.
The catchwords here are "to foster", "appreciation", and "employee orientation".	The catchwords here are "to demand", "added value", and "production orientation".

sense of personal supremacy and also of preventing it from slipping into anarchy or a welfare culture that would run counter to the actual purpose of the company.

Management and leadership means exerting influence and is thus a form of exercising power. Effectiveness here requires power, not only over the person being led, but also over the social and material environment. If we look at the two service functions of management, it becomes clear that in both cases power is required in a wide variety of forms. This is obviously true for the disciplinary function, and even at the level of self-management: "Do you have the discipline it takes to be a free spirit?" (von der Oelsnitz 2012, p. 90). Of course, the support function can also not be accomplished if the management actor does not have power, e.g., power over resources, work design, and counterproductive third parties. For good reason, it is standard practice in most organizations to structurally anchor much of this influence potential in the form of hierarchical positional power.

In principle, this applies to all management actors, but it is discussed specifically with regard to line manager positions (see Sect. 1.3.4). Concepts that aim to deprive leaders/managers of all hierarchical power and thus force them to permanently and laboriously fight for their influence in all directions are hardly ever functional. It should be noted that direct use of power generates resistance, and demonstratively celebrated power distance has a destructive effect. However, positional power tied to clearly defined service tasks is necessary and subtly shapes social relations in such a way that, for the most part, it does not even need to be acted out as positional power (see, for example, Scholl 2014). Nor is authoritarian leadership and management synonymous with appellative instructions, but should preferably be gentle through informal behavioral reinforcement and implicit communication (see Sect. 1.4.2 and 1.4.3).

2.3 Complementary Management Tasks: Leading as a Bundle of Tasks

The second core element of the Complementary Management Model consists of the complementary management tasks in which the two management functions introduced above are specified.

2.3.1 Theoretical Derivation: Task Models of Leadership

The theoretical bases for the element of management tasks are the task models of leadership and management of which there is no shortage in the literature (see excursus box). They describe leadership/management as a normative bundle of tasks or roles. The Complementary Management Model advances the established theoretical models in some respects. For one thing, it attempts to make the canon of tasks truly comprehensive and complete. Furthermore, it only formulates people management tasks while functional-technical tasks of corporate management are not the subject of the model (see Sect. 1.6.2). In addition, the tasks are described in such concrete terms that there is no room for doubt or interpretation when it comes to their specific content. And finally, elementary activities—communicating, decision-making, etc.—are not included as they are also relevant for many other activities and say nothing about the specific content of management and leadership. In essence, the Complementary Management Model follows the same logic as other task models, namely that of understanding and shaping leadership and management through concrete behavior. However, tasks are understood here as goals to be fulfilled; they are put into practice through specific leadership activities, another element of the model (see Sect. 2.5.3).

Excursus: Task-oriented Approaches to Leadership

The content of managerial behavior—i.e., its "what"—is likely the crucial aspect of organizational leadership and management (Katz 1955, p. 33; Malik 2000, pp. 38 f., 2007, p. 261; Kim and Mauborgne 2014, p. 63). Accordingly, most empirical research is concerned with the conduct and activities of leaders/managers (Yukl 2013, p. 390, 62 ff.). All other conceptual starting points may also contribute to the understanding of people management and leadership, but behavior is the key to improving its quality. Although other theoretical approaches also address aspects of this behavior, task models place it in the foreground. They describe leadership and management as a descriptive or normative set of tasks. Often, these recommended tasks are derived from the actual behavior of successful leaders and managers. The tasks are not always referred to as "tasks"; depending on the source, they are also referred to as "roles", "functions", or "practices". Often the conceptual differences between the tasks defined by the organization, the leader's subjective task conceptions, and the actual actions are blurred (see Hodgson et al. 1965, p. 231). Even the vast majority of "competence models" define nothing more than leadership/management tasks (namely those that leaders/managers are supposed to master) and thus ultimately also represent task models of leadership. There is no shortage of such task models in the literature (see Table 2.4; see Fleishman et al. 1991, pp. 247–252 for a very comprehensive overview of other models of this kind; see also the model by Yukl and Lepsinger 2005, p. 362 ff.). They are also frequently written about in the popular business press.

Defining its tasks is the silver bullet for designing leadership and management in organizations. This is because behavior can be significantly influenced by normatively defined leadership/management tasks (see, e.g., Pietschmann et al. 1999, p. 506; Weibler 2014, p. 276)—be it that managers orient themselves toward them on their own initiative or are made to do so by their organization. Thus, it is essential that corporate models of leadership and management define the leadership/management tasks that are considered decisive. Naturally, different categorizations and definitions can be created here. However, some leadership/management tasks can be quickly agreed

(continued)

Table 2.4 Task models of organizational leadership and management[a]; tabular summary: modified from Kaehler 2014a, p. 39 f.; © Boris Kaehler 2019. All rights reserved.)

Fayol (1916, p. 5 f.) was responsible for the classic canon of management tasks: (1) planning ahead, (2) organizing, (3) commanding, (4) coordinating, and (5) controlling. Indeed, this is still the central element of many textbook definitions of the term management. In the original text, however, it is clear that it is actually more of a broad categorization of about 10 management tasks, namely forecasting, planning, organizational design, staffing, defining and controlling work tasks, coordinating work activities, team building, performance feedback, and monitoring rule compliance.
Barnard (1938, p. 215 ff.) lists three functions of the senior manager in "The functions of the executive": (1) developing and maintaining a system of communication (under which he also subsumes aspects of organization, personnel selection, separation, and incentive design); (2) ensuring employee performance by establishing cooperative relationships between people and the organization; (3) formulating and defining the company's purpose and its goals and objectives.
In his book "The nature of managerial work" (1973, p. 59) and in his article "The manager's job—folklore and fact" (1975) Mintzberg describes ten managerial roles: The interpersonal roles of (1) figurehead, (2) leader and (3) liaison; the informational roles of (4) monitor, (5) disseminator and (6) spokesman; and the decisional roles of (7) entrepreneur, (8) disturbance handler, (9) resource allocator, and (10) negotiator. While the approach as such is descriptive, it makes the quasi-normative claim of highlighting the necessary activities and thus helping managers to better understand their jobs.
The book "The leadership challenge" (1987) by Kouzes and Posner has sold over 1.5 million copies according to its cover text. It recommends five "practices," each with two "commitments" (p. 26): Model the way: (1) Clarify values by finding your voice and affirming shared ideals (2) Set the example by aligning actions with shared values./Inspire a Shared Vision: (3) Envision the future by imagining exciting and ennobling possibilities. (4) Enlist others in a common vision by appealing to shared aspirations./Challenge the Process: (5) Search for opportunities by seizing the initiative and by looking outward for innovative ways to improve. (6) Experiment and take risks by constantly generating small wins and learning from experience./Enable Others to Act: (7) Foster collaboration by building trust and facilitating relationships. (8) Strengthen others by increasing self-determination and developing competence./Encourage the Heart: (9) Recognize contributions by showing appreciation for individual excellence. (10) Celebrate the values and victories by creating a spirit of community.
Fleishman et al. (1991, p. 260 f.) developed the following "leadership behavior dimensions" based on a very extensive literature review: (1) information search and structuring (acquiring information, organizing and evaluating information, feedback and control) (2) information use in problem solving (identifying needs and requirements, planning and coordinating, communicating information (3) managing personnel resources (obtaining and allocating personnel resources, developing personnel resources, motivating personnel resources, utilizing, and monitoring personnel resources (4) managing material resources (obtaining and allocating material resources, maintaining material resources, utilizing, and monitoring material resources).
In "Managing Performing Living" (2000, p. 338), Malik presents his task model which, in addition to leadership principles and tools, contains five management tasks: (1) managing objectives, (2) organizing, (3) decision-making, (4) monitoring/measuring/judging, and (5) developing people. He also describes seven "tools" used to perform these tasks (e.g., meetings, reports, and performance appraisals) and postulates certain basic principles. His catalog of tasks is almost consistent with Drucker's catalog of tasks in "Management—Tasks, Responsibilities, Practices" (1973, p. 400): (1) setting objectives, (2) organizing, (3) motivating/communicating, (4) measuring, and (5) developing people. This, in turn, is reminiscent of the old canon by Fayol (1916, p. 5 f.) mentioned above. Malik's book is a perennial bestseller in German-speaking countries and regularly appears in recommended reading lists, e.g., in the Handelsblatt list of the "50 most important business books of all time" (Handelsblatt, 12.10.2012, p. 65).

(continued)

Table 2.4 (continued)

In "The Leadership Code" (2008, pp. 14, 25, 53, 81, 105, 129), Ulrich, Smallwood, and Sweetman define five "rules", which in turn consist of a range of individual tasks. (I) Shape the Future: (1) Stay curious and develop a point of view about your own future. (2) Invite your savviest outsiders inside. (3) Engage the organization—no "one" knows enough. (4) Create strategic traction within the organization. (II) Make Things Happen: (1) Make change happen. (2) Follow a decision protocol. (3) Ensure accountability. (4) Build teams. (5) Ensure technical proficiency. (III) Engage Today's Talent: (1) Communicate, communicate, communicate. (2) Create aligned direction; connect the individual to the organization. (3) Strengthen others; ensure people have the competencies they need. (4) Provide people with the resources to cope with demands. (5) Create a positive work environment—practice spiritual disciplines at work. (6) Have fun at work. (IV): Build the Next Generation: (1) Map the workforce. (2) Create a firm and employee brand. (3) Help people manage their careers. (4) Find and develop next-generation talent. (5) Encourage networks and relationships. (V) Invest in Yourself: (1) Practice clear thinking: Rise above the details. (2) Know yourself. (3) Tolerate stress. (4) Demonstrate learning agility. (5) Tend to your own character and integrity. (6) Take care of yourself. (7) Have personal energy and passion.

In "Radikal führen" (2012, p. 51 ff.; own translation), Sprenger postulates a task model consisting of (1) organizing cooperation, (2) reducing transaction costs, (3) arbitrating conflicts, (4) securing future capability and (5) managing employees.

In the eighth edition of his landmark textbook "Leadership in Organizations" (2013), Yukl provides an overview of research approaches in the field of organizational leadership and develops the following task model as the "essence of effective leadership" (p. 406 f.): (1) Help interpret the meaning of events. (2) Create alignment on objectives and strategies. (3) Build commitment and optimism. (4) Build mutual trust and cooperation. (5) Strengthen collective identity. (6) Organize and coordinate activities. (7) Encourage and facilitate collective learning. (8) Obtain necessary resources and support. (9) Develop and empower people. (10) Promote social justice and morality.

Schmidt-Huber et al. (2014, p. 85; own translation) postulate an "evidence-based competency model" that, although empirically supported, primarily represents the integration of a range of established leadership theories at the level of leadership/management tasks: (1) Strategy orientation: (a) identifying market opportunities, (b) formulating future perspectives, (c) driving innovation; (2) Results achievement: (a) establishing objectives, (b) analyzing problems, (c) evaluating results; (3) Employee development: (a) delegating responsibility, (b) coaching employees, (c) providing feedback, (d) adopting perspectives; (4) Environment design: (a) communicating effectively, (b) providing resources, (c) managing conflict, (d) implementing change, (e) shaping working relationships; (5) People influence: (a) exuding confidence, (b) conveying authenticity, (c) managing ambiguity.

[a] Partly verbatim quotations (without quotation marks in the interest of readability)

upon. Work task definition, feedback, resource allocation, motivation, and conflict resolution are certainly among them. A brainstorming session among practitioners will quickly yield 10 to 20 additional tasks, some of which will be company- or division-specific, but many of which will be generally applicable. No matter how the task list of a particular organization is defined, henceforth there is clarity about the duties of leaders, and these duties can be requested and tracked.

(continued)

Regrettably, the established task models of leadership and management are not at all convincing in a number of respects. For example, at first glance, the task catalogs are almost always incomplete. The brainstorming method mentioned above quickly produces a multitude of necessary tasks, most of which are neglected or not fully represented in the literature. Many models also mix the tasks of functional-technical (= non-people) management with those of people management, which only makes sense if they are intended as corporate management models and not as pure people management models (see Sect. 1. 7.3). Furthermore, in some cases, there is simply a lack of logical consistency (e.g., if leading is to be considered a subcategory of leading). In addition, many tasks are described in rather general terms, leaving room for doubt and interpretation with respect to their actual content. Additionally, some tasks— communicating, deciding, organizing, etc.—are not leadership/management tasks at all, but general elementary activities or competencies that are also relevant for many other professional activities and give no indication about the specific content of the leadership/management influence. Finally, none of the established models differentiate between the management *tasks* and the management *activities* introduced in Sect. 2.5.3, which is indispensable if the model is to be put into practice:

> "[…] lists of managerial roles […] take the job apart without putting it back together. […] I was responsible for one of these lists. […] managers […] did not take particularly well to my list, or those of others (even if some academics did). As one manager commented: 'the descriptions are lifeless and my job isn't.' […]" (Mintzberg 2009, p. 44)

2.3.2 Integration into the Overall Context of People Management and Leadership

The task element of the Complementary Management Model represents an attempt to map in a normative manner the entire spectrum of tasks of people management and leadership in organizations. It answers the question of which tasks managers have to fulfill in order to ensure sustainable work performance on the part of their employees and to achieve work-related organizational goals. No work performance can be achieved—or it cannot be achieved sustainably and systematically—without work clarity, motivation, health, etc. Thus, behind the model's task element there is ultimately the postulate that generating work performance in organizations presupposes the fulfillment of all 24 management tasks.

As we shall return to below, people management and leadership is not the responsibility of the manager alone, but a collective process involving various management actors (including employees and the HR department). This circumstance is referred to as Shared Leadership in the leadership literature, but there it lacks a point of reference. In order to discuss the division of actors in a meaningful way, it is first necessary to determine what exactly needs to be divided. The complementary tasks provide this point of reference by describing which tasks are to be performed jointly by the management actors and which must be divided out among them.

The catalog of complementary tasks specifies the two complementary service functions. Each task contains both functions, i.e., both the disciplinary and the support function. For example, performance feedback is not only a means of enforcing performance requirements and behavioral regulations, but also, and even primarily, a means of assisting in the goal-oriented adjustment of behavior to the requirements of work, and thus a means of supporting the employee at work.

The Complementary Management Model describes management tasks as abstract goals that need to be fulfilled by concrete activities, i.e., management routines (see Sect. 2.5.3). In doing so, leaders/managers use the management instruments available in their respective companies, which are understood here to be formalized tools that support managing (see Sect. 2.5.4). Thus, managers carry out management tasks (e.g., performance feedback) by means of management routines (e.g., dialogs) and use management instruments (e.g., appraisal system and forms) to do so.

2.3.3 Overview of the Various Tasks

The Complementary Management Model describes eight task categories, each containing three tasks (Table 2.5). This is based on the premise that precisely these influences are required to generate sustainable human performance. The category "Setting HR norms" comprises the tasks of constitutive and strategic people management and leadership; the other seven categories are of an operational nature and are pre-structured by these norms.

The attentive reader will notice that task categories are sometimes divided into three tasks here that could just as easily be four or more individual tasks. The number of 24 management tasks is thus a concession to making the presentation look more pleasing; there could also be more. However, this does not imply any reduction in content, since each task is initially only a label and needs to be filled with content (see the detailed task descriptions in the last column). Whether, for example, employee selection and integration are combined in one task is ultimately irrelevant in terms of content; what is more important is that the task catalog is complete and that the individual tasks are consistently defined on a single logical level. Organizations can therefore also modify the catalog of tasks proposed here and define them differently. However, if people management and leadership is to be uniformly understood and optimally practiced within the whole organization, a catalog of tasks must be included in the corporate management model in the first place.

Defining a catalog of individual tasks is very useful for understanding and designing organizational leadership and management, as it provides a clear indication of which tasks are to be specifically pursued in order to ensure sustainable work performance and to achieve work-related organizational goals. However, it is a

Table 2.5 The tasks of people management and leadership in organizations according to the Complementary Management Model (modified from Kaehler 2014a, p. 82, 2017, p. 174; © Boris Kaehler 2019. All rights reserved)

Task category	Task	Task content in detail
Setting HR norms	To stipulate HR governance/HR strategies	• The operational leadership and management of the employee follows a coherent and functional internal HR governance consisting of the corporate management model as a metastructure and the HR infrastructure as a set of detailed regulations pertaining to structure, instruments, routines, and resources. • It also follows a coherent and functional HR strategy; all operational areas of HR management (= the other 21 management tasks) are backed up in this strategy by strategic goals and demand scenarios for the coming business period.
	To optimize organizational design/ processes	• All work processes, as well as the job and hierarchical integration of each employee, are optimized in terms of time, cost, and quality. • These processes and structures are documented in a comprehensible manner.
	To shape culture and diversity	• Clear cultural standards—shared values and appearances—applicable to the employee are set at the level of each organizational unit to which he or she belongs. • Clear diversity standards—welcomed differences and rules to protect them— applicable to the employee are set. • General rules of conduct (conduct, handling conflicts of interest, etc.) applicable to the employee are clearly defined.
Hiring, retaining, separating	To recruit and retain	• Applicant target groups with a high profile fit are defined. • All four sourcing areas (external and internal labor market, peripheral or pseudo workforces, and internal flexibility reserves) are considered with the defined target groups in mind. • Appropriate candidates are recruited. • Applicant relationships are systematically maintained. • Top performers are retained.
	To select and put onboard	• The requirement profiles of the positions are accurately recognized. • Personnel selection is carried out in an "end-to-end", process-oriented manner and by means of planned aptitude testing. • Jobs are filled exclusively with suitable and highly capable candidates. • New employees are systematically integrated.
	To dismiss and release	• Possible miscasts are dismissed. • Possible surplus personnel are reduced.

(continued)

Table 2.5 (continued)

Task category	Task	Task content in detail
		• Organizational arrangements are made for the event of unwanted attrition.
Ensuring administration	To handle HR administration	• The administrative work related to the employee is taken care of.
	To collect and analyze data	• The data relevant to the employee and his or her work are collected and evaluated in order to identify optimization potentials.
	To look after employee representatives	• Functional relationships exist with works councils as well as trade unions and other bodies representing staff.
Managing work tasks	To define work tasks and instructions	• The work tasks and work specifications of the employee are sensibly defined and known to him or her. • Development-oriented work task management is practiced, from small-scale leading with instructions to leading with objectives and self-control.
	To provide working time and resources	• The employee is provided with working time, material resources, and a financial budget in accordance with the tasks at hand.
	To evaluate performance and give feedback	• The work performance of employees is comprehensively appraised, and he or she knows how to properly judge it.
Arranging collaboration	To ensure coordinative communication	• Employee is continuously informed about the issues that are relevant to him or her. • The technical and functional need for coordination with the other group members is determined and the coordinative communication is conducted accordingly. • Wrong decisions and loss of creativity in groups are systematically prevented.
	To maintain relations and solve conflicts	• The employee assumes responsibility for relationships in all directions and maintains internal and external networks. • There is a constructive conflict culture. • Manifest conflicts are resolved quickly.
	To enhance group cohesiveness and identification	• There is an appropriately strong group cohesion. • The team members identify with the collective.
Fostering competence and development	To qualify	• Qualification gaps of the employee are identified and closed.
	To develop	• The employee's development potential is identified and systematically implemented. • Alternatives to a management career are also identified.
	To cultivate knowledge and innovation	• Existing knowledge of the employee is tapped and shared with others as needed.

(continued)

Table 2.5 (continued)

Task category	Task	Task content in detail
		• Divergent and convergent thinking achieves continuous improvement and innovation.
Granting care	To protect health and life balance	• Health hazards are minimized, and disaster, pandemic, and threat scenarios are in place. • The health and work-life balance of the employee are protected, and permanent work overload is prevented. • Resilience and the ability to cope with balance crises are strengthened.
	To create flow conditions	• The employee has a sense of control with respect to his or her work and its conditions. • Work design enables and promotes the phenomenon of flow.
	To explain and accompany change	• The employee understands the necessity and the context of upcoming changes. • Individual adaptation needs and requirements in connection with changes are taken into account.
Creating motivation	To consider needs and wants	• The permanent motive structures of the employee are recognized and taken into account. • The current motives of the employee are recognized and taken into account.
	To round off the incentive field	• The real existing field of inducements of the managed person is continuously analyzed. • Additional activity inducements, option inducements, social inducements, and monetary inducements are set in order to compensate for misaligned incentives and to generate additional motivation.
	To influence expectations/goals/impulse	• Performance, change, incentives, and justice expectations are consciously shaped. • The work activity is experienced as meaningful. • Goals and behavioral intentions correspond to work requirements. • The employee feels the necessary behavioral impulses to actually take action.

conceptual artifice, because the tasks can neither be clearly delineated from one another, nor are they independent of one another. Almost every designated task can be understood as a cross-cutting perspective of all the others. For example, almost all relevant aspects of work motivation result directly from other personnel management tasks. For this reason, Malik (2000, p. 237), for example, does not consider motivation to be a management task in the narrower sense, but rather the result of the fulfillment of other tasks. However, this also applies to all other leadership/

management tasks (e.g., work control, cooperation, and development), which are interwoven with each other and therefore build on each other to a good extent.

2.4   Complementary Management Actors: Leading as Shared Leadership

The third core element of the Complementary Management Model consists of the complementary management actors. All persons involved in managerial activities can be described as such (see Holtbrügge 2004, p. 33; Reiß 2011a, b).

2.4.1   Theoretical Derivation: Shared Leadership, Self-Leadership, and the Exception Principle

The theoretical basis of the model element of complementary actors is the theory of Shared Leadership (see excursus box). According to this approach, not all management tasks have to be performed by the line manager; rather, other actors also take on parts of these tasks. In Complementary Management, the established concept of Shared Leadership is enhanced in a number of respects. First, the totality of management tasks to be shared is specified and the complementary behavioral components and the derivation of practice-relevant specifications for the behavior of the individual actors are clearly defined. Second, Shared Leadership is not regarded as an emergent phenomenon of highly developed teams under specific conditions, but as a ubiquitous phenomenon that can be shaped by the specifications of corporate management/leadership guidelines. Third, the mode of interaction among complementary actors is specified using a compensatory mechanism. Fourth and finally, senior managers and human resources advisors are also considered to be management actors.

> **Excursus: Shared Leadership**
> Not all leadership activities have to be undertaken by the line manager; instead, various parties are involved in the leadership process. In the last two decades, this phenomenon has increasingly undergone scientific examination under the terms "Shared Leadership", "Distributive Leadership", and "Collaborative Leadership". The three concepts show a great deal of overlap, but are also distinguishable from one another (Perry et al. 1999; Pearce and Conger 2003; Pearce and Manz 2005; Raelin 2005; Crevani et al. 2007; Pearce et al. 2010; Gockel and Werth 2010; Kramer and Crespy 2011; Bolden 2011; Contractor et al. 2012; Ridder and Hohn 2012; Hoch and Dulebohn 2013; Piecha and Wegge 2014). The concept can be traced back to Katz and Kahn (1966, p. 331 ff.). In fact, even before this, Stogdill (1950, p. 12) had noted that

(continued)

leadership influence in organizations is exercised not only by one person, but by all organizational members, and that it is done to varying degrees on a personal and situational basis. The idea goes back even farther to Fayol:

> "Management, thus understood, is neither an exclusive privilege nor a particular responsibility of the head or senior members of the business; it is an activity spread, like all other activities, between head and members of the body corporate." (Fayol 1916, p. 6)

The academic discussion surrounding Shared Leadership clearly focuses on the shifting of individual aspects of leadership to team members, on lateral leadership by hierarchical equals, on the reciprocal influences and team effects of joint leadership, and on the situational alternation of leadership responsibility by the right specialist, especially in projects. Isolated sources also refer to the division of leadership responsibility among co-leaders of a management team (e.g., O'Toole et al. 2002). Conversely, literature and empirical research on Shared Leadership have so far neglected to define a totality of leadership activities to be shared, to clearly describe complementary behavioral components, and to derive practice-relevant guidelines for the actions and behavior of individual actors. Moreover, Shared Leadership is usually described as an emergent phenomenon, giving the impression that it is a special feature of highly developed teams under certain conditions. In reality, however, Shared Leadership is of course something quite common: managers have always delegated individual management tasks, have handed them over to informal leaders, or have temporarily swapped leadership and employee roles (e.g., in projects). The quantitative sharing of management tasks is also common (and not only where leadership is organized in part-time and a job-sharing model), because no one directly leads or manages 200 employees.

In leadership research, the concept of Shared Leadership and the move toward collective aspects of leadership may represent or initiate a paradigm shift; in organizational practice, however, it is a very common phenomenon (Werther 2013, pp. 76, 98, 125 f.; Werther and Brodbeck 2014, pp. 23 f.). Another point of criticism concerns the role of the leader. Admittedly, some sources emphasize the fact that Shared Leadership and Vertical Leadership complement each other or that selective intervention by the manager remains quite necessary (see, e.g., Pearce et al. 2010, p. 152; Ridder and Hohn 2012, p. 161; Blessin and Wick 2017, p. 367). However, the mode of interaction is not sufficiently specified. Furthermore, the literature neglects certain actors such as senior managers or the HR function.

(continued)

Despite this, the approach still fundamentally broadens the view of leadership and management by taking into account not only the leader and those being led, but also, for example, colleagues. It thus provides a good theoretical starting point for considerations on the strength-oriented composition of leadership teams, but above all for the description of interaction dynamics between management actors.

When it comes to defining the interaction of the actors in detail, it is useful to refer to the theoretical approaches of Self-leadership and Management by Exception. Self-leadership (see excursus box) should be the essential principle of people management and leadership. While often a rather vague concept in literature, in Complementary Management it is described quite specifically as the fulfillment of management tasks by the employees themselves.

Excursus: Self-management and Self-leadership

Self-leadership, self-management, self-direction, and self-control have always been the subject of basic research on leadership, and many authors of scholarly and practice literature also emphasize that leadership should ideally be a guiding toward self-management (e.g., Parker Follett 1930, p. 282; Skinner 1953, p. 227 ff; Manz and Sims 1989; Stayer 1990; Pearce and Manz 2005; Andreßen 2008; Sprenger 2007a, 2012, p. 277 ff; Stewart et al. 2011; von der Oelsnitz 2012, p. 86 ff; Yukl 2013, p. 237 ff; Furtner and Baldegger 2013; Poznanski 2014; Müller 2014; Furtner and Maran 2015). Management pioneer Peter F. Drucker places it at the center of his teaching with the concept of "management by objectives and self-control" (Drucker 1954, p. 121, 1973, p. 430). Here, the work to be done is controlled exclusively by objectives, while the path to the goal is left to the employee. Drucker himself aptly calls this "freedom under the law" and "management philosophy" (Drucker 1954, p. 135 f.).

Self-management is one of the basic forms of gentle influence and, as such, is highly significant in practice (see Sect. 1.4). As is so often the case, however, the relevant research findings are of little relevance to organizational practice, partly because the various aspects of (self-accomplished) leadership and management are not operationalized in a practice-oriented manner and, on the whole, questions are pursued that are rather removed from actual practice. In general, the different aspects and degrees of work-related self-management are not sufficiently differentiated (see Sect. 2.4.3). Moreover, the tenor is often to give employees complete control over their work (see, e.g., Becker and Holzmann 2013), which, based on experience, is bound to fail. Another aspect neglected in the literature is the question of why self-management occurs and how it can be brought about (see Skinner 1953, p. 240).

In fact, it would be naive to give all employees complete and unconditional control over their work, because it cannot realistically be expected that in a major organization all employees are always willing and able to exercise complete self-management in the interest of the company. Compensatory mechanisms are therefore necessary—otherwise, there would be no need for elaborate theoretical models or for line managers. One such regulatory mechanism is the intervention of other management actors, which can be designed in accordance with the approach of Management by Exception (see excursus box): other actors intervene only if and when the employee does not perform the management tasks himself. The principle of exception is thus concretely related here to the concrete management tasks and conceived as a collective process of several actors.

Excursus: Management by Exception
The "Exception Principle" ("Management by Exception") does not have a particularly good reputation. In the literature on personnel management, it appears almost exclusively in connection with the Transformational Leadership approach. There, it is regarded as a characteristic of "Transactional Leadership" and then primarily involves the use of punishments in the event of negative deviations from performance standards and the enforcement of rules to prevent errors (Densten and Gray 1998, p. 82 f.; Garman et al. 2003; Yukl 2013, p. 313 f.). However, the Exception Principle actually means setting limits of competence within which the employee controls his or her own work, which should be the case especially in routine operations. The manager then becomes active only in exceptional cases when authorization limits are exceeded. General management literature has always dealt with it in this way (see Taylor 1911, pp. 55 f., 65; Drucker 1973, pp. 219 f., 499; Bittel 1964; Scholz 2014, p. 1150; Steinmann et al. 2013, pp. 55 ff.; Schulte-Zurhausen 2014, pp. 224 f.). This can be based on two mechanisms that are not mutually exclusive: either employees are required to report unusual incidents of their own accord, which then become the responsibility of the manager; or the manager keeps an eye on what is happening and intervenes (only) if something goes wrong. Thus, almost all organizations today still work according to the principle of Management by Exception. It is presumably so self-evident and easy to understand that its importance is generally underestimated.

2.4.2   Integration into the Overall Context of People Management

There are several actors involved in the management process who work together in a complementary way. In order to describe this phenomenon, it is first necessary to define the reference point of the interaction. Building on the task models of leadership and management in general, and the task element of the Complementary Management Model in particular (Sect. 2.3), it makes sense to frame this complementarity in terms of tasks. The contributions of the actors can vary from task to task. This is roughly illustrated in Fig. 2.1 which shows a different actor distribution under each task category.

The Complementary Management Model thus describes people management and leadership as a collective phenomenon which manifests itself in the division of labor when performing the 24 management tasks. Since these tasks systematically serve to more narrowly define the two complementary management functions (see Sect. 2.2), all actors are committed to the guiding principle of dual service. By fulfilling parts of the defined management tasks, they act as service providers, i.e., they have to fulfill both the support function and the disciplinary function in the process. This applies to the line manager, the senior manager, the employee's colleagues, and the HR advisor, who simultaneously support and supervise the employee (and who do so in a compensatory manner, i.e., only when needed). But it also applies to the employee who, as a self-manager, ideally helps and disciplines him or herself.

The model recommended here makes the employee the reference point and demands a high degree of self-management (not always, but as a general objective), making it highly effective and leading to an optimum utilization of the company's existing employee potential. However, it is also culture-dependent in the sense that it contradicts a directive management culture. Even if this culture only affects a single team and has been shaped by a single, highly directive supervisor, considerable resistance from employees is to be expected in the event of change ("... now we are supposed to do the boss's work ... He should kindly tell us what to do and provide us with technical support ..."). This can be particularly dangerous for new managers, especially since such resistance often leads to oppositional behavior in a completely different area. It becomes even more difficult if such a team is embedded in an overall directive corporate culture with a high power distance, or if this mentality characterizes the entire national culture (as is the case, for example, in many Eastern European countries). Here, there is a generally held view that the boss's job description quite naturally includes exerting external control "from above". This management principle is made possible (and stabilized) by pronounced hierarchies with small spans of control; efficiency and effectiveness are secondary to this. Here, anyone who wants to take a different pathway must first build up an extraordinarily good position and then carefully change direction.

2.4.3 The Employee: Self-Management as a Goal

The essential principle of people management and leadership should be self-direction by the employee. Its importance cannot be overstated. Indeed, people management and leadership should be associated with the goal of giving employees the greatest possible freedom, as this increases their effectiveness. As a result, they should take over the largest share of leadership as possible themselves:

> "The job of the man higher up is not to make decisions for his subordinates, but to teach them how to handle their problems themselves, how to make their own decisions." (Parker Follett 1930, S. 282)

Complete self-determination is, of course, no more desirable in an organization than in a state. Just as citizens of a state have to respect the laws, membership in an organization requires subordination to its respective goals. Organizational self-management is therefore always only partial self-management, whereby a differentiation can be made between different degrees of self-management (see Table 2.6).

According to the model presented here, self-management simply means that employees accomplish leadership/management tasks on their own. Ideal employees understand their work tasks, organize their own processes, motivate themselves, obtain resources and feedback on their own, solve cooperation problems themselves, etc.; in other words, they practice self-management and require practically no intervention from the manager. Ideally, employees even recognize when they are in the wrong job and initiate the separation on their own initiative. In principle, the

Table 2.6 Degrees of self-management (modified from Kaehler 2017, p. 178; © Boris Kaehler 2019. All rights reserved)

Content-related scope of self-management	Self-leadership or self-management is defined here as the employee accomplishing management tasks him/herself. Accordingly, all or only some of them are performed entirely or only partially by the employee. For example, an employee can define his or her own work objectives (i.e., decide which to derive from the company's objectives), self-determine the procedure for achieving these objectives, and/or self-obtain the necessary work resources.
Decision-related scope of self-management	The accomplishment of leadership/management tasks is by no means dichotomous (in the sense of "all or nothing"), but requires decisions that can be taken in gradual stages: (a) employee makes decision freely and independently; (b) employee makes decision with the help of the manager (initial suggestion, suggestion for improvement); (c) manager makes decision with the help of the employee (initial suggestion, suggestion for improvement); (d) manager makes decision alone and gives directive (see Tannenbaum and Schmidt 1958).
Time-related scope of self-management	Employees can accomplish a leadership/management task on a permanent or temporary basis. An external or self-made decision can have a lasting effect (in the sense of a permanent rule) or temporary effect.

Table 2.7 Differentiation between self-management, participation, and execution of work (modified from Kaehler 2020, p. 200; © Boris Kaehler 2020. All rights reserved)

Autonomous execution of work (i.e., the actual content of the employee's work)	Participation in the line manager's management activities (dialogs, meetings, etc.)	True self-management by performing management tasks (e.g., "defining work tasks", "solving conflicts", "qualifying")
• The employee's genuine functional-technical work responsibilities • Line managers should not assume this work themselves	• Line manager participation is required • Preparation of and presiding over meetings and/or taking minutes may be delegated to the employee	• "Development-oriented" external influence by manager with the goal of maximum self-management (for line managers, this can mean fewer and shorter leadership activities) • Recruitment of employees with strong self-management skills • Compensatory intervention by the manager if necessary

perception of one's own leadership/management routines can also be understood as self-management. For example, many people withdraw from time to time and consider their future goals or solutions to certain self-steerage problems. However, since these self-management routines are usually of a rather informal nature and serve to complete leadership/management tasks, this aspect can be ignored. More relevant, from a practical point of view, is the participation in the leadership/management routines of the manager (see Sect. 3.1.5). If employees partially organize meetings or team discussions themselves, this is not self-management in the narrower sense, but it does relieve the manager of external management tasks. This does not, though, affect the core content of self-management. From a theoretical and conceptual point of view, it, therefore, seems sensible to reserve the terms self-leadership and self-management for the self-accomplishment of leadership/management tasks (Table 2.7).

From a systematic point of view, self-management must also be distinguished from the self-reliant completion of non-managerial tasks. This pertains to the functional-technical tasks performed by employees that represent their actual work. They lie within the employees' genuine scope of responsibility, even if they practice no self-management at all (i.e., do not assume any of the 24 personnel management tasks themselves). In practice, however, the lines become blurred because there is little difference between the employee deciding on the content of the work assignment (= functional work task) and the employee only defining the work assignment itself (= leadership/management task).

2.4.4 Other Participants in the Management and Leadership Process

The Complementary Management Model describes the interaction between the main actors of people management and leadership. These are not only the employee, the manager, and the specialized HR manager (see Holtbrügge 2004, p. 33; Völkl and Menzel-Black 2014), but also the employee's colleagues and the senior manager, i.e., the manager's superior. In practice, other stakeholders may also be involved in the organizational leadership process, e.g., the manager's colleagues, the works council, customers, external consultants, or even coaches and family members (see Holtbrügge 2004, p. 33; Reiß 2011a, b). However, it is difficult to systematically standardize their influence. Even though their influence may be helpful in individual cases, corporate management models should not assign them a decisive role. Instead, they should be designed in such a way that good and holistic leadership/management arises solely from the actions of the main actors. It is irrelevant whether these key players have permanent employment contracts or whether they are external contractors. Temporary workers supplied by agencies must ultimately be managed in the same way as regular employees; interim managers and external HR service providers, insofar as they are assigned management/leadership responsibility, act in the same way as genuine line managers. Usually, however, all main actors are permanent employees.

As desirable as employee self-management is, it is utopian for *every* member of a larger organization to *always* perform *all* leadership/management tasks themselves. A great quote from Robert Greenleaf relays this thought precisely:

> "Anybody could lead perfect people—if there were any." (Greenleaf 1970, p. 13)

Unfortunately, they do not exist, and that is precisely why organizations need line managers. Organizational people management and leadership is therefore by no means the responsibility of the employee alone, but also of his or her manager. As a compensatory entity, the line manager ensures that all (self) management/leadership tasks are fulfilled, but only intervenes if the employee is unable to accomplish this (Sect. 2.4.5). The line manager cannot relinquish this responsibility; it is an essential part of the job and makes him or her an important decentralized performer of personnel work:

> "Every manager is an HR manager." (Scholz 1996, p. 1081)

Because of the special importance of line managers in the context of the overall management structures, a separate chapter of this book is devoted to them (Chap. 3).

Management tasks can also be shifted to the team and divided among colleagues so that (in whole or in part) it is no longer the line manager who leads, but the collective or an individual employee. In terms of theory, this is addressed, in particular, by the theoretical approach of Shared Leadership (see Sect. 2.4.1). In practice, this collegial leadership (also: "lateral leadership") is ubiquitous and taken for granted. Many employees are guided, motivated, developed, etc. much more by colleagues than by their line-manager. In many places, there are "gray eminences" and "good souls" who perform large proportions of certain management tasks. This can take different forms. The Complementary Management Model provides two options here. On the one hand, the compensatory intervention of a colleague can be initiated by employees themselves as part of their self-management mandate. For example, employees who are unable to do a task on their own may ask a colleague to train them by providing guidance, or to mediate a conflict with a third party. On the other hand, line managers may delegate management tasks within the scope of their compensatory mandate without relinquishing management responsibility as a whole (see Sect. 2.4.5). In the aforementioned case, the manager would delegate the training task or conflict resolution to an employee's colleague. A common form of leadership and management among colleagues, but one not envisaged in the Complementary Management Model, is the establishment of informal leadership positions. In this case, individual employees acquire, in effect, the positional power of a line manager through communicative and micropolitical skills. This does not appear desirable because it runs counter to the systematic nature and transparency of formal management structures.

In larger organizations, most managers inevitably are subordinate to an even higher-level manager. These senior managers play an essential role in day-to-day management. However, this role is rarely discussed in the literature (see Weibler 2014; see also Antonakis and Atwater 2002) and will be described in more detail in Sect. 3.1.5. For example, senior managers perform additional leadership/management routines that can be described as leadership across hierarchies and involve exerting communicative influence on all employees at subordinate levels of the hierarchy. However, they are also immediately involved in "normal" people management and leadership by managing the line managers directly subordinate to them and, as a compensatory entity, they are responsible for managing the next level down in the hierarchy. This compensatory mandate follows the principle of self-management, i.e., the senior manager only intervenes if the subordinate manager fails to fulfill his or her (leadership) responsibilities.

In practice, the involvement of senior managers in people management and leadership is commonplace. In many companies, they naturally step up in the absence of the direct manager, act as a complaint authority for employees and/or participate in the fulfillment of certain management tasks, e.g., by setting additional incentives. A typical practical example:

> "[Many shift supervisors don't] dare conduct critique dialogs on their own. Instead, they call in their superiors, such as corporate or plant managers." (Hölzl 2014, p. 45; own translation)

The example of the inexperienced new manager who needs practical day-to-day help in almost all personnel management matters, from salary issues to separation interviews, immediately illustrates the special function of the "boss's boss". However, it is also not uncommon for experienced managers to demonstrate leadership weaknesses that are (or should be) compensated for by their senior managers in a complementary manner.

Another indispensable actor in people management and leadership is the human resources manager. This refers to the person in the HR function/personnel department who oversees the organizational unit of the respective employee and his or her line manager. In many companies, these actors are referred to as HR advisors, while others prefer the dazzling term "HR business partner" or the apt but misleading term "HR consultant." Such HR managers act as an additional compensatory entity in the management process—analogous to senior managers. Such an active leadership role of HR advisors, referred to here as "HR co-management" (Kaehler 2012; synonymous with "HR co-leadership"), is today largely rejected in the literature or not even considered. This may soon change, and it would be about time:

> "Some things in HR work can be subsumed under the somewhat unwieldy term 'management-related support tasks'. This is by no means just administrative support, but something like co-management or co-leadership." (Kern und Schneider 2017, p. 74; own translation)

Where people management and leadership really works in practice, there are almost always HR advisors involved as co-managers who support and supervise managers in operational matters. Analogous to the senior manager, the HR advisor, following the primacy of self-management, only has to intervene if the line manager does not fulfill his or her responsibility to the employee. This is absolutely necessary because in organizations with many line managers, there are always some that display occasional/situational or even massive leadership deficits.

Interestingly, while this strong advisory mandate of HR managers is, in effect, exercised in many companies, it is hardly ever formally standardized by the management/leadership model or structures. Instead, HR departments fight for their corresponding position of authority in the shadowy realm of micropolitics through privileged access to key people and resources. In many cases, people management and leadership only function because HR informally oversteps its actual role and intervenes in the management process in tacit agreement with the units in charge. This makes perfect sense, but it contradicts the idea of transparent and systematically designed management/leadership structures. The role of the HR function is dealt with in detail in Chap. 4, where other activities are also discussed—including participation in strategic issues and the development and administration of HR instruments.

2.4.5 Compensatory Interaction Between the Leadership Actors

So various actors are involved in the management process. The essential principle of people management and leadership should be self-management. Ideally, employees know what work needs to be done, they motivate themselves, resolve conflicts on their own, acquire new knowledge on their own if this is required, and so on. This means that they perform the corresponding leadership/management tasks themselves

Table 2.8 Intervention options of the line manager (here illustrated by the example of the management task "resolving conflicts") (modified from Kaehler 2017, p. 182; (© Boris Kaehler 2019. All rights reserved)

Corrective intervention	The line manager induces the employee to fulfill the leadership/ management task (i.e., in this case, resolving an existing conflict with colleagues him/herself).
Joint intervention	The line manager supports the employee in performing the leadership/ management task (i.e., in this case, in resolving the conflict).
Delegative intervention	The manager arranges for a colleague of the employee or for the HR advisor to fulfill the leadership/management task (i.e., in this case, to mediate the conflict). This can be used to compensate for the line manager's own time or competence deficits. "The ideal manager is the man who knows exactly what he is not capable of doing himself, and who gets the right people to do it" (Attributed to Philip Rosenthal).
Substituting intervention	The manager takes on the leadership/management task him/herself (and mediates the conflict).

and thus fulfill both the support function of self-help and the order function of self-discipline. However, since experience shows that not all employees are always willing and able to exercise self-steerage in the interest of the company, a regulator is required.

This is where the compensatory mechanism of Complementary Management comes into play. At its core is the line manager as the essential compensatory entity. In relation to each particular management task, line managers must constantly assess the extent to which the individual employee is already performing these tasks on his or her own and take compensatory action (only) in the event of deficits. If employees know their assignments and are aware of their performance, for example, the line manager no longer needs to explain this to them; if not, the line manager must intervene. There are several intervention options (Table 2.8) that can also be combined. Intervention takes place with the full authority and positional power of classic authoritarian leadership/management, but should preferably be exercised gently, e.g., via informal behavioral reinforcement and implicit communication (see Sect. 1.4).

The role of the line manager as a compensatory entity is therefore to ensure that all management tasks are performed in relation to those being managed/led. This is done within the framework of leadership/management routines (e.g., in regular work dialogs). Admittedly: The fact that line managers have to perform various leadership/management routines while keeping an eye on many different leadership/management tasks may seem complicated at first. In practice, however, the concept can be easily implemented since the tasks and routines are not extravagant undertakings, but merely systematized facets of typical managerial work. No line manager is overburdened by having to conduct regular work dialogs, team meetings, etc., while paying attention to multiple aspects such as work assignments, performance feedback, revision, and conflicts. Compare the principle to the requirements of any job, from chef to pilot: Are a dozen activities, each made up of two dozen tasks, anything out of the ordinary?

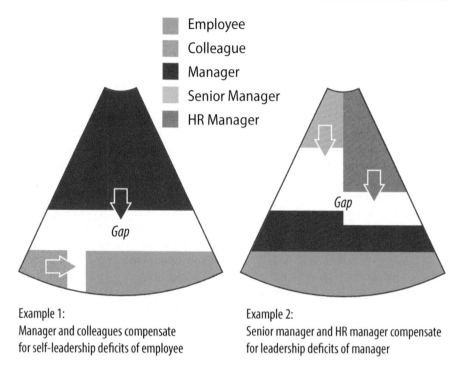

Example 1:
Manager and colleagues compensate
for self-leadership deficits of employee

Example 2:
Senior manager and HR manager compensate
for leadership deficits of manager

Fig. 2.2 Compensatory situational interaction of the management actors (own graphic based on Kaehler 2014b, p. 460; modified from Kaehler 2017, p. 183; © Boris Kaehler 2017. All rights reserved)

Just as not all employees always and fully lead and manage themselves, not all line managers are always and fully willing and able to fulfill their compensatory responsibilities. For this reason, other actors must be involved in the leadership process who, in turn, act as higher-level compensatory entities. These are the senior manager and the HR advisor, who intervene in a compensatory manner with respect to the line manager according to the same principles as the line manager intervenes with respect to the employee (see Sects. 3.1.3 and 4.2.3).

The principle is illustrated in Fig. 2.2 using two unspecified leadership/management tasks as examples. In the first case, a colleague and the manager compensate for the task-related self-management deficits of the employee. In the second example, the line manager does not fulfill his mandate and only partially compensates for the employee's self-management deficits; here, the senior manager and the HR advisors intervene in a compensatory manner. In principle, the superordinate entities only become active when deficits exist, i.e., they only fill the "gap" that the respective subordinate entity allows to arise.

This compensatory mechanism ensures that all management tasks relating to an employee are actually performed even if the line manager is inactive, thus ensuring effective people management. At the same time, the multilevel system prevents abuse of power by the line manager. This means that all four actors have a permanent leadership/management responsibility. The respective superordinate entities are responsible for ensuring that none of the 24 leadership/management tasks are neglected and intervene as soon as deficits arise. People management and leadership is therefore neither the task of managers nor the task of the HR department, but a collective process.

So far, a dynamic distribution of the participants has been assumed, in which the compensatory entities react situationally to deficits or needs. This is indeed necessary because it is the only way to ensure situational-based distribution. A static distribution can, however, also be established. This is often the case when it is obvious from the outset that the subordinate actor is unwilling or unable to perform a leadership/management task. In this case, compensatory influence takes place proactively, i.e., the higher-level entity intervenes on its own initiative. For example, the superordinate actors typically provide very strong proactive support to new managers and new employees and only gradually withdraw over time.

In principle, it is also possible to permanently leave individual parts of a management task not to the employee, but rather to another specific party. For example, the line manager may claim the right to optimize the work processes of all employees him or herself, or a colleague or an HR advisor may be the one who always organizes the integration of new employees. Of course, such a fixed distribution calls into question the general primacy of self-management. It is certainly possible to permanently keep employees "on a short leash" with regard to certain or even all leadership/management tasks. However, the clearly more efficient and effective principle lies in comprehensive self-management, which should therefore be the long-term aim. The principle of the development-oriented management of work tasks can thus be generalized in the sense of development-oriented external management that is only temporary. Here, too, it is advisable to resort to informal behavioral reinforcement and implicit communication (see Sect. 1.4).

For the sake of theoretical clarity, a systematic reference is again indicated here: The distribution of management tasks among the actors must be systematically separated from the distribution of management routines. The latter is determined on a company-specific basis, e.g., in the course of introducing a corporate model of leadership (see Sect. 2.6). For example, a particular company may stipulate that only managers, only HR advisors, or both are to participate in the management routines "annual performance review" and "separation project". The decisive factor here is to divide up the routines in such a way that all compensatory actors have the opportunity to keep track of all management tasks for the routines assigned to them. The distribution of management routines among the actors, therefore, does not determine the division of management tasks.

A further demarcation concerns the genuine functional-technical work tasks of the employee. These tasks are purely executional in nature and are the employee's genuine responsibility, even if he or she does not practice self-management/self-leadership in any way (i.e., does not completely take over any of the 24 personnel management tasks). Here, too, interventions may occur because, as a rule, the line manager cannot completely escape responsibility for the functional-technical work.

The mechanism of choice here is the "exception principle" or "management by exception," according to which the manager only assumes responsibility for tasks in cases of escalation and disruption (see Sect. 2.4.1). Both types of intervention are of a compensatory nature, but from a systematic point of view, people management and leadership (= steering influence) must be kept separate from the execution of work (conducting/performing work). In practice, however, the lines are blurred because there is little difference between the employee deciding on the content of the work order (= functional work task) or only on the definition of the work order itself (= personnel management task).

2.5   The Four Implementation Elements

The core model of Complementary Management presented in the previous sections has three elements (management functions, tasks, and actors) and describes the fundamental aspects and mechanisms of people management and leadership in organizations. In order to understand and actually design real leadership/management processes, additional model elements are required that describe the actual implementation of the core model.

2.5.1   Systematic Relationship Between the Core Model and Implementation Elements

Figure 2.3 shows these four implementation elements (management unit design, management routines, management instruments, management resources) which are explained in more detail below.

The systematic relationship can be summarized as follows: Managers fulfill management tasks (e.g., performance feedback) by performing management routines (e.g., interviews), apply management instruments (e.g., work schedules), require management resources (e.g., business information), and do all this on the basis of the management unit design (e.g. their span of control). Table 2.9 clarifies this distinction.

It should be noted that the model elements are not clearly delineated building blocks with clearly delineated content, but rather different perspectives on one and the same object of observation. All seven perspectives are needed to comprehensively understand and implement organizational leadership and management. When implementing the theory in corporate leadership and management models, it is entirely possible to replace the individual elements with alternative concepts. Even corporate models that omit some elements altogether can be effective, since the missing perspectives are not non-existent, but simply not explicitly regulated. It is thus perfectly possible for leaders to, for example, perform routines or mobilize resources even if these are not defined in a corporate model. However, holistic corporate models of leadership and management should, of course, take up and develop all seven elements (see Sect. 2.6).

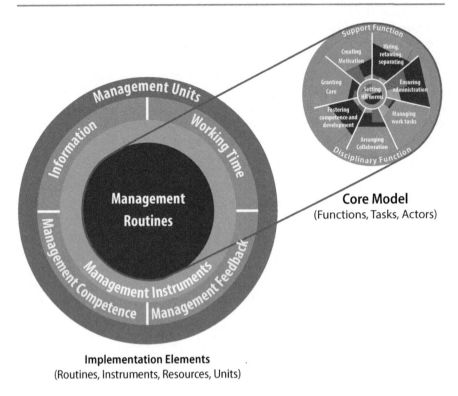

Core Model
(Functions, Tasks, Actors)

Implementation Elements
(Routines, Instruments, Resources, Units)

Fig. 2.3 Core model and implementation elements of Complementary Management (modified from Kaehler 2017, p. 317; © Boris Kaehler 2019. All rights reserved)

The four implementation elements of the Complementary Management Model (structure, routines, instruments, and resources) are structures that are needed to put the core model into practice. When implementing a corporate model of management and leadership, these elements are designed specifically for the company and distributed among the individual management actors (also see Sect. 2.6). In the process, the logical as well as the personal levels overlap. Since the leadership/management actors are not only leaders but also led themselves, the task element of the Complementary Model must also be applied to them. And because the catalog of 24 leadership/management tasks theoretically aims to describe the prerequisites of human performance, the implementation elements are in fact already included in it, because leadership work is of course also work. Strictly speaking, the implementation elements only represent substantive specifications: the design of the management unit specifies the management task of "optimizing organizational design", the management routines and instruments relate to the management tasks of "optimizing processes" and "defining work tasks and instructions", and the four management resources refer to the management tasks of "providing working time and resources", "ensuring coordinative communication", "evaluating performance and giving feedback", and "to qualify". The fact that only these seven of the 24 leadership/

Table 2.9 Delineation between core elements and implementation elements (modified from Kaehler 2017, p. 318; © Boris Kaehler 2019. All rights reserved)

	Element	Content	Object of observation
Core model	Management functions	Support function and disciplinary function	"What is leadership for?"
	Management tasks	Eight task categories with three tasks each (e.g., performance feedback)	"What is to be accomplished?"
	Management actors	Employee, line manager, senior manager, colleagues, and HR advisor	"Who leads?"
Implementation elements	Management unit design	Organizational units involved in leadership and their distribution of tasks/authorities	"What units are there and who does or is authorized to do what?"
	Management routines	Concrete activities (e.g., conducting dialogs)	"What concrete behavioral actions have to be taken?"
	Management instruments	Formalized systems, programs and forms (e.g., working time system)	"What tools should be used?"
	Management resources	Management competence, management information, management working time, management feedback	"What do leaders need?"

management tasks are designed as implementation elements can be explained by the fact that these tasks require leadership-specific solutions and are so critical to success that they require a uniform, formalized design. In principle, all other leadership/management tasks are also relevant, but for pragmatic reasons they are not designed as separate model elements here due to their lesser importance. Systematically, therefore, the four implementation elements of the Complementary Management Model are really only specifications of the management tasks in relation to the work of management. As confusing as these statements may be at first glance, they cannot be omitted here for reasons of systematic transparency. However, they are of no significance for the practical implementation of leadership models.

The systematic differentiation of tasks, routines, and instruments makes the topic of people management and leadership complex because, in addition to a few dozen management tasks, there are about as many management routines and management instruments needed to achieve the tasks. Some authors therefore resort to radical abbreviation. However, it is common knowledge that many different activities (workshops, meetings, a range of employee discussions) and tools (systems, plans, documentation, etc.) are inevitably used in the fulfillment of the various leadership/management tasks (work control, cooperation, motivation, etc.) in everyday corporate life. Resources and structures are also naturally involved. Accordingly, conceptual theorists and practical users are required to deal with all of the core and implementation elements, even if this appears confusing at first glance. Once again, we can fall back on the metaphor of driving a car, an activity consisting of numerous subtasks and many different activities, for which dozens of instruments are required—from the starter motor to the warning vest. Yet no one seems overwhelmed by this.

2.5.2 Management Unit Design

The management unit design is understood here to mean the organizational setup that shapes the scope of action of the management actors. This relates to the structure and hierarchical integration of the organizational units involved in people management and leadership (jobs, groups, departments, divisions, etc.). Also associated with this, however, is the distribution of tasks among the actors and the respective powers (in the sense of authorizations). Like all other organizational activities, leadership/management activities should be systematically anchored in the organizational structure. Thus, the general principles of organizational design also apply here.

The management unit design, like the other elements of the model, does not represent a subarea of leadership/management, but constitutes a particular perspective on it. As such, it cannot be viewed separately from the overall model. Without permanent unit structures, processes of influence certainly take place, but this no longer has any bearing on goal-oriented organizational leadership and management. Although the Complementary Management Model leaves room for tasks and activities to be widely distributed among the actors, its elements provide a rough structural framework. For example, an HR department that, for lack of authorization, neglects one of the two complementary service functions (support/discipline) or refuses to engage in compensatory HR co-management would be incompatible with the Complementary Management Model.

How people management and leadership works in an organization depends largely on how the unit is designed. Conversely, the unit must be designed in such a way that functional people management and leadership is possible. The organizational structures of the management actors are mutually dependent: the responsibility of one unit does not need to be assigned to another anymore. According to the Complementary Management Model, several actors share responsibility for fulfilling the defined leadership/management tasks. Accordingly, the design of staff positions should take into account the duty and authorization for self-management, which must also be reflected in job descriptions, for example. The design of line management and HR advisor positions, on the other hand, should establish their roles as compensatory entities (see Sect. 2.4.5). The structure of line management positions is discussed in more detail in Sect. 3.1.4. The organizational structure of the HR department is the subject of Sect. 4.2.3.

One of the key aspects of management unit design is the definition of the span of control, i.e., the number of staff positions reporting directly to a line manager. Although on the surface it only concerns the design of line management positions, it inevitably also affects the job assignments and responsibilities of the other

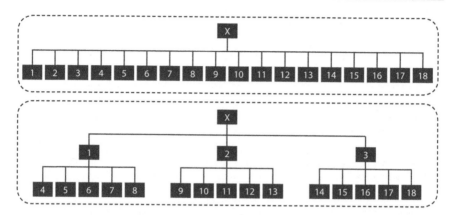

Fig. 2.4 Relationship between span of control and depth of control (from Kaehler 2014a, b, p. 58; own graphic based on Carzo/Yanouzas 1969, p. 181; © Boris Kaehler 2014. All rights reserved)

leadership/management actors. The span of management results from the principle of hierarchy, i.e., the formal subordination or superordination of organizational units (departments, jobs, etc.). The decisive factor is that there is a negative correlation between span of control and depth of control, i.e., the smaller the span of control, the greater the number of hierarchical levels (for the same number of employees) (Simon 1946, p. 56; see Fig. 2.4).

With this in mind, the omnipresent talk of "flat hierarchies" and "hierarchy reduction" is misleading. An organization needs exactly as many hierarchy levels as are necessary to ensure that the span of control at the level of the organizational units is not too large (= no longer manageable), but also not too small (= unnecessary interfaces). The issue of the right span of control is discussed in more detail in Sect. 3.1.4. However, the margin is quite limited, with around 15 being the maximum. The next time someone proudly tells you that they have 30 or more employees in their direct reporting line, ask them about the actual distribution of specific leadership/management tasks. It will almost always turn out that a) essential leadership/management tasks are actually not being performed at all, that b) it involves an extremely well-structured workplace in which process specifications largely standardize work behavior, or that c) informal leadership/management positions have been established that just do not officially appear in the organizational chart. The same also applies to all concepts of (allegedly) hierarchy-free leadership and management, which have already been criticized in Sect. 1.7.6. At any rate, where a "flat hierarchy" is mentioned, it is usually not really the hierarchy that is meant, but the organization's power distance and communication/decision culture.

2.5.3   Management Routines

In order to put management tasks into practice, concrete management activities such as discussions and meetings are required. These can aptly be described as routines because they are, at minimum, potentially recurring, represent an expected behavior, and should be tested or practiced. Leadership routines are leadership-related activities or actions that, together, make up the leadership activity of a specific actor—i.e., the concrete application of leadership and management:

> "What then is leadership [. . .]? The first thing to say about it is that it is work." Peter F. Drucker (1992, p. 101)

For some, the term "routine" may take some getting used to as it can be used in a rather negative way in the sense of mindless, repetitive work. This is, of course, not what is meant though, and with appropriate communication, the term can certainly acquire a positive connotation in corporate jargon. If necessary, it can be replaced by an alternative term like "leadership/management activities". While Ulrich (1978, p. 214, own translation) really addresses the (not necessarily congruent) construct of "methods", he expresses the underlying approach well and even closely linguistically:

> "Methods directly serve to regulate the behavior of managers, they suggest to them a certain approach to solving their management tasks. Methods as specific procedures for solving problems play an outstanding role in all human spheres of action; the learning of appropriate methods forms an essential part of school education, learning and experience. Every human being acquires 'routines' during the repeated execution of similar actions, which he uses from then on; the self-evident mastery of such methods represents a tremendous facilitation of work. Since the beginning of industrial psychology, however, it has been known that the 'routines that arise by themselves' are rarely also the most economical ones."

In terms of management theory, this model element is based on the established concept of organizational routines (see excursus box). These are repetitive, recognizable patterns of independent actions by multiple actors in the organizational context. Formal business processes, which, after all, also include a sequence of activities, may be understood as a form of organizational routines. The concept of organizational routines goes beyond them, however, in that it addresses not only the idealized, schematic form of the sequence, but also the patterns that are actually lived. Organizational routines can be influenced by behavioral prescriptions, but they cannot be completely determined. The Complementary Management Model takes up this approach because leadership/management activities are indeed patterns since they can also be established informally, and because they can be influenced in part but not in their entirety by behavioral prescriptions. For this reason, they can be integrated into business processes, but not completely mapped. For example, it is advisable to define the approximate frequency and objectives of team meetings and to make formal/content-related recommendations for them. However, the actual course of the meeting cannot be meaningfully described as a process.

Excursus: Organizational Routines

According to most definitions in what is quite inconsistent literature, organizational routines are repetitive, recognizable patterns of independent actions by multiple actors in an organizational context (see Feldman and Pentland 2003; Becker 2004, p. 644 ff.). They can be viewed as an organizational analogy to individual habits (Hodgson 2009, p. 26). They may serve the organization as a method or technology, while at the same time representing organizational capabilities or potentials (Nelson 2009). As such, they can be a source of organizational inertia and inflexibility, but also an important framework for flexible situational action (Feldman and Pentland 2003, p. 94); the existence of a routine says nothing about its degree of regulation and situational flexibility. Organizational routines have coordinating, stabilizing, complexity-reducing, and knowledge-binding functions (Becker 2004, p. 662). Organizational science has increasingly dealt with them in recent decades (see in particular Nelson and Winter 1982; Feldman and Pentland 2003; Becker 2004; Becker et al. 2005; Pentland and Feldman 2005; Becker and Lazaric 2009; Nelson 2009; Hodgson 2009; Pentland et al. 2010, 2012; Hansen and Vogel 2011; Kaiser and Kozica 2013; Kozica et al. 2014; Geiger and Schröder 2014; Beverungen 2014; see also Ulrich 1978). Formal business processes, which also involve a sequence of activities, may be understood as a form of organizational routine. However, the concept of organizational routines goes beyond this by addressing not only the "ostensive" aspects of the process, i.e., its idealized, schematic form, but also the "performative" aspects, i.e., the patterns that are actually lived experiences. In this context, organizational routines can be influenced by the ostensive specifications but cannot be completely determined (Feldman and Pentland 2003; Pentland and Feldman 2005, pp. 796 f., 2008; Beverungen 2014, p. 215). The design of organizational routines can thus be viewed as a hierarchical construction process as well as a social construction process (Beverungen 2014, p. 217).

Looking at the publications available on the topic of organizational routines, it is noticeable that it is a rather diffuse theoretical construct that provides few concrete starting points for how routines can be concretely dealt with in practice (Kaiser and Kozica 2013, p. 18). The literature clearly focuses on organizational analysis, i.e., organizational routines are understood as a way to understand organizational circumstances. In principle, however, the concept can also be used for the systematic design of leadership and management structures, insofar as organizations assign leaders certain predefined activities (e.g., occasion-related discussions) that are to be implemented by them according to specific action maxims.

A closer look at the management tasks contained in typical task models quickly reveals that they are not concrete activities but rather tasks, i.e., objectives to be achieved (see Sect. 2.3.1). Determining work assignments, solving conflicts,

Table 2.10 Types of management routines (modified from Kaehler 2017, p. 323; © Boris Kaehler 2019. All rights reserved)

Continuous routines (on a weekly or monthly basis)	Individual work dialogs; team meetings, short workplace visits
Annual routines	Annual employee dialogs; annual team events (strategy workshop; team building workshop; community event)
On-demand routines	Problem talks for misconduct/conflict; illness/crisis intervention; on-the-job guidance; hiring project, separation project, etc.

providing motivation, etc. are not concrete activities, but rather people-related results to be achieved through the influence of management and leadership. This also applies to the catalog of tasks of the Complementary Management Model described in Sect. 2.3.3. It is, therefore, necessary to introduce a further element in addition to the tasks, which specifies the concrete activities through which the management/leadership influence is exercised. This distinction between tasks and activities is unusual, but actually quite obvious. Hodgson et al. (1965, p. 231) already distinguished between mere task expectations and the actions actually exhibited, albeit using misleading terminology. Complementary Management theory accounts for this with the implementation element of management routines. The management tasks are part of the core model and, in fact, designate goals ("What is to be accomplished?"); management routines as an implementation element, on the other hand, describe concrete activities ("What exactly is to be done?").

In terms of their defined rhythm, management routines can be divided into continuous routines, annual routines, and on-demand routines (Table 2.10). Certain routines must be performed on an ongoing basis, others only within the rhythm of business periods, and still others only when required.

Management routines cannot be assigned 1:1 to management tasks so that a particular routine would serve to achieve a particular management task. Rather, there are many overlaps and duplications. For example, the management routine of the weekly work dialog implements almost all 24 management tasks. The spectrum of other management routines is not quite as broad, but they all serve to fulfill multiple management tasks.

Many activities that are discussed in the literature are actually not management activities at all, but only their fundamental basis. Some of them are completely unspecific and occur as part of practically all of life's activities. Communicating, observing, reflecting, praising, etc., must be done by everyone who is active in any way or who deals with people. They are not specific and are just as relevant when going to the zoo or having a coffee, both of which have nothing to do with organizational leadership/management. Others are definitely specific for managing organizations, but not for managing people. Planning, decision-making, organizing, instructing, and controlling are examples. If we follow the management definition outlined in Sect. 1.1, leadership and management is a steering influence on business operations which can and should also be exercised as self-management. In this sense, planning, etc. is definitely a management activity. If you plan the preparation of your

Sunday omelet, you are managing yourself; the frying and the enjoyment of the egg dish, on the other hand, would be considered the execution. Managing one's breakfast, of course, is not organizational leadership either. Thus, planning is an elementary activity, a building block. It is practiced when leading/managing organizations, but also when raising children, selling ice cream, cutting hair, or lifeguarding. It is of course practiced in people management and leadership in order to fulfill specific tasks. However, it does not constitute people management and leadership and is not a complex routine, but merely its basis, its behavioral building block. Leadership routines are thus nothing more than framework activities within which the many elementary activities necessary for the performance of management tasks and their elementary tasks take place. For example, the management task "to round off the incentive field" consists, among other things, of the elementary task "praise", which is fulfilled by the elementary activity "communicate" within, e.g., the routine "work meeting". Table 3.4 in Sect. 3.4.3 clarifies the distinction and explains its implications using the line manager as an example.

Management routines are actor specific, i.e., specific routines are to be defined for each management actor. However, as a rule, several actors are involved in each management routine. A work dialog, for example, is by no means only a line manager's activity but at least as much an activity of the employee. Thus, it is a routine of both the line manager and the employee. Many routines also involve colleagues, senior managers, or HR advisors. The exact proportion of the actors in the routines depends on the company. Thus, in the course of introducing a corporate leadership model, the routines must first be defined and specified. These specifications can then be narrowed down on an individual basis, with the manager assigning certain parts of certain routines to a specific employee. This results in a bundle of responsibilities for each actor, which forms his or her management activity.

Corporate models of leadership and management can make very different arrangements in this respect. For example, in some companies only the HR department is responsible for recruitment projects or termination dialogs, in others only the responsible line manager, and in still others both together. In principle, an actor's shares in routines always add up to the totality of his or her management job. Once the actor-specific parts of routines have been determined, they cannot be delegated in any meaningful way. The actors must therefore participate in their respective routines. However, they do not necessarily have to be in charge of organizing and executing the routines themselves. For example, taking minutes at meetings and in work dialogs can be the responsibility of either the employee or the line manager; the line manager or the HR advisor can conduct job interviews, and so on. From a theoretical and conceptual perspective, this is because a routine is usually assigned to several actors and thus not everyone can perform all sub-activities themselves. It is of practical importance because it offers the possibility of shifting work volumes between the actors (e.g., it can relieve the line manager from taking minutes or conducting interviews).

In addition to the people management routines described below, the management actors generally work in other areas and take on other routines, such as conducting/

executing non-managerial work or non-people management routines. This is explained in more detail in Sects. 3.1.5 and 4.2.5 in relation to the line manager and the HR department. A systematic peculiarity lies in the fact that some management routines—above all the permanent routine "work dialog"—also contain functional-technical components. These are therefore not purely people-related, but also, at least in part, functional-technical management routines. This has a conceptual and theoretical significance for defining self-management (see Sect. 2.4.3) and the distinction between people and non-people management routines (see Sect. 3.1.5). In practice, however, the lines become blurred because there is little difference between making a decision on the content of the work assignment (= factual-technical task) and only defining the work assignment itself (= personnel management task).

The definition of management routines is, or should be, an important component of corporate models of leadership and management. Organizations have significant latitude in shaping their own model, which they must utilize if a common understanding is actually to be achieved. Under no circumstances should they merely define a catalog of management tasks and leave it up to the discretion of the management actors or the arbitrary interpretation of leadership trainers. Experience shows that the most diverse—and unfortunately often dysfunctional—ideas take hold in such cases. For this reason, the routines should be clearly defined as part of leadership and management structures (see Sect. 2.6).

Depending on the specific design of the corporate model of leadership and management, the individual actors are responsible for certain parts of certain routines. In order to ensure that the defined management routines are actually put into practice, appropriate normative prescriptions are required. It has proven useful to implement these specifications in guidelines that also contain concrete recommendations for action, descriptions of behavior, and tips. For example, a guideline for weekly work dialogs can contain recommendations for different phases of conversation and how to deal with common difficulties. In this context, it may be helpful to describe the required behavior not only positively but also negatively, i.e., to also give examples of leadership mistakes and behaviors that should be refrained from (Schilling 2005, p. 130; Armbrüster and Hehn 2011). In any case, the principle of compensatory intervention, including the various intervention options, should be explained. It should be conveyed that authoritarian influence is necessary under certain circumstances, but that it is not synonymous with appellative instructions (Instead, it should preferably be gentle, using informal behavioral reinforcement and implicit communication, see Sect. 1.4).

Since most routines involve multiple actors, it makes little sense to frame such guidelines and recommendations as secret documents for executives. Rather, they should be made available to all members of the organization. It is true that they primarily serve as a basis of information and training for managers. However, employees should also have access to them; after all, they also play an active role in the line manager's routines. Good leadership and management thrive on all the actors involved sharing a common understanding of it. Moreover, especially in a working world dominated by digital media, communication materials such as guidelines or seminar documents must always be expected to reach the internal or even external public. Transparency is, therefore, on the whole, more advisable here than secrecy.

2.5.4 Management Instruments

The term "management instrument" (also: "leadership instrument", "HR instrument", and "management tool") is widely used in the literature, but is usually overstretched to include routines, i.e., activities (e.g., Malik 2000, pp. 242 ff., Malik 2007, p. 75 ff; Weise and Selck 2007; Weibler 2016, pp. 365 ff). In the context of Complementary Management theory, it is reserved for formalized tools that support people management and leadership, e.g., sets of rules, systems, programs, and forms. The management instruments available in a particular organization are applied by the leader in the management routines. Only a selection of particularly important or widespread management instruments is discussed below. In principle, however, every formalized tool counts, from the travel expense account form up to the legally mandatory reports. The term thus covers a broad spectrum of very different formalisms and there may be problems of demarcation, e.g., with regard to the question of whether external coaching or outplacement is more likely to be counted as a tool or as an activity. From a pragmatic point of view, however, such issues do not really matter. What is important is that the management actors know which tools to use. To ensure this, organizations are well-advised to systematize them.

Management instruments are usually designed by the HR function (see Sect. 4.2.5), but other management actors may also be involved. They are part of governance, i.e., the regulatory framework of corporate management and leadership (Sect. 2.6). Formalisms, such as early retirement or working time regulations, which are standardized by legislation, regional collective agreements, or similar agreements, can also be considered instruments insofar as they are used as tools in an organization. Instruments must therefore be systematically distinguished from the legal sources and corporate norms—programs, guidelines, company agreements, collective agreements, laws, etc.—in which they are formally laid down.

Similar to management tasks and management routines, management instruments encompass a whole catalog of relevant tasks. Not every organization uses every management instrument. Also an instrument can take on very different forms and degrees of complexity. For example, the working time system may only encompass the statutory regulations, as is the case in many very small companies; in large companies, on the other hand, elaborate sets of rules are typical, which provide comprehensive and detailed variants for dozens of occupational groups and are codified in works agreements. However, certain topics are covered by instruments

Table 2.11 The main management instruments ()

Information and controlling system (e.g., personnel information system, personnel files, and HR controlling including employee surveys)
Organization manual (e.g., structure and process documentation, quality systems, codes of conduct, and control systems)
Compensation system; working time system
Recruitment and selection tools (e.g., staffing plan, applicant management system/career portal, personnel marketing mix, and candidate pools)
Personnel selection instruments (e.g., assessment center and test procedures)
Personnel development tools (e.g., training programs and external training courses, development/ promotion programs, and knowledge management systems)
Separation instruments (e.g., personnel reduction instruments, outplacement, and partial retirement)
Performance management systems (e.g., objective agreements, performance appraisals, and rewards)

almost everywhere, if only because labor and tax regulations make this compulsory. Table 2.11 provides an overview of the main management instruments.

The conceptual differentiation between routines and instruments has significant implications. Leadership and management is not exercised by the instrument (e.g., a salary system or appraisal procedure), but always by its specific application. Good instruments are sometimes devalued by poor application. Conversely, dysfunctional and poorly designed HR instruments can be put into perspective in the course of their application—a question of management quality, but certainly also a question of the internal distribution of roles and power. For example, many companies have formalized bonus systems that work as incentive instruments, but in practice trigger massive mis-steerage (e.g., one-sided fulfillment of sales goals while neglecting risk, innovation, and social behavior). Within the context of management routines, the line manager has to apply the instrument, while at the same time round off the incentive field by setting additional incentives (e.g., praise/reproach).

Consequently, few aspects of human resource work are criticized as massively as these tools. In many places, they have developed into bureaucracies that hinder good people management and leadership instead of promoting it, and which degenerate into unproductive self-employment. The problem here is not the formalization as such, but the formalization of ineffectual procedures that are not related to actual management tasks and routines. Another problem is the often excessive rigidity of the standardization, which does not allow for decision-making leeway or exceptions. And finally, many management instruments suffer from a lack of evaluation and do not adapt to changing contextual conditions. This prompts the three antidotes: strict alignment with management tasks and routines, implementation of decision latitude and exceptions, and ongoing review and adaptation based on user feedback. All three ensure that the people management and leadership tools actually provide assistance (Kaehler 2016, p. 25).

2.5.5 Management Resources

The four implementation elements of the Complementary Management Model are actually nothing more than specifications of the content of certain management tasks with regard to management and leadership as work. This results from an overlapping of person-related levels: management actors are not only managers of others, but also managers of themselves. Thus, the task element of the Complementary Model can also be applied to their own (management) work. In this context, the four management resources—information, feedback, working time, and competence embody the four management tasks of "ensuring coordinative communication", "giving feedback", "providing working time", and "training".

The fact that only these four management tasks are resources is due to the pragmatic design of the model. Working time, information, competence, and feedback are highlighted simply because people management and leadership so often fails in practice because of these very resources. Strictly speaking, however, they have more or less been arbitrarily taken from the catalog of 24 management tasks (or the requirements of human performance depicted in the management tasks, which are of course also decisive for management work). In principle, the health or motivation of management actors, for example, could also be labeled as a resource. This reduction primarily makes it easier for the model to be handled. Again, it should be noted that these are clarifications in the sense of systematic and theoretical transparency. They are not significant for the practical implementation of the model.

The first of the four management resources is information. Whether crafting strategies, defining work tasks, or providing motivation—ultimately, no management task can be mastered without knowing the superordinate frame of reference and having information about the current situation. Of course, this applies to everything and everyone within an organization. There is no doubt that all management actors need comprehensive information, for instance, on the company's purpose, the strategies chosen, the current situation (market, revenues, costs, etc.), and the existing structures. This need must be continuously met. Typically, information is passed from one hierarchical level to another. Equally important, however, are the tools that allow those concerned to constantly arm themselves with relevant information. Knowledge management systems can make a valuable contribution here. It is advisable to systematically analyze the information needs of the management actors and to develop an information system tailored to these needs. However, information is by no means synonymous with hard accounting data and market-related facts. "Soft" factors, which are more likely to be picked up at the watercooler than taken from manuals and controlling reports, are also relevant:

> "The managers I studied seemed to cherish soft information. Gossip, hearsay, and speculation form a good part of the manager's information diet." (Mintzberg 2009, p. 26)

Feedback on management performance from those being managed and other management actors is the second management resource. Just as employees need feedback on the quality of their work, all management actors need feedback on their performance. Since management feedback is commonly discussed in relation to line managers and is particularly important for their development and performance, it is discussed in more detail in Sect. 3.4.4 in the context of manager development. In any case, normative structures are needed:

> "The art is to make feedback as independent as possible from the courage and goodwill of individuals by anchoring it in regulated processes and structures." (Doppler 2009, p. 12; own translation)

In order to perform management routines and fulfill management tasks, all management actors must have or utilize the third resource: time. This sounds obvious, but it is an often-ignored factor. In fact, the most effective single measure for improving the quality of leadership and management in organizations is probably to give the actors sufficient time to manage. Those who demand good people management and leadership must ensure that everyone is given the time resources that are actually required for this purpose. This important aspect of time is examined in more detail in Sect. 3.1.7, using the line manager as an example.

Management also requires the fourth resource: specific competencies. Once again, the real problem lies in understanding it. As long as what constitutes good leadership and management is not clearly defined, it is difficult to carry out effective needs analyses and qualification measures. As a result, there must first be a corporate model that defines, among other things, the required activities, tasks, and instruments of leadership and management. Only from this can the necessary competencies initially be derived and then implemented in training and development measures. These consist of action competencies (i.e., skills to successfully perform management routines), which in turn are based on non-managerial, elemental competencies (e.g., communication, analysis, assessment, and decision-making). This last implementation element, management resources, is of cause also relevant for all management actors; anyone who is to do something must have the necessary skills. However, because the topic is particularly relevant for line managers, a separate section is devoted to it under manager development (Sect. 3.4).

2.6   Conversion into Corporate Management Models

The Complementary Management Model is intended to be of scientific use and to serve as an orientation for leaders. However, its main purpose is to provide a theoretical basis for corporate models of management and leadership.

2.6.1 Purpose and Content of Management Models in Organizations

In this book, corporate models of leadership and management are equated with management principles and guidelines (see Sect. 1.7.3). These are fundamental stipulations relating to leadership and management in a specific organization in the sense of a constitution of personnel work. They define why, by whom, and how a specific organization or organizational unit (including its personnel) is to be managed and led (see Kaehler 2017, pp. 63 f., 387 f.; Kaehler and Grundei 2019, pp. 41 f.). Even though management principles/guidelines can also be understood to be theory-like guiding principles that merely describe leadership and management in general terms, they are also management models—just superficial ones. It would be non-sensical to limit a corporate management model to people management because it represents precisely the link between functional-technical management and people management (see Sect. 2.2.2). It is a subset of both, i.e., it has personnel-related and non-personnel-related aspects. Strictly speaking, therefore, only the personnel-related part of the management model falls under HR governance. In practice, it is not possible to achieve a high level of leadership and management quality throughout the organization in any other way than by means of a corporate model of leadership and management. This normative approach was justified and explained in detail in Sect. 1.7.5.

The management model must be distinguished from the management infrastructure. The latter comprises detailed regulations that cannot be meaningfully assigned to the management model as a metastructure. This demarcation is of a purely pragmatic nature and thus in some respects arbitrary. Here, it is suggested that the management model purely names and roughly specifies the management functions, tasks, actors, instruments, routines, resources, and unit structures that are required by a company. The management infrastructure then consists of the concrete design of these seven elements of Complementary Management in detail. In principle, it is possible to categorize the relevant aspects of the infrastructure differently and, for example, to name only the management instruments and the management unit design as fields of action; the rest would then be dealt with implicitly in this context. In corporate practice, however, it has proven useful to structure the regulations of management/leadership on the basis of the these elements.

As it was developed specifically for this purpose, the Complementary Management Model can serve as a structuring aid for corporate models of leadership and management. In principle, however, such corporate models can also be conceptualized on a different theoretical basis. Models that do follow the Complementary Management Model contain indeed seven elements with numerous differentiations. This raises the fundamental question of the extent to which such complexity can be reasonably imposed upon the people involved. Unfortunately, all too many practitioners have become accustomed to the fact that leadership and management in books and seminars is hidden beneath a theatrical fog of intricacy and myth and is presented in a less differentiated manner than the simplest activities of daily life. Here again, a reference to the theoretical complexity of making coffee

Table 2.12 Possible implementation approaches (modified from Kaehler 2017, p. 390; © Boris Kaehler 2019. All rights reserved)

Alternative A: Minimum solution	People management and leadership is defined in job descriptions, etc., as an essential task of management positions. Following on from this, managers are granted or demand the corresponding working time for this purpose. In many places, the number one management problem is simply a lack of time on the part of managers (see Sect. 3.1.7).
Alternative B: Small partial solution	In addition to approach A, the principle of leadership and management as a service with its two components—the disciplinary and the support function —is propagated in the company in an appropriate manner (see Sect. 2.2). This removes the possibility of autocratic and destructive leadership and management. At the same time, it is advisable to standardize the principle of self-management, which encourages all employees to take responsibility for their own performance process (see Sect. 2.4.1).
Alternative C: Large partial solution	In addition to approaches A and B, a canon of management routines—work dialogs, team meetings, conflict dialogs, etc.—is defined, which specifies the personnel management activities of managers and also makes them verifiable to some extent (see Sect. 2.5.3). Recommendations should be developed for implementing the routines.
Alternative D: Complete solution	All seven elements of the Complementary Management Model are adapted to the circumstances of the organization and implemented as an overall organization-specific model. This is, without doubt, the best and most sensible approach.

or driving a car may be helpful. How many elements would these have to be broken down into? The expectation that a useful corporate model of leadership and management can be dealt with in a few sentences and made comprehensible without delving into it further is just as unrealistic as explaining how to drive a car using a similar format.

If there is a well-founded worry that an overly complex model will overburden the company's managers and employees, a more rudimentary concept of the types described in Table 2.12 may be more appropriate as an initial step. A simplistic but lived management model is better than a comprehensive one that has not been applied to everyday life. In principle, however, good and effective management and leadership require an approach for all seven elements of the Complementary Management Model. It is advisable not to hastily create simplistic models, but to consider how a model of appropriate complexity can be professionally communicated. In many cases, a well-thought-out, simplified presentation already solves the problem of acceptance (see Sect. 2.6.2). Indeed, the following applies: "You shall expect humankind to put up with the truth." (Attributed to Ingeborg Bachmann, own translation)

Anyone who has understood the Complementary Management Model—reading this book should suffice—can convert it into an organization-specific management model with the help of the procedure described here. Hence, internal HR experts and project specialists may take over handling the entire project and manage without external support. Many companies, on the other hand, tend to offload most of the corresponding work packages to external service providers and buy in the corresponding consulting services. Both paths—"make" or "buy"—are viable. However, it is not advisable to simply adopt management models from other companies (Knebel and Schneider 1994, p. 45 f.; Pietschmann et al. 1999, p. 507 f.). At best, structural suggestions can be borrowed from them, which then have to be adapted based on the special requirements of one's own organization.

However pragmatically one may proceed, the introduction of a new management and leadership model involves some effort. Given the importance of personnel in the corporate context and the great leverage that such corporate models can provide for improving performance and cost results, this investment of time and energy is more than justified. Nevertheless, there will be organizations that shy away from the effort in general, or at least at the present time. However, even these should not completely abandon the idea of developing a new management model or revising their existing one, but rather should simply be selective in its implementation. Four alternatives are conceivable in line with the starting points for improving the quality of leadership and management described in various sections of this book (Table 2.12).

Having a management model is one thing, living it is another. One of the advantages of the Complementary Management Model over other theoretical foundations is that it already contains elements of mutual reinforcement and control. Thus, employees who are informed about the model will insist on the intended management routines actually taking place and demand latitude to self-manage themselves. For their part, line managers will demand and support this self-management of employees within the management routines. The HR advisors and senior managers, in turn, will intervene in a compensatory manner as needed and also support the management process with formalized instruments. This multilevel system greatly increases the likelihood that the understanding of leadership and management envisaged by the corporate model will actually be practiced on a day-to-day basis. Furthermore, training, appraisal, and selection must be used to ensure that line managers receive support and in-depth qualification and that competent line managers are regenerated (see Sect. 3.4). In addition, compensatory co-management by HR advisors and senior managers is also important here (see Sect. 2.4.5) as "on-the-job" management support, so to speak. The evaluation envisaged in the project plan must ensure that the degree of actual application of the management model and its effectiveness are regularly reviewed. This is ultimately a problem of HR metrics, since it concerns defining, collecting, and evaluating key data necessary for steerage. Aspects to be taken into account are, in particular, work performance and costs, the workforce structure (body of personnel), and the satisfaction of all relevant stakeholders in personnel work, including employee satisfaction. The results of the evaluation serve as starting points for a continuous improvement of the management model.

2.6.2   Project to Develop and Implement a Corporate Model of Leadership and Management

Introducing a new management model in organizations or organizational units is nothing more than just a project, i.e., a management activity. A project like many others, one might add, because once the actually decisive question of the theoretical basis has been clarified, the rest follows a pattern that could just as well be applied to the development and implementation of other concepts. In this respect, the procedure proposed here is in large part not specific to the Complementary Management Model. Those who do not like it may alternatively follow other suggestions for introducing management models (e.g., Knebel and Schneider 1994, p. 46 f.; Pietschmann et al. 1999, p. 508 f.) or be guided, for example, by the common procedure for developing mission statements (see, e.g., Stolzenberg and Reiners 2012; Weh and Meifert 2013). Certainly, a lot can go wrong in the context of developing and implementing leadership principles. In practice, however, acceptance problems arise much more frequently from the weakness and one-sidedness of the content than from an unfortunate project design (see Knebel and Schneider 1994, p. 44; Schilling 2005, p. 128).

The development and implementation of corporate models of leadership and management is nothing more than fundamentally structuring all of a company's managerial work. A correspondingly prudent and systematic approach should be taken here. A procedure that uses five project phases is recommended (see Fig. 2.5), which will be explained in more detail below.

Phase 1 consists of creating a model design. As is well known, at the beginning of any project there should be a clarification of the task. This is also the case here: "Why

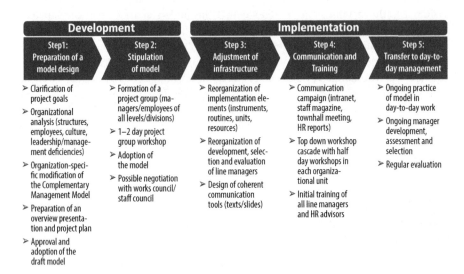

Fig. 2.5 Phases of model development and implementation (Modified from Kaehler 2017, p. 388; © Boris Kaehler 2019. All rights reserved)

and for what purpose do we need a new management model?" Often, the initiative to create a new corporate management model does not come from the top management of the respective organization or organizational unit, but from the human resources department. It is often the first to recognize the need for a new model, whether it is because management/leadership deficiencies are becoming apparent or because management selection, development, or compensation measures are creating new requirements. In these cases, the clarification of the mandate should, on the one hand, ascertain the interests and goals of the initiators and, on the other hand, also address the interests of the top management, which must ultimately support the project. The same applies to the works council, due to the need for a communication culture, but also because parts of the related management infrastructure—at least under German law—are subject to corporate co-determination (e.g., "assessment principles" with regard to leadership). In general, a comprehensive stakeholder analysis should be carried out and it should be checked to see which supporters and opponents the project has.

Organizational interventions should also always be preceded by a survey of the initial state in the form of a context and needs analysis. In the literature, this is called an "organizational analysis" or "organizational diagnosis", with one of the two terms usually being chosen arbitrarily and then serving as an umbrella term for the three steps of "data collection—analysis—diagnosis" (see Bartscher and Stöckl 2011, p. 110 ff.). Admittedly, some sources limit themselves to the purely psychological perspective (like Werner and Elbe 2010, p. 11) or only consider organizational structures (like Künzli 2013). In general, however, a holistic analysis approach is propagated, which includes as comprehensive an inventory as possible. Employee sensitivities, characteristics, behavior, and expectations are analyzed alongside the design parameters of the organizational, project, and process structures; the organizational culture; the leadership structures; and relevant aspects of the external environment, strategic positioning, and organizational results (see, e.g., Titscher et al. 2010, pp. 22 f., 27; Nerdinger 2014; Rosenberger 2014; Doppler and Lauterburg 2014, p. 270; see also Felfe 2014). All conceivable methods of observation, document analysis, and communication/relationship analysis can be used (Titscher et al. 2010, p. 42). However, the central method is usually a survey of employees and managers at all levels. If necessary, external stakeholders and experts can help with additional individual/group interviews, hearings, diagnostic workshops, and/or written questionnaires (see Titscher et al. 2010, p. 42; Doppler and Lauterburg 2014, pp. 269, 271 f.; Rosenberger 2014, p. 105; Felfe 2014, p. 413). The purpose of an organizational analysis is to determine findings about the current state of an organization, to identify neuralgic points, and to describe and evaluate the collected findings (Rosenberger 2014, p. 104). This is also especially indicated for an intervention as far-reaching as the implementation of a new management model:

"Every human organization is a complex and sensitive organism. Those who fiddle around with it without considering the inner connections risk doing harm rather than improving conditions." (Doppler and Lauterburg 2014, p. 267; own translation)

Of course, the data required by the project managers is necessary for the ongoing strategic and operational steerage of people management and leadership anyways. It is therefore advisable not to conceive of the organizational analysis as a one-off action, but to consider it right away as the initial spark for a permanent professionalization of HR metrics. Organizations that do not conduct regular employee surveys and have no knowledge of internal and external factors relevant to personnel (including management and performance problems) are hardly helped by one-off surveys. A pragmatic approach, limited to the essential information relevant to management and leadership, which is continued later and can thus also be used to evaluate the project, is always more practical than an overcomplex snapshot.

Drawing on the findings from the goals clarification and the organizational analysis, the Complementary Management Model is then modified to suit the specific organization. First to be dealt with is the conceptual implementation and graphic presentation. Every company has its own language and presentation culture, and all too often individual terms (e.g., "management tasks," "management routines," and "management instruments") or certain graphic representations are already associated in some way. But adjustments must also be made to the content. It is true that the seven elements of the Complementary Management Model cannot be exchanged or changed at will. However, they can and must be adapted to the respective circumstances: Which routines are envisaged, what the individual management tasks entail in detail, and how they are to be divided among the actors varies from organization to organization.

Furthermore, not all elements necessarily have to be addressed when launching the model. For example, although management unit design and management instruments inevitably play an important role in the management process, they can also be left out of the project (i.e., in this case, the status quo is maintained and serves as a reference point). This applies in particular to the management unit design, changes to which regularly go beyond the scope of such a project due to the associated power claims and jeopardize the introduction of the model as a whole. In this case, it often makes sense to merely adjust the job profiles of the actors a little and leave out the basic setup of organizational structures. If the management model proves to be viable, any sensible changes to the organizational structures are usually addressed in other contexts at the appropriate time. The result of the modification is a draft model that already reveals all the key points of the future management model.

Once this important preliminary conceptual work has been completed, an overview presentation of the draft model must be prepared, which can serve as a basis for discussion for decision makers and project participants. Particular care is required here because conceptual errors, incomprehensible/implausible content, or micropolitically clumsy formulations can significantly delay and hinder the launch. It is advisable to test the presentation several times on non-specialists with a short attention span and to correct any weak points. A project plan—including a time and budget framework—as well as an evaluation concept must also be drawn up in accordance with the respective in-house regulations. The initiators will first obtain approval for the draft model, after which the draft model and project plan must generally be approved by the overall management. During the decision-making

Table 2.13 Essential components of a workshop for developing a corporate leadership and management model (modified from Kaehler 2017, p. 394; © Boris Kaehler 2019. All rights reserved)

Activation of the participants' previous experience with linkage to the results of the organizational analysis
Presentation of the model design
Structured discussion of the model components including the participants' experiences
Joint modification of model components
Adoption of the new management model by the project group

process, additional discussion loops and further changes may naturally occur and it is advisable to plan time buffers for this from the outset.

Phase 2 of the project consists of stipulating the subsequent management and leadership model. Such models live from their implementation in everyday management. Simply introducing the draft model developed "on the drawing board" makes little sense. Instead, it is strongly recommended that the draft model be discussed critically and modified further in a project group workshop. This enables any remaining conceptual deficiencies to be ironed out, after which supplementary ideas can be incorporated and stakeholders can participate in the design of management structures. Employees and managers from all levels and areas should be represented in the project group. Participation by the top management ensures that the workshop has an appropriate status within the group and the company. HR advisors and manager developers from the HR department should participate in addition to the divisional line management. To facilitate later negotiations, it is advisable to invite (if there are any) representatives of the works council. In this way, the project group quickly reaches 20 to 30 members.

In a one to two-day workshop, the project group transforms the draft model into the actual management model. A prerequisite for the success of the event—not least because of the size of the group and the different interests involved—is a fully developed model design and a professionally well-prepared and well-moderated workshop. The essential components of the event are shown in Table 2.13. The result of the workshop is the finished corporate model of leadership and management.

Before the management model can actually be implemented, a corresponding resolution by top management is usually required. It may also be necessary to amend codified agreements with the works council, which requires negotiations. If significant changes are made at this stage, the project group will have to be reconvened so as not to jeopardize the participatory element of the project and expose the model to criticism. To avoid this and to make the process more elegant, it is advisable not only to include representatives of the top management and the interest groups in the project group, but also to ascertain their requirements when the project goals are initially clarified.

Phase 3 of the project adapts the corporate management infrastructure. When doing so, it is necessary to ensure that the inevitably abstract model elements are translated into practical measures and linked to existing HR policy measures (see, e.g., Schilling 2005, p. 130). Whether or not the model needs to adapt naturally depends on which management elements the actual corporate model includes and which deviations these require in relation to the status quo. The main need for adaptation usually arises in the fields mentioned below. In order to ensure that the newly defined management routines are actually put into practice, appropriate specifications are required. After all, depending on the design of the corporate model, the individual actors are responsible for certain aspects of certain routines. It has proven useful to translate these specifications into corresponding guidelines that also contain concrete recommendations for action and tips (e.g., recommendations for different discussion phases of weekly work dialogs and for dealing with typical difficulties). Since several actors are usually involved in the routines and transparency is certainly desirable, it is advisable not to make these guides actor specific. Section 2.5.3 discusses them in more detail.

The content of all formalized management instruments (systems, programs, forms, etc.) must be reviewed to determine the extent to which they are still in harmony with the other elements of the corporate model. If necessary, i.e., if the management model provides for it, the development of new instruments must be initiated. Section 2.5.4 entails a systematic overview of the main instruments that could be used.

Changes to the management model generally require changes to the structure of the departments and organizational units involved, i.e., the management structure. Naturally, the corresponding structure documentation of the individual management actors must also be adapted. Sections 3.1.4 and 4.2.4 go into detail on how this is to be accomplished in the case of line management positions and HR departments. In particular, the time required by the actors for their personnel management activities under the new model must also be taken into account. As described above in the paragraph on modification, management unit design is often a power-political issue; if necessary, major adjustments should therefore be deferred until the management model has proven itself.

The four essential management resources—working time, information, competence, and feedback—should be mentioned in management models because this increases the probability that they will actually be made available. To this end, infrastructural adjustments must be made here as well, if necessary. In the case of working time, this means that if the layout of line management positions changes, personnel planning of line managers must also be adjusted. Those who are expected to spend more time on people management and leadership, can, for instance, take on fewer additional functional-technical tasks. Thus, additional manpower must be planned to provide relief. In terms of directional and situational information, it is advisable to rethink the appropriate information channels, media, and information cycles. With regard to competencies and feedback, it is also necessary to ensure that the corresponding concepts and practices are adapted to the new model. Traditionally, the focus has been on manager/leader development, selection, and assessment (including feedback systems). Section 3.4 provides an overview of the key aspects of this activity. However, since all other management actors also require management

Table 2.14 Communication tools to convey a shared understanding of management and leadership (modified from Kaehler 2017, p. 396; © Boris Kaehler 2019. All rights reserved)

Brochure or compendium	Brief introduction on the topic of people management (definition, service functions, actors, etc.), essential overviews and explanations of management tasks, management routines, and management instruments
Sample presentation slides	All elements of the management model are presented in graphical form
Sample texts	Appropriate summary and, if necessary, set pieces of the model for use in internal and external communication as well as for implementation in personnel and manager development

competence and feedback, the general personnel development structures must also be adapted accordingly.

Communicating the new management model and its implications efficiently and effectively to the members of the organization requires a professional means of communication. Of course, it would not be in the interest of the project to have the model be presented in different ways by different participants and communicated in a correspondingly inconsistent manner. For this reason, sample texts, presentation graphics, and brochures must be created that can be used in different media and event formats, especially those used in leader development. Particularly in the case of multilayered models, every effort must be made to convey them well didactically. The management routines should be placed in the foreground, because these ultimately form the actual people management activities of the actors. The question arises as to whether the means of communication should be directed at specific actors in each case, e.g., the line managers. This seems obvious, but is not necessarily advisable. Good leadership and management thrives on all actors involved sharing the same understanding of leadership. Moreover, especially in a working world dominated by digital media, it is always to be expected that communication materials, such as brochures or seminar documents, will reach the internal or even external public. Transparency is generally more sensible than secrecy. The means of communication should therefore be designed in such a way that it can serve as a basis of information for all departments involved (see Table 2.14).

Like any major corporate change, a new management model requires a concerted communications campaign. The issue of leadership affects everyone in the organization because they are all actors in the management process (Sect. 2.4). Every so often, the following applies:

> "Expect to share a message ten times for every one time that it will be heard and understood." (Ulrich et al. 2008, p. 86)

The new management model should therefore not only be discussed in internal seminars, but it should be communicated to the workforce using all available media—from the intranet to employee magazines, staff reports, and (regular) company meetings. In order to anchor the importance of the topic and the key points of the improvements deeply in the collective consciousness, storytelling is the method of choice (see, e.g., Frenzel et al. 2013). Project group participants can be used as "internal ambassadors." All organizational members should have the opportunity to comment on the model as needed; appropriate contact persons should be designated for this purpose. More importantly, the campaign should demonstrate that feedback on management and leadership is desired in day-to-day work and it should explain when and how this can be provided. Ideally, a descending workshop cascade ("top-down") is carried out with half-day workshops in each organizational unit. Here the model is presented, and moderated discussions take place.

All of this not only represents a mere dissemination of information, it already has the character of a genuine intervention in terms of content. The ideas and expectations that employees and line managers have with regard to leadership and management shape their actions in day-to-day business life. If it is possible to communicate a uniform image of leadership to all members of the organization, a major step has already been taken toward improving the management quality. In particular, the communication campaign should also be used to align the related perceptions and expectations of employees and line managers. Most organizations communicate official leadership/management principles to the workforce in "marketing speak." Rarely, however, do they also communicate to employees the real perspective and real dilemmas of line managers. Thus, it is not surprising when many of them rashly rail against "those up there." As Weilbacher puts it (2012, p. 24; own translation):

> "The HR director [...] is probably not so wrong when he says that the negative comments about leadership that you hear more often in company hallways are uttered quickly [...] because some employees often don't see the forces at work behind them."

The fourth and final phase of the project consists of communication and training as well as implementing the model in day-to-day management. The main pillars of the model and its implementation are naturally the line managers. A mere information campaign is not enough to communicate the intricacies of the model to all line managers; instead, it requires training. A useful format for the initial training of all line managers could be a one-day classroom event focusing on practicing management routines (work dialogs, annual reviews, etc.). This is prepared through knowledge transfer via e-learning and rounded off by the offer of optional coaching. Low-threshold day-to-day coaching can also be provided by HR advisors, who should first go through the training package described for this purpose. For the sake of completeness, implementation in everyday management is described above in Fig. 2.5. It is presented as the fifth project phase, but is of course no longer part of the actual project.

2.7   Summary

This chapter introduced a new theoretical model of leadership and management. The core model of Complementary Management consists of three elements, each of which has complementary (i.e., supplementary) components that lend the model its name. The model describes people management and leadership as a bundle of specific tasks that represent preconditions of human performance. The two service functions of support and discipline are concretized in each of the tasks. Ideally, the employee fulfills all of these tasks in their entirety as a self-manager. As a complementary actor, the line manager intervenes in a compensatory manner only when the employee is unable to fulfill these management tasks. If this does not happen, senior managers and HR advisors step in. Implementing this core model requires four further implementation elements.

The first element of the core model consists of the complementary management functions. Organizational people management and leadership is understood to be an internal service. This service has two functions with respect to the personnel in an organizational unit. The support function is to help individual employees perform their jobs. The catchwords "to foster", "appreciation", and "employee orientation" illustrate this. The disciplinary function is to discipline and supervise the performance of individual employees. The catchwords here are "to demand", "added value", and "production orientation". In terms of management and leadership theory, the model element thereby ties in with the approach of "management as a service" and the classic duality of "employee orientation" vs. "production orientation". It has the status of a fundamental principle and is primarily of practical value: The idea of management as a dual service provides orientation for managers and prevents destructive leadership.

The complementary management tasks form the second model element. People management and leadership consists of 24 tasks that can be grouped into eight categories: "Setting HR norms", "Hiring, retaining, separating", "Ensuring administration", "Managing work tasks", "Arranging collaboration", "Fostering competence and development", "Granting care", and "Crafting motivation". This is based on the premise that precisely these influences are required to generate sustainable human performance. The model is thus in the theoretical tradition of normative task models of leadership and management. However, the management tasks are not understood as activities, but as abstract goals to be realized within the framework of concrete activities ("management routines"). All 24 tasks together complement each other to form the overall task of people management and leadership. In each task, both the disciplinary and the support functions are specified.

The third element of the core model encompasses the complementary management actors. People management and leadership is the responsibility of several key players: the employee, his or her colleagues, the line manager, the senior manager, and the HR advisor. The primary management principle should be self-management, i.e., the employee should ideally take on all leadership/management tasks him or herself. Since not all employees always do this, the line manager must intervene in a compensatory manner when necessary. If he or she does not, it is up to the senior manager and the HR advisor acting as "HR co-manager" to intervene in a compensatory manner. These interventions can be corrective, joint, delegative, or substitutive. The complementary actors thus complement each other and collectively perform the 24 management tasks. This compensatory mechanism ensures, on the one hand, that all management tasks are actually performed with regard to each individual employee even if the line manager is inactive, thus ensuring that work is performed. On the other hand, this multi-entity system is suitable for preventing an abuse of power by the line manager. In terms of management and leadership theory, the element of complementary management actors takes up the "Shared Leadership" approach, which is combined with the concept of self-management and with a vertical hierarchical exercise of authority based on the principle of exception.

This core model of Complementary Management describes basic mechanisms of people management and leadership in organizations. Implementing it requires four further model implementation elements: management unit design, management routines, management instruments, and management resources. The systematic relationship can be summarized as follows: Managers fulfill management tasks (e.g., performance feedback) using management routines (e.g., interviews), apply management instruments (e.g., work schedules), require management resources (e.g., business information), and do all this on the basis of the management unit structure (e.g., the design of their job).

The management routines, understood as concrete activities, serve as a way to implement the management tasks. For example, performance feedback is initially only an abstract task that must be implemented in regular employee dialogs, among other things. A distinction must be made between annual routines (e.g., annual employee reviews), continuous routines (e.g., weekly work dialogs), and on-demand routines (e.g., crisis interventions or hiring projects). The theoretical basis of this element of the management model is the established construct of organizational routines. Those for whom the term has a negative connotation (in the sense of getting stuck in a rut) may replace it with "management activities". Organizations should clearly define which management routines are to be performed, which actors are involved, and what the frameworks are. The shares each actor has in the routines add up to the totality of their people management activities. This puts management responsibilities into very concrete terms: Has an actor actually carried out the routines incumbent upon him or her and thereby achieved the defined management tasks? If, for example, a line manager does not conduct regular work dialogs, he or she is simply neglecting his or her professional duties.

Within the framework of management routines, management actors use the management instruments available in their respective companies. These are formalized tools that support employee management and leadership, in particular, rules, systems, programs, and forms. The conceptual differentiation between routines and instruments has significant implications. Leadership and management is not exercised through the instrument (e.g., a salary system or appraisal procedure), but always through its specific application. Good instruments are sometimes devalued by their inadequate use in everyday management. Conversely, dysfunctional and poorly designed HR instruments can be relativized in the course of their application and misguided decisions can be avoided—a question of management quality and certainly also a question of the internal distribution of roles. Above all, however, it becomes clear that HR instruments must be designed in such a way that they effectively support day-to-day people management and leadership.

The management unit design encompasses the organizational structures in which the various management actors are integrated. This relates to the structure and hierarchical integration of the organizational units involved in people management and leadership (jobs, groups, departments, divisions, etc.). However, the distribution of tasks among the actors and their respective powers are also connected with it. The general principles of organizational science form the theoretical basis here. The management unit design, like the other elements of the model, does not represent a sub-area of management and leadership, but provides a special perspective on it. Thus, it cannot be considered separately from the overall model. Influencing processes certainly take place without permanent management structures, but this has little to do with systematic organizational leadership and management. The Complementary Management Model leaves room for different distributions of tasks among the actors, but its elements provide a rough structural framework. For example, a human resources department that refuses to accept compensatory "HR co-management" would not be compatible with the model. The same applies to management positions without disciplinary authority or with an overstretched management span. Functioning people management and leadership requires a functional management unit design.

In the Complementary Management Model, the implementation element of management resources represents a purely pragmatically reasoned selection of management prerequisites critical to success. In practice, leadership and management often fail because of four essential problematic resources—so much so that it is worth highlighting them prominently by means of a separate element. First: the working time required to perform management routines, which many leaders do not have or do not take. Second, management competencies are required. These consist of action competencies (i.e., skills to successfully perform management routines), which in turn are based on non-managerial elemental competencies (e.g., communication, analysis, assessment, and decision-making). Third, management actors need comprehensive directional and situational information. And finally, holistic management feedback is required. All four resources are necessary to enable effective people management and leadership in the first place.

Even though the Complementary Management Model is also intended to be of scientific use and to serve as an orientation for leaders, its main purpose is to provide a theoretical basis for corporate models of management and leadership (=principles, guidelines). These are fundamental stipulations relating to leadership and management in a specific organization in the sense of a constitution of personnel work. They define why, by whom, and how a specific organization or organizational unit (including its personnel) is to be managed and led. Organizations designing such corporate models may use some or all elements of Complementary Management and should progress with the project in five phases.

References

Albach, Horst (1977): Mitarbeiterführung – Text und Fälle; Gabler 1977.

Allport, Floyd H. (1962): A Structuronomic Conception of Behavior: Individual and Collective – I. Structural Theory and the Master Problem of Social Psychology; Journal of Abnormal and Social Psychology 1/1962 (Vol. 64); pp. 3–30.

Alvarez, José/Svejenova, Silviya/Vives, And Luis (2007): Leading in Pairs; MIT Sloan Management Review Summer 2007; pp. 10–14.

Andreßen, Panja (2008): Selbstführung im Rahmen verteilter Führung; Dissertation VS Research 2008.

Antonakis, John/Atwater, Leanne (2002): Leader distance: a review and a proposed theory; The Leadership Quarterly 2002 (13); pp. 673–704.

Armbrüster, Thomas/Hehn, Roland (2011): Kein Platz für humanistische Ideale; Human Resources Manager Juni/Juli 2011; pp. 78–79.

Bales, R. F./Slater, P.E. (1969): Role Differentiation in Small Decision-Making Groups; in Gibb, Cecil A.: Leadership; Penguin 1969; pp. 255–276.

Barnard, Chester I. (1938): The Functions of the Executive; Neuauflage Harvard University Press 1968 (first edition 1938).

Bartscher, Thomas/Stöckl, Juliane (2011) (Hrsg.): Veränderungen erfolgreich managen – Ein Handbuch für interne Prozessberater; Haufe 2011.

Becker, Markus C. (2004): Organizational Routines: a Review of the Literature; Industrial and Corporate Change 4/2004 (13); pp. 643–677.

Becker, Markus C./Lazaric, Nathalie (2009): Advancing Empirical Research On Organizational Routines: Introduction; in Becker, Markus C./Lazaric, Nathalie: Organizational Routines – Advancing empirical research; Edward Elgar 2009; S. 1–7.

Becker, Markus C/Lazaric, Nathalie/Nelson, Richard R/Winter, Sidney G (2005): Applying organizational routines in understanding organizational change; Industrial and Corporate Change 5/2005 (14); pp. 775–791.

Becker, Wolfgang/Holzmann, Robert (2013): Selbstkontrolle von Mitarbeitern fördern; zfo 2/2013; pp. 96–102.

Beverungen, Daniel (2014): Über das Zusammenwirken der Gestaltung und Emergenz von Geschäftsprozessen als Organisationsroutinen; Wirtschaftsinformatik 4/2014; pp. 209–222.

Bittel, Lester R. (1964): Management by Exception – Systematizing and Simplifying the Managerial Job; McGraw-Hill 1964.

Blessin, Bernd/Wick, Alexander (2017): Führen und Führen lassen; 8th edition UVK-Lucius/UTB 2017.

Bolden, Richard (2011): Distributed Leadership in Organizations: A Review of Theory and Research; International Journal of Management Reviews 2011 (13); pp. 251–269.

Bradt, George (2012): Lessons In Complementary Leadership From Disney And Coca-Cola; http://www.forbes.com/sites/georgebradt/2012/05/30/lessons-in-complementary-leadership-from-disney-and-coca-cola/ (Accessed 01/05, 2022).

Bühner, Rolf/Horn, Peter (1995): Mitarbeiterführung im Total Quality Management; in Bruhn, Manfred (ed.): Internes Marketing: Integration der Kunden- und Mitarbeiterorientierung; Grundlagen – Implementierung – Praxisbeispiele; Gabler 1995; pp. 652–678.

Bühner, Rolf (1998): Mitarbeiterführung im Dienstleistungsunternehmen; in Bruhn, Manfred/Meffert, Heribert (eds.): Handbuch Dienstleistungsmanagement; Gabler 1998; pp. 734–749.

Carzo, Rocco/Yanouzas, John N. (1969): Effects of Flat and Tall Organization Structure; Administrative Science Quarterly, 1969-06-01, Vol.14 (2), pp.178-191

Contractor, Noshir S./DeChurch, Leslie A./Carson, Jay/Carter, Dorothy R./Keegan, Brian (2012): The Topology of Collective Leadership; The Leadership Quarterly 2012 (23); pp. 994–1011.

Crevani, Lucia/Lindgren, Monica/Packendorff, Johann (2007): Shared Leadership: A Postheroic Perspective on Leadership as a Collective Construction; International Journal of Leadership Studies 1/2007 (3); pp. 40–67.

Densten, Lain L./Gray, Judy H. (1998): The Case for Using both Latent and Manifest Variables to Investigate Management-by-Exception; The Journal of Leadership Studies 3/1998 (5); pp. 80–92.

Dierendonck, Dirk van (2011): Servant Leadership – A Review and Synthesis; Journal of Management July 2011 (37); pp. 1228–1261.

Dierendonck, Dirk van/Stam, Daan/Boersma, Pieter/de Windt, Ninotchka/Alkema, Jorrit (2014): Same difference? Exploring the differential mechanisms linking servant leadership and transformational leadership to follower outcomes; The Leadership Quarterly 2014 (25); pp. 544–562.

Doppler, Klaus (2009): Über Helden und Weise – Von heldenhafter Führung im System zu weiser Führung am System; Organisationsentwicklung 2/2009; pp. 4–13.

Doppler, Klaus/Lauterburg, Christoph (2014): Change Management – Den Unternehmenswandel gestalten; 13th German edition Campus 2014.

Dreyer, Nils/Schlippe, Arist von (2008): Nachfolge in Pionierunternehmen; zfo 5/2008; pp. 324–331.

Drucker, Peter F. (1954): The Practice of Management; Neuauflage HarperCollins 2006 (first edition 1954).

Drucker, Peter F. (1973): Management – Tasks, Responsibilities, Practices; Neuauflage Harper Business 1993 (first edition 1973).

Drucker, Peter F. (1992): Managing for the Future; Butterworth Heinemann 1993 (Erstveröffentlichung 1992).

Einstein, Albert (1934): On the Method of Theoretical Physics; Philosophy of Science April 1934 (1); pp. 163–169.

Etzioni, A. (1965): Dual Leadership in Complex Organizations; American Sociological Review 5/1965, (30); pp. 688–698.

Etzioni, A. (1969): Dual Leadership in Complex Organizations; in Gibb, Cecil A.: Leadership; Penguin 1969; pp. 386–406.

ESG Elektroniksystem- und Logistik-GmbH (2014): Leitbild/Leitsätze; www.esg.de/unternehmen/leitbild/ (Accessed 17.7.2015).

Fayol, H. (1916). General and industrial management (English edition 1949). London: Sir Isaac Pitman & Sons Ltd (first published in French in bulletin de la sociéte de l'industrie minérale 1916).

Feldman, Martha S./Pentland, Brian T. (2003): Reconceptualizing Organizational Routines as a Source of Flexibility and Change; Administrative Science Quarterly March 2003 (48); pp. 94–118.

Felfe, Jörg (2014): Organisationsdiagnose; in Schuler, Heinz/Moder, Klaus (eds.): Lehrbuch Organisationspsychologie; 5th German edition Verlag Hans Huber 2014.

Ferrary, Michel (2001): Pour une théorie de l'échange dans les réseaux sociaux; Cahiers Internationaux de Sociologie Juillet–Décembre 2001 (111); pp. 261–290.

Fleishman, Edwin A./Mumford, Michael D./Zaccaro, Stephen J./Levin, Kerry Y./Korotkin, Arthur L./Hein, Michael B. (1991): Taxonomic Efforts in the Description of Leader behavior: A Synthesis and Functional Interpretation; Leadership Quarterly 2 (4), 1991; pp. 245–287.

Fournier, Cay von (2006): Führung als Dienstleistung – 10 Tipps für den 'perfekten' Chef; Portal Perspektive Mittelstand 25.1.2006; http://www.perspektive-mittelstand.de/Personalfuehrung-10-Tipps-fuer-den-perfekten-Chef/management-wissen/281.html (Accessed 17.7.2015).

Frenzel, Karolina/Müller, Michael/Sottong, Hermann (2013): Storytelling – Das Praxisbuch; Hanser 2013.

Fuchs, Jürgen/Stolarz, Christian (2001): Produktionsfaktor Intelligenz – Warum intelligente Unternehmen so erfolgreich sind; Gabler 2001.

Furtner, Marco/Baldegger, Urs (2013) Self-Leadership und Führung – Theorien, Modelle und praktische Umsetzung; Springer Gabler 2013.

Furtner, Marco/Maran, Thomas (2015): Self Leader führen besser – Selbstführung als Grundlage von Mitarbeiterführung; Personalführung 1/2015; pp. 36–40.

Garman, Andrew N./Davis-Lenane, Deborah/Corrigan, Patrick W. (2003): Factor Structure of the Transformational Leadership Model in Human Service Teams; Journal of Organizational Behavior 6/2003 (24); pp. 803–812.

Gebert, Diether/Kearney, Eric (2011): Ambidextre Führung – Eine andere Sichtweise; Zeitschrift für Arbeits- und Organisationspsychologie 2/2011 (55); pp. 74–87.

Geiger, Daniel; Schröder, Anja (2014): Ever-changing Routines? Toward a Revised Understanding of Organizational Routines Between Rule-following and Rule-breaking; sbr Schmalenbach Business Review April 2014 (66); pp. 170–190.

Gockel, Christine/Werth, Lioba (2010): Measuring and Modeling Shared Leadership – Traditional Approaches and New Ideas; Journal of Personnel Psychology 4/2010 (9); pp. 172–180.

Greenleaf, Robert K. (1970): The Servant as Leader; new edition The Robert K Greenleaf Center 1991 (first edition 1970).

Grün, Anselm (1998): Menschen führen, Leben wecken – Anregungen aus der Regel Benedikts von Nursia; 6. edition dtv 2010 (first edition Vier-Türme Verlag 1998).

Halpin, Andrew W./Winer, B. James (1957): A Factorial Study of the Leader Behavior Descriptions; in Stogdill, Ralph M./Coons, Alvin E. (eds.): Leader Behavior – Its Description and Measurement; Ohio State University Business Research 1957; pp. 39–51.

Hansen, Nina Katrin/Vogel, Rick (2011): Organizational routines: a review and outlook on practice-based micro-foundations; Economics, Management, and Financial Markets 3/2011 (6); pp. 86–111.

Heidelberger Institut für Systemische Forschung und Therapie e. V. (2017): Dienende Führung: Von der Gier zum Wir – Symposion vom 7.–8. Juni 2018 (Website); https://www.dienende-fuehrung.de/ (Accessed 5.4.2019).

Hemphill, John K./Coons, Alvin E. (1957): Development of the Leader Behavior Description Questionnaire; in Stogdill, Ralph M./Coons, Alvin E. (eds.): Leader Behavior: Its Description and Measurement; Ohio State University Business Research 1957; pp. 6–38.

Hinsen, Ulrich E. (2012): Komplementäre Führung; http://www.management-radio.de/komplementare-fuhrung/ (Accessed 01/05, 2022).

Hoch, Julia E./Dulebohn, James H. (2013): Shared leadership in enterprise resource planning and human resource management system implementation; Human Resource Management Review 1/2013; pp. 114–125.

Hodgson, Geoffrey M. (2009): The Nature and Replication of Routines; in Becker, Markus C./Lazaric, Nathalie: Organizational Routines – Advancing Empirical Research; Edward Elgar 2009; pp. 26–44.

Hodgson, Richard C./Levinson, Daniel J./Zaleznik, Abraham (1965): The Executive Role Constellation – An Analysis of Personality and Role Relations in Management; Harvard University 1965.

Holch, Christine (1997): Handel und Dienstleister versuchen, ihr Personal auf mehr Kundenfreundlichkeit zu trimmen – Die Offensive des Lächelns; Die Zeit 28.2.1997; http://www.zeit.de/1997/10/kunde.txt.19970228.xml (Accessed 2022/01/5).

Holtbrügge, Dirk (2004): Personalmanagement; Springer Gabler 2004.

Hölzl, Hubert (2014): Eine bunte Truppe führen; Personalwirtschaft 5/2014; pp. 45–47.

Hunter, Emily M./Neubert, Mitchell J./Jansen Perry, Sara/Witt, L.A./Penney, Lisa M./Weinberger, Evan (2013): Servant Leaders Inspire Servant Followers – Antecedents and Outcomes for Employees and the Organization; The Leadership Quarterly 2013 (24); pp. 316–331.

Jacobi, Jens-Martin (1990): Qualitätszirkel als Führungsaufgabe; Personalführung 3/1990; pp. 172–182.

Jacobi, Jens-Martin (1991): Die Führungskraft 2000; in Feix, Wilfried E (ed.): Personal 2000 – Visionen und Strategien erfolgreicher Personalarbeit; Gabler 1991; pp. 485–506.

Jacobi, Jens-Martin (1993): Qualitätsmanagement; in Strutz, Hans (ed.): Handbuch Personalmarketing; 2nd edition Gabler 1993; p. 443–455.

Jäger, Janine (2014): Kooperativer Führungsstil – Führung als Dienstleistung; UZ UnternehmerZeitung 4/2014; pp. 48–49; https://www.fhnw.ch/plattformen/iwi/2014/03/31/kooperativer-fuehrungsstil/ (Accessed 01/05, 2022).

Judge, Timothy A./Piccolo, Ronald F./Ilies, Remus (2004): The Forgotten Ones? The Validity of Consideration and Initiating Structure in Leadership Research; Journal of Applied Psychology 1/2004 (89); pp. 36–51.

Kaehler, Boris (2012): Komplementäre Führung – Ein Beitrag zur Theorie und konzeptionellen Praxis der organisationalen Führung; epubli 2012.

Kaehler, Boris (2013): Aufgabenorientierte und komplementäre Führung – Grundzüge eines integrativen Modells; Personalführung 7/2013; pp. 30–37.

Kaehler, Boris (2014a): Komplementäre Führung – Ein praxiserprobtes Modell der organisationalen Führung; 1st edition Springer Gabler 2014.

Kaehler, Boris (2014b): Komplementäre Führung – Ein neues Führungsmodell; Arbeit und Arbeitsrecht 8/2014; pp. 459–461.

Kaehler, Boris (2016): Die Rolle der Personalfunktion im Unternehmen: Grundsatzfragen und aktuelle Herausforderungen – Wege aus der ewigen Strategiediskussion; Zeitschrift Personalführung 2/2016; p. 20–26.

Kaehler, Boris (2017): Komplementäre Führung – Ein praxiserprobtes Modell der Personalführung in Organisationen; 2nd edition Springer Gabler 2017.

Kaehler, Boris (2019): Führen als Beruf: Andere erfolgreich machen; 1st edition Tredition 2019.

Kaehler, Boris (2020): Komplementäre Führung – Ein praxiserprobtes Modell der Personalführung in Organisationen; 3rd Auflage Springer Gabler 2020.

Kaehler, Boris/Grundei, Jens (2018): HR-Governance im Führungs-Kontext: Der normative Rahmen des Personalmanagements; ZCG Zeitschrift für Corporate Governance 5/2018, pp. 205–210.

Kaehler, Boris/Grundei, Jens (2019): HR Governance – A Theoretical Introduction; Springer 2019.

Kaiser, Stephan/Kozica, Arjan (2013): Organisationale Routinen – Ein Blick auf den Stand der Forschung; Organisationsentwicklung 1/2013; pp. 15–18.

Katz, Robert L. (1955): Skills of an Effective Administrator; Harvard Business Review January/February 1955; pp. 33–42.

Katz, Daniel/Kahn, Robert L. (1966): The Social Psychology of Organizations; John Wiley & Sons 1966.

Kern, Dieter/Schneider, Nalah (2017): Gute Führung macht den Unterschied; Human Resources Manager Februar/März 2017, pp. 72–74.

Kim, Chan/Mauborgne, Renée (2014): Blue Ocean Leadership; Harvard Business Review 5/2014; pp. 60–72.

Knebel, Heinz/Schneider, Helmut (1994): Führungsgrundsätze – Leitlinien für die Einführung und praktische Umsetzung; 2nd edition Sauer-Verlag 1994.

Königswieser, Roswita/Lang, Erik/Wimmer, Rudolf (2009): Komplementärberatung – Quantensprung oder Übergangsphänomen?; Organisationsentwicklung 1/2009; p. 46–53.

Kouzes, James M./Posner, Barry Z. (1987): The Leadership Challenge; 4th edition Jossey Bass 2007 (Erstveröffentlichung 1987).

Kozica, Arjan/Kaiser, Stephan/Friesl, Martin (2014): Organizational Routines: Conventions as a Source of Change and Stability; sbr Schmalenbach Business Review July 2014 (66); pp. 334–356.

Kramer, Michael W./Crespy, David A. (2011): Communicating collaborative leadership; The Leadership Quarterly 2011 (22); pp. 1024–1037.

Krell, Gertraude (2001): Zur Analyse und Bewertung von Dienstleistungsarbeit – Ein Diskussionsbeitrag; Industrielle Beziehungen 1/2001; pp. 9–37.

Krost, Markus/Kaehler, Boris (2010): Servant Leadership – Die Führungskraft als Diener?; Personalführung 6/2010; pp. 54–56.

Krusche, Bernhard (2012): Führung 2.0– nein danke! Warum wir keine Managementinnovationen brauchen; zfo 2/2012; pp. 102–103.

Künzli, Benjamin (2013): Szenariotechnik – Zukunftsbilder entwickeln und für strategische Vorhaben nutzen; zfo 1/2013; p. 46–48.

Laszlo, Ervin/Leonhardt, Claus-Peter (1994): Evolutionäres Management – Marketing in instabilen Systemen; Absatzwirtschaft 7/1994, pp. 34–38.

Liden, Robert C./Wayne, Sandy J./Liao, Chenwei/Meuser, Jeremy D. (2014): Servant Leadership and Serving Culture: Influence on Individual and Unit Performance; Academy of Management Journal 5/2014 (57); pp. 1434–1452.

Malik, Fredmund (2000). Managing performing living: Effective management for a new era (English edition 2006). Frankfurt am Main: Campus (first published in German 2000).

Malik, Fredmund (2007): Management – das A und O des Handwerks (Band 1 der Serie Management – Komplexität meistern); Neuauflage Campus 2007.

Manz, Charles C./Sims, Henry P. (1989): SuperLeadership – Leading Others to Lead Themselves; Prentice Hall Press 1989.

Müller, Günter F. (2014): Führung durch und zur Selbstführung; in Sauerland, Martin/Braun, Ottmar L.: Aktuelle Trend in der Personal- und Organisationsentwicklung – Tagungsband; Windmühle 2014.

Mazzarol, Tim/Reboud, Sophie (2008): The Role of Complementary Actors in the Development of Innovation in Small Firms; International Journal of Innovation Management June 2008 (12); pp. 223–253.

Merkle, Hans L. (1979): Dienen und Führen – Anmerkungen zur Abwertung von Begriffen; in Merkle, Hans L.: Dienen und Führen – Erkenntnisse eines Unternehmers; 2001 Hohenheim Verlag; pp. 159–173

Miles, Stephen A./Watkins, Michael D. (2007): The Leadership Team – Complementary Strengths or Conflicting Agendas?; Harvard Business Review April 2007; pp. 90–98.

Mintzberg, Henry (1973): The Nature of Managerial Work; Harper & Row 1973.

Mintzberg, Henry (1975): The manager's job – folklore and fact; Harvard Business Review July/August 1975; pp. 49–61.

Mintzberg, Henry: Managing; 2009; San Francisco: Berret-Koehler Publishers.

Nelson, Richard R. (2009): Routines as technologies and as organizational capabilities; in Becker, Markus C./Lazaric, Nathalie: Organizational Routines – Advancing Empirical Research; Edward Elgar 2009; pp. 11–25.

Nelson, Richard R./Winter, Sidney G. (1982): An Evolutionary Theory of Corporate Change; Belknap Press/Harvard University Press 1982.

Nerdinger, Friedemann W./Rosenstiel, Lutz von (1996): Führung und Personalwirtschaft bei dezentralisierten Kompetenzen; in Lutz, Burkart/Hartmann, Matthias/Hirsch-Kreinsen, Hartmut (eds.): Produzieren im 21. Jahrhundert: Herausforderungen für die deutsche Industrie – Ergebnisse des Expertenkreises Zukunftsstrategien Band I; 1996 Campus Verlag; pp. 295–323.

Nerdinger, Friedemann W. (2014): Organisationsdiagnose; in Nerdinger, Friedemann W./Blickle, Gerhard/Schaper, Niclas (eds.): Arbeits- und Organisationspsychologie; 3rd German editon Springer 2014; pp. 133–142.

Neuberger, Oswald (2002): Führen und führen lassen; 6. edition UTB Lucius & Lucius 2002.

von der Oelsnitz, Dietrich (2012): Einführung in die systemische Personalführung; Carl Auer Verlag 2012.

O'Toole, James/Galbraith, Jay/Lawler, Edward E. III (2002): When Two (or More) Heads are Better than One: The Promise and Pitfalls of Shared Leadership; California Management Review Summer 2002 (44); pp. 65–83.

Parker Follett, Mary (1930): Some Discrepancies in Leadership Theory and Practice; in Metcalf, Henry C./Urwick, L.: Dynamic administration – The Collected Papers of Mary Parker Follett; Harper & Brothers 1942 (Erstveröffentlichung 1930); pp. 270–294.

Pearce, Craig L./Conger, Jay A. (2003) (eds.): Shared Leadership – Reframing the Hows and Whys of Leadership; Sage 2003.

Pearce, Craig L./Manz, Charles (2005): The New Silver Bullets of Leadership: The Importance of Self- and Shared Leadership in Knowledge Work; Organizational Dynamics 2/2005 (34); pp. 130–140.

Pearce, Craig L./Hoch, Julia Elisabeth/Jeppesen, Hans Jeppe/Wegge, Jürgen (2010): New Forms of Management – Shared and Distributed Leadership in Organizations; Journal of Personnel Psychology 4/2010; pp. 151–153.

Pentland, Brian T./Feldman, Martha S. (2005): Organizational Routines as a Unit of Analysis; Industrial and Corporate Change 5/2005 (14); pp. 793–815.

Pentland, Brian T./Hærem, Thorvald/Hillison, Derek (2010): Comparing Organizational Routines as Recurrent Patterns of Action; Organization Studies 7/2010 (31); pp. 17–40.

Pentland, Brian T./Feldman, Martha S./Becker, Markus C./Liu, Peng (2012): Dynamics of Organizational Routines: A Generative Model; Journal of Management Studies December 2012 (49); pp. 1484–1508.

Perry, Monica L./Pearce, Craig L./Sims, Henry P. (1999): Empowered Selling Teams: How Shared Leaderships Can Contribute to Selling Team. Outcomes; Journal of Personal Selling & Sales Management 3/1999 (19); pp. 35–51.

Piccolo, Ronald F./Bono, Joyce E./Heinitz, Kathrin/Rowold, Jens/Duehr, Emily/Judge, Timothy A. (2012): The Relative Impact of Complementary Leader Behaviors: Which Matter Most?; The Leadership Quarterly 2012 (23); pp. 567–581.

Pichler, Martin (2006): Was ist Komplementärberatung?; Wirtschaft und Weiterbildung 11/12 2006; pp. 18–23.

Piecha, Annika/Wegge, Jürgen (2014): Shared Leadership in Teams; in Felfe, Jörg (2015) (ed.): Trends der psychologischen Führungsforschung – Neue Konzepte, Methoden und Erkenntnisse; Hogrefe 2015; pp. 79–88.

Pietschmann, Bernd P./Huppertz, Silke/Ruhtz, Vanessa (1999): Was macht Führungsgrundsätze erfolgreich?; Personal 10/1999; pp. 506–510.

Pircher Verdorfer, Armin/Peus, Claudia (2014): The Measurement of Servant Leadership Validation of a German Version of the Servant Leadership Survey (SLS); Zeitschrift für Arbeits- und Organisationspsychologie 1/2014 (58), pp. 1–16

Pircher Verdorfer, Armin/Peus, Claudia (2015): Servant Leaderhip; in Felfe, Jörg (2015) (ed.): Trends der psychologischen Führungsforschung – Neue Konzepte, Methoden und Erkenntnisse; Hogrefe 2015.

Poznanski, Karin (2014): Eigene Handlungsmöglichkeiten erweitern – Wie Mitarbeiter Selbstführung lernen; Personalführung 11/2014; pp. 70–75.

Raelin, Joseph (2005): We the Leaders: In Order to Form a Leaderful Organization; Journal of Leadership and Organizational Studies 2/2005 (12); pp. 18–30.

Reiß, Michael (2011a): Vernetzte Führung zwischen Kooperation und Konkurrenz – Ansätze für ein erweitertes Führungsmodell; Personalführung 7/2011; pp. 22–28.

Reiß, Michael (2011b): Kooperation und Konkurrenz; Personal Heft 03/2011; pp. 10–12.

Ridder, Hans-Gerd/Hohn, Christina (2012): Führung in Teams – Geteilte Führung als Beitrag zum Führungsprozess; in Bruch, Heike/Krummaker, Stefan/Vogel, Bernd (eds.): Leadership – Best Practices and Trends; 2. edition Springer Gabler 2012; pp. 157–164

Rivkin, Wladislaw/Diestel, Stefan/Schmidt, Klaus-Helmut (2014): The positive relationship between servant leadership and employees' psychological health: A multi-method approach; Zeitschrift für Personalforschung, 1–2/2014 (28); pp. 52–72.

Rosenberger, Walter (2014): Der Einsatz und Nutzen einer Organisationsanalyse; in Rosenberger, Bernhard (eds.): Modernes Personalmanagement: Strategisch – operativ – systemisch; Springer Gabler 2014; pp. 104–108.

Schall, Ellen/Ospina, Sonia/Godsoe, Bethany/Dodge, Jennifer (2004): Appreciative Narratives as Leadership Research: Matching Method to Lens; in David Cooperrider and Michel Avital (eds.): Advances in Appreciative Inquiry Vol 1: Constructive Discourse and Human Organization; Elsevier Science; https://www.researchgate.net/publication/235297357_APPRECIATIVE_

NARRATIVES_AS_LEADERSHIP_RESEARCH_MATCHING_METHOD_TO_LENS (Accessed 01/05, 2022).

Scheiring, Hermann/Mattheis, Carmen (2008): Motivation (Präsentationsfolien); http://www.colegio-humboldt.edu.pe/refo/refo-2008/Materialien/08-2008%20Materialien/17%20Motivation%20Management%20und%20Leadership.pdf (Accessed 01/05, 2022).

Schilling, Jan (2005): Inhalte von Führungsgrundsätzen unter der Lupe – Ergebnisse und Perspektiven; Zeitschrift für Personalpsychologie, 3/2005 (4); pp. 123–131.

Schmidt-Huber, Marion/Dörr, Stefan/Maier, Günter W. (2014): Die Entwicklung und Validierung eines evidenzbasierten Kompetenzmodells effektiver Führung (LEaD: Leadership Effectiveness and Development); Zeitschrift für Arbeits- u. Organisationspsychologie 2/2014 (58); pp. 80–94.

Scholl, Wolfgang (2014): Führen und (sich) führen lassen; Personalmagazin 7/2014; pp. 22–24.

Scholz, Christian (1996): Die virtuelle Personalabteilung – Ein Jahr später; Personalführung 12/1996; pp. 1080–1086.

Scholz, Christian (2014): Personalmanagement – Informationsorientierte und verhaltenstheoretische Grundlagen; 6th edition Vahlen 2014.

Schulte-Zurhausen, Manfred (2014): Organisation; 6th edition Vahlen 2014.

Simon, Herbert A. (1946): The Proverbs of Administration"; Public Administration Review, Vol. 6, No. 1 (Winter), pp. 53-67

Sprenger, Reinhard K. (2007a): Prinzip Selbstverantwortung – Wege zur Motivation; 12th edition Campus 2012.

Sprenger, Reinhard K. (2007b): Vertrauen führt – Worauf es im Unternehmen wirklich ankommt; 3rd edition Campus 2007.

Sprenger, Reinhard K. (2012): Radikal führen; Campus 2012.

Skinner, B. F. (1953): Science and Human Behavior; The Free Press 1953.

Stayer, Ralph (1990): How I Learned to Let My Workers Lead; Harvard Business Review November-December 1990; pp. 66–83.

Steinmann, Horst/Schreyögg, Georg/Koch, Jochen (2013): Management – Grundlagen der Unternehmensführung; 7th edition Springer Gabler 2013.

Stewart, Greg L./Courtright, Stephen H./Manz, Charles C. (2011): Self-Leadership – A Multilevel Review; Journal of Management 1/2011; pp. 185–222.

Steyrer, Johannes/Meyer, Michael (2010): Welcher Führungsstil führt zum Erfolg? 60 Jahre Führungsstilforschung – Einsichten und Aussichten; zfo 3/2010; pp. 148–155.

Stippler, Maria/Moore, Sadie/Rosenthal, Seth/Dörffer, Tina (2011): Führung – Überblick über Ansätze, Entwicklungen, Trends; Bertelsmann Stiftung 2011.

Stogdill, Ralph M. (1950): Leadership, Membership and Organization; Psychological Bulletin 1/1950 (47); pp. 1–14.

Stolzenberg, Kerstin/Reiners, Heiner (2012): Werkzeugkiste 33. – Visions- und Leitbildentwicklung; Organisationsentwicklung 4/2012; pp. 80–85.

Streich, Richard K. (2013): Fit for Leadership – Entwicklungsfelder zur Führungspersönlichkeit; Springer Gabler 2013.

Sun, Peter Y.T. (2013): The servant identity: Influences on the cognition and behavior of servant leaders; The Leadership Quarterly 2013 (24); pp. 544–557.

Tannenbaum, Robert/Schmidt, Warren H. (1958): How to Choose a Leadership Pattern; Harvard Business Review 36; March/April 1958; pp. 95–101.

Taylor, Frederick W. (1911): Shop Management; Neuauflage Nu Vision Publications 2008 (Erstveröffentlichung 1911).

Taylor, Frederick W. (1912): The Principles of Scientific Management; in Dartmouth College (ed.): Addresses and Discussions at the Conference on Scientific Management; Dartmouth College 2012; p. 22–55; https://archive.org/details/addressesdiscuss00dart (Accessed 01/05, 2022).

Tenney, Matt (2014): Serve to Be Great: Leadership Lessons from a Prison, a Monastery, and a Boardroom; Wiley 2014.

Titscher, Stefan/Mayrhofer, Wolfgang/Meyer, Michael (2010): Zur Praxis der Organisationsforschung; in Mayrhofer, Wolfgang/Meyer, Michael/Titscher, Stefan: Praxis der Organisationsanalyse – Anwendungsfelder und Methoden; Facultas/UTB 2010; pp. 17–44.

Trompenaars, Fons/Voerman, Ed (2009): Servant-Leadership across cultures; Infinite Ideas Ltd. Oxford 2009.

Ulrich, Hans (1978): Unternehmungspolitik; Verlag Paul Haupt 1978.

Ulrich, Dave/Smallwood, Norm/Sweetman, Kate (2008): The Leadership Code; Harvard Business School Press 2008.

Völkl, Christian/Menzel-Black, Christin (2014): Nach Bedarf designt; Personalmagazin 6/2014; pp. 35–37.

Weh, Saskia-Maria/Meifert, Matthias T. (2013): Etappe 8 – Kulturmanagement; in Meifert, Matthias T. (Hrsg.): Strategische Personalentwicklung – Ein Programm in acht Etappen; 3rd edition 2013; pp. 315–330.

Weibler, Jürgen (2014): Führung der Mitarbeiter durch den nächsthöheren Vorgesetzten; in von Rosenstiel, Lutz/Regnet, Erika/Domsch, Michel E. Führung von Mitarbeitern – Handbuch für erfolgreiches Personalmanagement; Schäffer-Poeschel 2014; pp. 271–283.

Weibler, Jürgen (2016): Personalführung; 3rd edition Vahlen 2016.

Weise, Carolin/Selck, Andreas (2007): Fehlende Orientierung? Führungsinstrumente richtig einsetzen; Arbeit und Arbeitsrecht; pp. 712–717.

Werner, Christian/Elbe, Martin (2010): Therapie ohne Diagnose?; in Werner, Christian/Elbe, Martin (eds.): Handbuch Organisationsdiagnose; Herbert Utz Verlag 2013.

Werther, Simon (2013): Geteilte Führung – Ein Paradigmenwechsel in der Führungsforschung; Dissertation Springer Gabler Research 2013.

Werther, Simon/Brodbeck, Felix (2014): Geteilte Führung als Führungsmodell: Merkmale erfolgreicher Führungskräfte; Personal Quarterly 1/2014; pp. 22–27.

Without author (1992): KARRIERE-Gespräch mit Ploenzke-Geschaeftsführer Juergen Fuchs über den Abschied von der Karriere – Im Netzwerkverbund zaehlen Dienstleistung und Teamgeist mehr als Dienstgrad und Titel; Handelsblatt 25.09.1992; p. k01/Karriere.

Yukl, Gary (2013): Leadership in Organizations; 8th edition Pearson 2013.

Yukl, Gary/Lepsinger, Richard (2005): Why Integrating the Leading and Managing Roles Is Essential for Organizational Effectiveness; Organizational Dynamics 4/2005; pp. 361–375.

Zimmermann, Alexander/Welling, Christian (2010): Auf dem Weg zum 'janusköpfigen Manager'? Komplementäre und integrierte Führungsstrukturen in Zeiten des Wandels; in Kunisch, Sven/Welling, Christian/Schmitt, Ramona (eds.) (2010): Strategische Führung auf dem Prüfstand; Springer 2010; pp. 113–126

The Role of Line Managers in Complementary Management

3

3.1 The Line Manager in the Context of Management and Leadership Structures

This chapter describes the role of line managers in the context of the Complementary Management Model as outlined in Chap. 2. It is aimed at those interested in the theoretical aspects of management and leadership, particularly corporate models of management and leadership. The benefit of such corporate models is to provide orientation for management actors on relevant issues, thereby shaping their behavior. To do this, the models must be understood, especially by the line managers who ultimately play a key role in the leadership process. Therefore, a well-thought-out presentation is required. However, before a corporate model can be communicated, it must be designed; the theoretical foundations, e.g., the Complementary Management Model, must be adjusted and adapted to the corresponding corporate circumstances (see Sect. 2.6). This, in turn, requires an in-depth examination of the entire solution space. Thus, when describing in detail (below) all seven elements of the Complementary Management Model in terms of their implications for line managers, experts dealing with such conceptual issues of management and leadership are the ones being addressed—not the line managers as "end users". The book "Führen als Beruf" (Kaehler 2019) can be recommended for the latter, an English edition of which is planned for 2022.

3.1.1 Management Functions: Line Managers as Dual Service Providers

People management and leadership is not an end in itself, but is a part of corporate management, defined as a steering influence on market, production, and/or resource operations that may address both people and non-people issues with the aim of achieving the unit's objectives (Sect. 1.1.1). Apart from possible special cases, organizations maintain workforces not for their own sake, but as a resource, because they need the work performance to achieve their organizational goals. Accordingly, people management and leadership must be designed to influence people in terms of their contributions to the organization's purpose and business success. It serves as a way to achieve the unit's goals by generating work performance and meeting other requirements. People management and leadership thus serves to enable and promote the actual business. This could certainly also be described as its "function".

The functionality of people management and leadership in relation to the organizational unit, as explained above, can be distinguished from its functionality in relation to an organizational unit's personnel. The Complementary Management Model addresses this through its element of complementary management functions. This starts with the recognition that leadership is nothing other than a service, which was explained in detail in Sect. 2.2. Like all other service professions, the line manager's job requires two functions to be fulfilled simultaneously which stand under a certain degree of tension with respect to one another: the support function and the disciplinary function. On the one hand, the line manager helps the person being managed/led to take up and sustainably achieve his or her work performance; on the other hand, he or she ascertains order by ensuring that the rules and requirements of the corporate community are enforced. Just as waiters, teachers, policemen, or salespeople have to provide clearly defined assistance while also ensuring order, line managers have to both support employees and supervise them. The important thing to note here is that line managers act purely as compensatory service providers, i.e., they only step in when an employee is unable to help and discipline him or herself—something which they ideally should do.

Such service-providing management is by no means to be regarded as an unlimited servantship. Instead, its contents can be precisely demarcated like any other service. This demarcation takes place by defining the complementary management tasks which represent the actual management requirements and in which the two service functions are specified. Both functions are realized within a particular management task. For example, it is difficult to reasonably establish whether sorting out unclear work assignments is more of a support for the disoriented employee or an enforcement of the organization's performance requirements—it is simultaneously both to different degrees depending on the situation.

When there is a criticism of poor management and leadership, it is usually because the line manager is practicing what can be described as self-referential or destructive management and seen by the respective line managers as a mandate of domination, with "his or her" employees being a personal resource. Often enough management fails because line managers see their position as a privilege, good manners as superfluous, and employees as personal servants. Nothing is better suited to encourage such line managers to adopt more appropriate and productive behavior than the service idea. They have to justify to their own superiors (plus the human resources department, the auditing department, etc.) how this behavior fits with their job description, since it falls neither under the support nor the disciplinary function and is more like that of a little king than of an effective service provider. At every available opportunity, organizations should explicitly and consistently communicate to the entire workforce the principle of management as a dual thrust service. Once embedded as a philosophy, it shapes mutual expectations and removes the tendency towards autocratic leadership and management. No single measure—perhaps with the exception of providing line managers with enough time to work—has a greater impact on improving unsatisfactory management/leadership quality than the message "we're not here for ourselves, we're here for others."

Anyone who deduces from the principle of servant leadership that status symbols must be abolished will generally fail. Former Chief Human Resources Officer of Deutsche Telekom, Thomas Sattelberger, on the subject of failure:

> "In a service company, leadership and management must have a pronounced servant component and not be exercised as positional power. Our surveys show that this has improved somewhat. But a broad understanding is not yet part of the corporate culture. I've taken away title levels, stripped epaulettes, cut parking spaces and phone numbers - which are all signals of hierarchies. Even for the executive board. Without resounding success. I asked myself: Was I too radical, was I too superficial, was the approach wrong? Obviously, I didn't get it right." (Quoted from Straub and Jessl 2012, p. 13; own translation).

Indeed, leading as a service cannot be enforced by reducing status symbols, but only through effective management structures that meaningfully concretize the abstract principle of service. Status symbols are not detrimental to this; on the contrary, they can form an important incentivizing component to keep service-based leadership and management attractive to future talent. Moreover, most employees are presumably only marginally interested in the privileges and status symbols of their bosses, but eagerly desire the support of effective management.

3.1.2   Management Tasks: Clear Definition of People Aims

The second element of the Complementary Management Model is the catalog of management tasks which attempts to map the entire spectrum of organizational employee management tasks in normative terms. This aims to establish which people-related tasks have to be performed in order to ensure sustainable work performance on the part of those being managed/led. As such, management tasks are not understood as concrete acts, but as people-related goals that require practical implementation within the framework of management routines (for more information, see Section 3.1.5).

An overview of the various tasks is provided in Table 2.5 under Sect. 2.3.3. Organizations can, of course, modify the catalog of tasks proposed there and define them differently. There is a certain conceptual arbitrariness anyways in grouping numerous detailed tasks into exactly eight task categories, each containing exactly three tasks. Many detailed tasks can undoubtedly also be divided differently. However, including a catalog of tasks in corporate models of leadership and management is necessary to ensure that people management and leadership is understood uniformly and practiced optimally within the company. It is true that experienced line managers themselves often have useful implicit management theories with respect to tasks. However, the idea that all members of an organization would independently develop a helpful canon of management tasks for themselves that would meaning-fully reflect what needs to be done in the field of people management seems naïve.

3.1.3 Management Actors: The Line Manager as a Part of the Whole

The third core element of the model consists of the complementary management actors. These are all of the people involved in the process. (Sect. 2.4 goes into more detail on this.) People management and leadership is thus also, but not only, the task of the line manager. Indeed, it is not even primarily the line manager's task, because the employees' self-management should be the essential principle of people man-agement. The senior manager, HR advisor, and, where applicable, the employee's colleagues also play a role in this nexus.

The employee's self-steerage is indeed a key to good, efficient, and effective leadership and management. Ideally, employees are self-aware of what work needs to be done, motivate themselves, resolve conflicts alone, autonomously acquire new knowledge when required, etc. This means that they perform the relevant manage-ment tasks themselves and fulfill both the support function of self-help and the order function of self-discipline. However, a compensatory mechanism is required since experience shows that not all employees are always willing and able to fully exercise self-direction in the interest of the company. Were that the case, leadership and management would be child's play and neither elaborate theoretical models nor line managers would be needed:

"Anybody could lead perfect people – if there were any." (Greenleaf 1970, p. 13)

As a compensatory entity, the line manager must first judge—in relation to each single management task—the extent to which the employee already fulfills this task on his or her own, and then (only) take compensatory action in the event of deficits. For example, if an employee knows his or her work tasks and work performance, the line manager no longer needs to explain them. If this is not the case, the line manager must intervene. If a line manager detects that an employee is not fulfilling a certain management task, several intervention options are available (Table. 3.1; repetition of Table 2.8), which can also be combined. Intervention takes place with the full authority and positional power of classic authoritarian management but should preferably be exercised gently via informal behavioral reinforcement and implicit communication (see Sect. 1.4).

The line manager therefore generally responds to situational requirements. Only in cases where it is clear from the outset that the employee is unwilling or unable to fulfill a management task is compensatory management carried out proactively, i.e., the line manager takes action on his or her own initiative. Normally, however, the line manager takes reactive compensatory intervention.

The line manager's role as a compensatory entity is to ensure that all management tasks are performed with respect to all those being managed/led. This is done within the framework of established management routines, e.g., dialogs (see Sect.

Table. 3.1 Intervention options of the line manager (illustrated here by the example of the management task "resolving conflicts") (modified from Kaehler 2017, p. 409; © Boris Kaehler 2019. All rights reserved)

Corrective intervention	The line manager induces the employee to fulfill the leadership/management task (i.e., in this case, resolving an existing conflict with colleagues him/herself)
Joint intervention	The line manager supports the employee in performing the leadership/management task (i.e., in this case, in resolving the conflict)
Delegative intervention	The manager arranges for a colleague of the employee or for the HR advisor to fulfill the leadership/management task (i.e., in this case, to mediate the conflict). This can be used to compensate for the line manager's own time or competence deficits. "The ideal manager is the man who knows exactly what he is not capable of doing himself, and who gets the right people to do it." (Attributed to Philip Rosenthal)
Substituting intervention	The manager takes on the leadership/management task him/herself (and mediates the conflict)

3.1.5). Note: This concerns the employee-related management tasks, not the genuine work tasks of the employee (which are not management, but mere execution).

Just as all employees do not always fully lead themselves, all line managers are not always and comprehensively willing and able to take compensatory action. This is why it is so important to involve other actors in the process, who in turn act as higher-level compensatory entities. These entities are the senior manager and the HR advisor, who intervene in a compensatory manner with respect to the line manager according to the same principles as the line manager intervenes with respect to the employees. This interaction between management actors has already been explained in more detail and illustrated in Sect. 2.4.5. On the one hand, the compensatory mechanism ensures that all management tasks relating to the employees are actually performed even if the line manager is inactive, thus ensuring effective people management and leadership. On the other hand, such a multilevel system is suitable for preventing abuse of power by the line manager. The fact that, in addition to senior managers, HR advisors also play a compensatory role in this process and thus engage in "HR co-management" is explained in detail in Sect. 4.2.3.

> **Excursion: The Role of Senior Managers**
>
> The role of senior line managers is an issue that deserves special attention as it is very much neglected in the literature (see Weibler 2014). First of all, it should be noted that senior managers also practice "normal" people management and leadership of those reporting directly to them. It takes place in a cascading manner, i.e., top managers influence middle managers, who then influence employees through lower management levels (see Yukl 2013, p. 21; Weibler 2014, pp. 273 f., 277). Senior managers do not manage the line managers reporting directly to them any differently than the latter manage

(continued)

their direct reports (Weibler 2014, p. 280). Thus, all of the maxims established above for normal management and leadership work apply, in particular the compensatory role with regard to self-management. If, for example, the subordinate line manager does not know what work to do, is not motivated, not able to solve own conflicts with colleagues, or otherwise fails to perform the management tasks that relate to him or her, the senior manager must intervene.

What can make the situation slightly confusing is the fact that a good part of the subordinate line manager's work consists of people management and leadership. This means that the compensatory mandate of the senior manager also includes the higher-level leadership and management of the employees reporting to the directly subordinate management level. Just as the line manager regularly talks to his or her team members about their job duties, the senior manager talks to the subordinate line manager about his or her management/leadership work and the individual employees being managed. And just as the senior manager intervenes when the employee does not know, master or complete his or her work assignments, the senior manager intervenes when the line manager fails to intervene in cases of self-management deficits of the employee. And of course, in doing so the senior manager also has the options of corrective, joint, delegative, or substitutive intervention (see Sect. 3.1.3). This higher-level management of employees is thus ultimately only a derivative of the direct management of a senior manager in relation to the subordinate line manager. In the system of Complementary Management, however, it is an important building block because higher-level leadership adds another important management actor and thus an additional compensatory entity to the game.

In this context, the senior manager should avoid acting without consulting the line manager (even though this is known to happen in practice) because this generally undermines the latter's authority and motivation. It goes without saying, however, that in many companies senior managers take over for line managers in their absence, act as a complaints authority for employees, and/or participate in the fulfillment of some management tasks, e.g., by setting additional incentives. Hölzl gives a typical example:

> "[Many shift supervisors don't] dare to conduct critique meetings on their own. So they call in their superiors such as corporate or plant managers." (Hölzl 2014, p. 45)

Another example is that of the new, inexperienced line manager who needs active day-to-day help in almost all people management matters, from salary issues to termination dialogs. This is a good illustration of the special function of the "boss's boss". However, it is not uncommon even for experienced line managers to have their management weaknesses compensated for by complementary senior managers, and this is indeed how it should be.

3.1.4 Management Unit Design: Job Design for Line Management Positions

The Complementary Management Theory's four implementation elements—unit design, routines, instruments, and resources—describe the management structures required to implement the core model in concrete terms. The associated systematic issues have already been explained in more detail in Sect. 2.5 and do not need to be addressed again here.

One of the four implementation elements is the management unit design in the sense of the design of the positions of those responsible for people management. In an organizational context, leadership and management is a professional activity (Drucker 1954, pp. 6–17; Malik 2000, pp. 46 ff., 2007, pp. 38, 67; Kaehler 2019; critically Kellerman 2012, pp. 191 f). Following this assertion, one will have to consider what concrete work this consists of, i.e., what particular activities are to be bundled in a line management position. This is essentially a classic question of organizational design ("job creation"). In practice, however, the configuration of management positions usually results simply from situational requirements, i.e., these break out in an uncontrolled manner. As a result, the job holders themselves act as buffers in the sense that they take additional time when needed. The overload of many line managers is a sign in many places that too much work tends to be bundled into one position.

In fact, this absence of systematic structuring in the design of line management positions—in addition to coordination difficulties, which also represent an organizational failure—is the reason why part-time leadership widely does not work (see Karlshaus and Kaehler 2017). How should something be shared in a meaningful way that is not systematically defined and requires such large buffers? In principle, of course, part-time leadership is certainly organizationally feasible, because any job is always the result and a component of the division of labor and is therefore, in turn, always further divisible (Andreas Hoff, cited in Dellekönig 1995, p. 96). In any case, the configuration of management positions should not be left to chance or the free play of forces any more than the configuration of other jobs.

As in any other type of job, very different work tasks and activities can be bundled in line management positions. However, the understanding of holistic management and leadership advocated here implies that there are certain areas of activity which are generally indispensable for a functional governance. First of all, it should be noted that organizational leadership and management almost always consists of two major areas of activity: management of functional-technical matters and management of people. The distinction between the two is not as trivial as it might seem—details can be found in Section 1.6.2. In any case, qualified work must be performed in both areas, which presupposes the corresponding resources and qualifications. A third area of activity is inevitably self-management. This differentiation is often conceptually disregarded, but in fact is neither new nor unusual (see the three pillars of the "BMW Management House" in Hoffmann and Jäckel 2011, p. 34).

Fig. 3.1 Areas of activity of the line manager (modified from Kaehler 2014a, p. 56, 2017, p. 411; (© Boris Kaehler 2019. All rights reserved)

In all three subareas, it is possible to identify indispensable activities that form the core of the management occupation, and others that are additional and can be easily dispensed with (Fig. 3.1). The core activities of people management, management of functional-technical matters, and self-management must be considered in any case when designing line management positions. In contrast, the three additional activity fields are not necessarily part of such jobs. It may well make sense to assign such additional activities to a particular line management position. However, if too many other tasks are already bundled in a position, (only) these additional tasks should be eliminated.

Excursion: Flat Hierarchies and the Right Span of Control

Few management buzzwords are as widespread and, at the same time, as absurd as that of the "flat hierarchy." After all, there is a negative correlation between span of control (also: management span) and depth of control (also: hierarchy depth), i.e., the smaller the span of direct reports, the greater (for the same number of jobs) the number of hierarchy levels (Fig. 2.4 in Sect. 2.5.2). An organization, therefore, needs exactly as many hierarchy levels as are necessary to ensure that the span of control is neither too large (= no longer manageable) nor too small (= unnecessary management interfaces). Like all things, hierarchies have, by no means, only negative aspects, but also positive ones (Sprenger 2008, p. 91; Sanner and Bunderson 2018). Furthermore, where the "flat hierarchy" is invoked, it is often not an organizational hierarchy that is meant at all (i.e., an organizational super−/subordination of jobs and units), but rather the lived power distance and communication/decision-making culture that build social hierarchies.

(continued)

Obviously, the question of the right span of control cannot be answered in a generalized way (Gutenberg 1979, pp. 255–256). It is possible to widen the span through good process organization as well as by relieving line managers of non-management-related tasks and supporting them in management tasks and activities. However, the scope here is definitely limited; in most cases, a leadership span of 6–12 employees is realistic (see Penning 2012). Even Jack Welch, an avowed supporter of the flat hierarchy, recommends only 10–15 employees (Welch and Welch 2005, p. 134). According to an old practitioner's rule of thumb, the average line manager needs about 5% of his or her working time to lead an average employee. This figure seems quite plausible. Where 30 or more employees are allegedly managed/led in a direct reporting line or (ostensibly) entirely without hierarchy, this is almost always explained by one to three factors. The first is that essential management tasks are simply not being performed. If an understanding of management and leadership is used that reduces the range of management tasks, the span of control can of course also be increased: "[. . .] while a manager can typically supervise only about seven people, he or she can coach close to thirty." (Hammer and Champy 1993, p. 78 f.) A second possibility is that it involves extremely well-structured workplaces in which work and management behavior are largely standardized by process specifications. The third factor may be that informal management positions have been established that just do not appear in the organizational chart.

In recent years, many companies have reduced the middle and lower management levels beyond what is objectively justified in the course of restructuring and "organizational efficiency" campaigns, thus expanding the management spans. This has inevitably led to an increased workload for the remaining line managers (Claßen and Sattelberger 2011, p. 59; Kern, cited in Schrehardt 2012; Goldschmidt cited in Link 2015, p. 113; Straub with a positive assessment, as cited in Hergert 2012). As a result, many line managers simply no longer have time for proper people management and leadership (see Sect. 3.1.7).

In order to make the chosen organizational design known within the organization, it must be documented. This is done through job descriptions and organizational charts. Regardless of the fact that these are often poorly drawn up and hopelessly outdated, they serve a fundamentally important function as information and steerage instruments. It is advisable to use *management tasks* to describe people management work in job descriptions, which makes the presentation more meaningful (Table 3.2). In principle, however, reference can also (or only) be made to *management routines* (conducting employee dialogs, chairing meetings, etc.). The decisive factor is to send a clear message to the company that people management and leadership is an important and extensive part of the management occupation. More detailed implementation specifications are reserved for guidelines, i.e., regulations

Table. 3.2 Possible conversion of management task categories into job descriptions (modified from Kaehler 2017, p. 413; © Boris Kaehler 2019. All rights reserved)

Task Category (Details Sect. 2.3.3)	Clause in job description
Managing work tasks	"Ensuring productive and accurate performance of subordinate employees through task delegation, resource allocation and performance feedback"
Setting HR norms	"Strategic and constitutive management; optimization of process and organizational structure; shaping of culture and diversity in the team"
Ensuring administration	"Gathering and evaluation of personnel data, handling of personnel administration requirements; liaison with representative bodies"
Hiring, retaining, separating	"Participation in employee recruitment and maintenance of applicant relationships; participation in personnel selection and integration; retention of top performers"
Arranging collaboration	"Regulating coordinative communication; resolving conflicts and promoting professional team relations; strengthening team cohesion and identification"
Fostering competence and development	"Qualifying and developing subordinate employees; managing existing and required knowledge; promoting innovation"
Granting care	"Protecting health and enabling contractional work-life balance; creating flow conditions; providing support in change processes and crisis situations"
Crafting motivation	"Motivating employees through holistic performance incentives based on individual needs and existing incentive instruments; supporting performance impulses; communicating realistic performance, incentive, target, and equity expectations"
Additional clause for senior managers	"Designing management instruments; communicating across hierarchies; higher-level people management by guiding subordinate line managers"

and recommendations for continuous, annual, and on-demand management routines (see Sect. 2.5.3). The aim should be to have documentation that is always up to date and actually used by the addressees. This can best be achieved by observing users in action. Pure formal documentation, which is only created on the occasion of upcoming job advertisements, audits, or quality management campaigns, is of no help to anyone.

Excursion: Positional Power of Managerial Positions

It has already been emphasized several times that self-management should be the overriding principle of people management and leadership. When, however, the literature often concludes that modern line managers no longer need any formal authority at all, this is simply misleading because there are of course situations in which they do need it (Foss and Klein 2014). In organizational practice, therefore, line managers still almost always have a pronounced

(continued)

positional power. "By virtue of their office," for example, they exercise the employer's right of direction and are entitled to issue instructions to employees and to impose or initiate sanctions. Even where this authority to issue directives is not made explicit in any way, cultural patterns almost always operate in such a way that employees informally ascribe such prerogatives to their line managers and rank the gain or loss of their boss's social recognition as particularly important. Certainly, it is an extremely clumsy form of communication and rather a sign of weakness when line managers assert their influence by constantly referring to formal entitlements, because such exercising of power generates resistance (see Sect. 1.4.1). However, it is not even necessary, because the theoretical and, at best, selectively demonstrated possibility normally makes actual use unnecessary (see, e.g., Scholl 2014). The mere existence of authorizing and sanctioning powers ensures that unfair conduct is prevented from the outset or can be averted at the outset. The underlying principle is US President Theodore Roosevelt's motto: "Speak softly and carry a big stick" (Roosevelt 1901). However, since this inevitably entails the risk of abuse of power, a clear definition of the authority of management positions is required. At the same time, a multilevel system of different, mutually complementary actors is recommended. One such mechanism is the compensatory mechanism of the Complementary Management Model, which combines the principle of self-management with the needs-based intervention of the respective higher-level actors (Sect. 4.4.4). This compensatory mechanism means that the line manager intervenes on the part of the employee in the event of self-leadership deficits—and this certainly requires corresponding powers. However, while authoritative leadership and management is necessary in certain circumstances, it is not synonymous with appealing instructions and should preferably be gentle, using informal behavioral reinforcement and implicit communication (see Sect. 2.4).

Ultimately, all functions and tasks of the line manager are rooted in conferred formal authority in the sense of positional power (see already Mintzberg 1975, p. 54). It follows from this that where management positions are not granted any positional power in terms of organizational structure, i.e., through job and process design, the line management position loses its supporting role within the framework of the management architecture (it then degenerates into that of a mere moderator) or must laboriously fight for it in the shadowy realm of micropolitics (this will be discussed in Section 3.2). No matter how you slice it: Line managers need a robust and well-defined mandate for authoritarian intervention because the unlimited self-determination of all employees is unrealistic. To this end, management icon Hans L. Merkle writes:

(continued)

"Managing implies delegation, but by no means consists of it. I know of few greater platitudes in management theory than the term 'management by delegation'—a common coin, but a term not taken to its logical conclusion, because you cannot lead by handing over leadership thoughtlessly, so to speak. It was not a joker but a serious practitioner who proposed to say 'management by managers'." (Merkle 1983, p. 182)

Giving and limiting this mandate at the same time is an important aspect to be taken into account in the organizational design of the management units.

3.1.5   Management Routines: Concrete Activities of Management and Leadership

The first aspect to discuss in connection with the management routines of line managers is the concept as such. In order to practically implement management tasks, which are ultimately only goals, concrete management activities are required—e.g., conversations and meetings. These can be aptly described as "management routines" because they are, at minimum, potentially recurring, involve an expected course of action, and should be tested or practiced. Sect. 2.5.3 goes into more detail on the derivation of the concept and Fig. 3.1 shows a graphical representation of the three essential activity fields. Management routines are nothing more than complex activities within which the many elementary activities take place that are necessary to perform the management tasks and their elementary tasks. For example, the management task "to round off the incentive field" consists of, among other things, the elementary task "praise", which is fulfilled by the elementary activity "communicate" within the routine "work dialog". Organizations should not leave it up to line managers to decide which management routines they consider useful because experience shows that there is a wide range of, unfortunately, often dysfunctional views in this regard. Rather, the routines should be clearly defined as part of the management structures and backed by detailed implementation recommendations. It has proven useful to categorize them into continuous routines, annual routines, and on-demand routines.

The main people management routines were already presented in detail in Sect. 2.5.3. This non-actor-specific presentation was chosen because, as a rule, several management actors are involved in the routines. Even in corporate settings, the expected management routines should not be presented as the sole responsibility of a single actor. An employee dialog, for example, is by no means the responsibility of the line manager alone, but is shaped at least as much by the employee, and possibly by other management actors as well. In the course of introducing a corporate management model, the routines as such must first be defined and the responsibilities of the actors specified (see Sect. 2.6). Only then does this result in a bundle of responsibilities for each actor, which he or she has to fulfill within the framework of the routines.

Corporate models of leadership and management can make very different stipulations in this respect. For example, in some companies only the HR department is responsible for hiring projects or dismissal dialogs, in others only the line manager is involved, and in still others both together. In principle, the routine parts an actor performs always add up to the totality of his or her people management activities.

Once established, the actor-specific parts of the routines cannot be delegated in a meaningful way. Line managers must therefore and by all means participate in their own routines. However, they do not necessarily have to be in charge of organizing and carrying out the routines themselves. For example, taking minutes at meetings and in work dialogs can be delegated to the employee, or leading interviews can be delegated to an HR advisor. This is of practical importance because it offers the possibility of shifting work volumes between actors (e.g., it can relieve the line manager from taking minutes or leading conversations). The question of what line managers actually have to do in relation to their employees can therefore be answered quite simply: they must perform their defined share of the designated management routines, e.g., participate in work dialogs and meetings. Within the framework of these management routines, line managers must ensure that the management tasks are fulfilled and must apply the existing management instruments. From the line manager's point of view, management routines are the focal point of the entire process of management and leadership.

The second aspect to discuss in connection with the management routines of line managers is the compensatory dynamic of interventions. The role of the line manager as a compensatory entity was already the subject of the paragraph on management actors (Sect. 3.1.3). It became clear that the line manager only has to intervene if and to the extent that an employee shows self-leadership/self-management deficits, i.e., does not take on management tasks him or herself. Not everyone is capable of it, and even those who manage themselves do not always do so all the time and for every task. This is exactly why there are line managers at all! Intervention always relates to concrete management tasks—e.g., defining the work to be done, resolving conflicts, and maintaining health—and takes place within the framework of management routines.

It follows from this that, in conversations and contact situations of all kinds, the line manager must first find out where the employee stands in relation to a particular management task. It is an equally frequent and unnecessary mistake for a manager to try to impose solutions on employees that they have already found for themselves. The opposite mistake is not to intervene and not to offer solutions even when this is objectively necessary. It is no wonder that, to this day, many trainers and authors are trying to teach managers to listen (see, for example, Ferrari 2012; Groyberg and Slind 2012). After all, "As long as you talk yourself, you learn nothing." (Attributed to Marie von Ebner-Eschenbach).

The various people management routines provide the framework for both the ongoing monitoring of employees with regard to their self-management, and for compensatory interventions in the event of respective deficits. A skillful combination of continuous, annual, and on-demand routines and their anchoring in the management structures must ensure that there is sufficient contact between line managers and employees and that all management tasks are covered in terms of content.

The third aspect to discuss in connection with the management routines of line managers are the routines for the "management of functional-technical matters". Leadership and management has both non-people and people-related components. In established literature, however, only the distinction between management/leadership tasks and functional-technical tasks is common, referring to steerage tasks on the one hand and executing functional-technical tasks on the other (e.g., Gutenberg 1979, p. 243; Malik 2007, pp. 65, 90 ff.; Steinmann et al. 2013, p. 7 f.). However, the performance of these functional-technical tasks is not management or leadership at all:

> "Most managers spend most of their time on things that are not "managing." A sales manager makes a statistical analysis or placates an important customer. A foreman repairs a tool or fills out a production report. A manufacturing manager designs a new plant layout or tests new materials. A company president works through the details of a bank loan or negotiates a big contract [...] All these things pertain to a particular function. All are necessary and have to be done well. But they are apart from the work which every manager does whatever his function or activity, whatever his rank and position, work which is common to all managers and peculiar to them." (Drucker 1973, p. 399 f.)

Most management positions in organizations are designed in such a way that their holders not only perform functional-technical management routines, but also other functional-technical activities of a non-managerial nature that could well be delegated. This applies to involvement in higher-level organizational projects (e.g., in the case of corporate acquisitions) or the support of important customers, projects, or central functions. Such additional business tasks can be permanently reallocated or temporarily assigned to other positions, which is advisable, e.g., when the jobholder is overloaded. Another large block of functional-technical matters are those tasks that the line manager should actually delegate to employees, but, in fact, withholds and handles alone. The term "retained work" is proposed here for these non-delegated work tasks. This does not refer to management tasks, such as defining work assignments or solving conflicts, which ideally should be carried out by the employee as a self-manager. Rather, these are purely execution activities (conducting/performing functional-technical work) that are or should be a genuine part of the employee's primary job. Many line managers have a pronounced tendency to take over such work from employees or not to pass it on to them at all. However, this often leaves them with insufficient time to perform their actual core management activities. To make matters worse, these line managers are often under the illusion that they are supporting their employees and thus providing good people management and leadership—even though they are actually only performing non-managerial functional tasks. What is needed here are guidelines that clarify which activities are core components of the management position and which are not. In this context, one might refer to a quotation from Mary Parker Follett from 1930 (!):

"The job of the man higher up is not to make decisions for his subordinates, but to teach them how to handle their problems themselves, how to make their own decisions." (Parker Follett 1930, S. 282)

The genuine management activities also have large functional-technical, i.e., non-people components. Whereas the personnel-related and functional-technical aspects of *operational* management are so closely linked that they cannot be meaningfully separated; the greater part of *strategic* and *constitutive* management has no direct reference to personnel. It is therefore purely functional-technical management work—determining business areas and financing strategies is not people management. These activities include the strategic steerage of all business areas that do not involve personnel (sales, production, other resources), as well as the constitutive management of these areas, i.e., the projects and workshops that serve to define non-people standards such as the external corporate mission or the technical management and controlling system. This was explained in detail in Sect. 1.6. Unfortunately, it cannot be expressed very elegantly in terms of language. The somewhat clumsy term "management of functional-technical matters" may denote the parts of constitutive and strategic management which do not concern the management of personnel. Like people management, they involve a set of specific management routines. While the line manager can certainly call on help in completing these indispensable functional activities, responsibility as such cannot be relinquished. Note that the management of functional-technical matters also includes external representation. The higher the position in the hierarchy, the more important it is to represent the organization externally, i.e., to the public and external stakeholders. The leadership and management of an organizational unit therefore always has a functional-technical component. In this respect, the idea of line managers as "full-time coaches" (Jenewein and Halder 2018, p. 83) is not an accurate or complete picture of their job.

A systematic peculiarity lies in the fact that some management routines—above all the continuous routine "work dialog"—also contain functional-technical components. These are therefore not purely people management routines, but also, at least in part, routines for the management of functional-technical matters. With regard to operational *management* tasks, it has already been established that the two aspects cannot be separated here anyway. As far as the *execution* tasks of the employees' primary job are concerned, the responsibility for this lies, as already stated, in the genuine responsibility of this employee, even if he or she does not lead/ manage himself in any way (i.e., does not take over any of the 24 management tasks him or herself). Only rarely, however, will the line manager be able to withdraw entirely from responsibility for such functional-technical issues. The mechanism of choice here is the "exception principle" or "management by exception", according to which the line manager only assumes responsibility for tasks in cases of escalation and disruption (see Sect. 2.4.1) and which should be used as rarely as possible. From a systematic point of view, this is also part of the "management of functional-technical matters" and must therefore be theoretically and conceptually separated from people management. In practice, however, the lines become blurred because there is little difference between the employee deciding on the content of the work assignment (= functional work task) and the employee only defining the work assignment itself (= leadership/management task).

The fourth aspect to discuss in connection with the management routines of line managers are the *self*-management routines of line managers. By its very nature, the principle of self-management of course does not only apply to the staff level. Just as employees should ideally fulfill as many management tasks as possible themselves, line managers cannot expect superordinate positions to relieve them of all (self-) management tasks. A line manager therefore has to lead and manage not only others, but also him or herself, with ultimately the same tasks needing to be fulfilled. Ideal line managers understand their work tasks, obtain feedback for themselves, are self-motivated, etc.; in other words, they do not leave this up to their superior, but manage/lead themselves. The 24 management tasks form the core of this self-management. They are carried out within the framework of the management routines where the line manager is the one being managed/led (e.g., work dialogs between the line manager and the senior manager).

Furthermore, additional routines can, again, be performed here. For many line managers today, these additional self-activities include their own correspondence and office organization. In the course of computerization, many companies have decided to do away with traditional secretarial positions and let line managers, at least those at lower and middle levels, handle their own secretarial work. At the latest when all line managers show symptoms of overload, one should think about whether this step was sensible. Other additional tasks arise from housekeeping duties, etc. in the private sphere. Here it is possible to relieve line managers of private work, e.g., through laundry services, catering, or transport facilitation, which is becoming increasingly common.

The fifth and last aspect to discuss in connection with the management routines of line managers are the additional routines of senior managers. Section 3.1.3 covered the special role of senior managers, which includes higher-level management in addition to "normal" management. On top of this, the senior manager is naturally also responsible for all hierarchical levels below the two levels directly subordinate to him. This hierarchy-spanning management comes with two main types of additional routines. Firstly, there are routines of communication across the hierarchy (e.g., mass communication and interaction with workforce representatives). These routines connect the senior manager communicatively with the corporate base and vice versa. In this way, they supplement the hierarchical communication cascade, which is indispensable, but are always accompanied by information losses according to the principle of the "telephone" game (UK: "Chinese whispers") and therefore requires corrective measures. These routines, too, must be defined specifically for each organization as part of the management structures and can be designed as continuous, annual, or on-demand routines. The higher the hierarchical position of the senior manager, the higher the number of employees that need to be managed across the hierarchy. Former CEO of Deutsche Bahn, Rüdiger Grube, claims to have received advice from the long-time CEO of Deutsche Lufthansa, Jürgen Weber, who said that a CEO should spend half of his working time dealing with his employees (Fockenbrock 2014, p. 75). This may seem realistic; however, in light of the fact that the normal and higher-level management of the two directly subordinate levels already demands a good part of this time, it will only be sufficient if the subordinate levels also participate in hierarchy-spanning communication.

The other type of additional routines of senior managers involves participation in the development and administration of formal management instruments, such as guidelines, systems, programs, and forms. This is usually assigned to the HR department as the lead function. Nevertheless, senior managers are generally involved as either internal sponsors, co-developers, or users. Given the widespread tendency of management instruments to take on a life of their own, as described in Sect. 2.5.4, this is not only desirable but necessary. For senior managers, it means additional, instrument-related management routines. Since the HR department is usually responsible for the greater part of this, more detailed considerations can be found in Sect. 4.2.6.

3.1.6   Management Instruments: Tools or Obstacles?

Management instruments are understood here to be formalized tools that support people management; Sect. 2.5.4 discusses them in more detail. These include, in particular, rules, guidelines, systems, programs, and forms. These management instruments are to be distinguished from the management routines discussed above (e.g., employee dialogs). Although these may follow formalized rules, they are themselves not instruments, but rather activities. The concept of management instruments is established in the literature, but is usually overstretched to include routines (see, e.g., Malik 2000, pp. 243 ff. ("tools"), 338, 2007, p. 75 ff.; Weise and Selck 2007; Weibler 2016, p. 365 ff.).

By performing the management routines, the line manager ensures that the 24 management tasks are fulfilled and applies the management instruments available in that particular company. Sect. 2.5.4 presents the main management instruments. In practice, line managers are seldom free to decide which instruments they wish to use. Instead, guidelines, which are themselves formalized instruments, dictate when and how the existing instruments are to be implemented throughout the organization. This makes sense and is unproblematic as long as they are functionally designed and aligned with the management structures; as such they make effective tools that support good people management and leadership. However, it is not uncommon for complex HR tools, such as compensation systems, performance agreements, training programs, or appraisal procedures, to become bureaucratic monsters that hinder rather than support effective management and leadership. In such cases, line managers often systematically undermine personnel instruments, i.e., they deviate from them, do not use them at all, or apply them only pro forma. This is usually to be interpreted as self-defense and a cry for help.

Organizations have two options to avoid such shortcomings. First, they should rely on lean and pragmatic HR tools that are functionally aligned with the other management structures and are continuously improved with the help of user feedback. Secondly, they should ensure that their corporate management models and guidelines differentiate between instruments and routines as recommended here. The instrument is then not simply deployed but applied within the framework of management routines in such a way that it corresponds to the spirit of the management tasks to be performed. This prevents outdated HR instruments or those that are poorly designed from the outset from having a negative impact on people management and leadership. Many companies have, for example, formalized bonus systems that work as incentive instruments but in practice trigger massive misdirection (e.g., one-sided fulfillment of sales goals while neglecting risk, innovation, and social behavior). Thus, within the framework of management routines, the line manager has to apply the instrument and at the same time round off the incentive field by setting additional incentives (e.g., praise or reprimand).

3.1.7   Management Resources: What Line Managers Need

The implementation element of management resources comprises four resources that are essential to the line manager's work. The first resource is directional and situational information. To lead and manage effectively, line managers must be well informed. This applies to the overarching constitutive framework (e.g., corporate mission, legal regulatory framework, legal/organizational form, organizational structures, business model, stakeholder interests, planning, management, and controlling system). It also applies to the overall functional-technical business strategies in the areas of marketing, production and resources, and to the human resource strategies. Information on the current situation, including the market, earnings, costs, and plans, is also important. Typically, line managers receive much of this information from their own (senior) managers. Equally important, however, are tools that allow them to continually supply themselves with relevant information. Knowledge management systems can make a valuable contribution here. It is advisable to systematically analyze the information needs of an organization's line managers and to develop an information system tailored to these needs. This can include newsletters, morning briefings, press reviews, and events, in addition to the aspects mentioned above (see Meifert 1999). All of this is needed by the line manager first and foremost for him or herself. Which of this information is to be passed on to employees, and how, can be one of the most difficult decisions line managers have to make. It is therefore advisable to provide them with clear rules and recommendations for passing on this information and to train them to carry out this management task in a situationally appropriate way as part of their management routines.

Another indispensable resource is feedback on management performance from those being managed and other management actors. Just as employees need feedback on their work performance, line managers need feedback on their management and leadership performance. This resource is so significant to the line manager's performance and development that it is worth addressing separately. The section on manager development (Sect. 3.4) will therefore cover it in more detail.

The third and probably most important resource is the working time that line managers have at their disposal to conduct their management and leadership activities. In order to find out which time resources the holder of a management position requires under the given conditions, three key factors must be taken into account: firstly, the job design, i.e., the definition of which functional-technical (non-people) and people-related activities as well as self-management activities a position has to perform in the first place (see Sect. 3.1.4); secondly, the distribution of management tasks and routines among the management actors, including the question of how far the activities of the employees are pre-structured by central process specifications (see Sect. 3.1.3), and thirdly, the span of control (see Sect. 3.1.4). Conversely, these three factors can also be regarded as adjustment screws that can be used to adjust the management activity to the working time resources that are actually available. In the one case, working time would be the variable that is shaped (additional work), in the other it would be the work itself (handing over tasks). Of course, it is also possible to make adjustments to both at the same time. However, there are usually limits to the expansion of working hours. After all, e.g. 26.6% of full-time employees in headship positions in Germany already report working more than 48 hours per week (compared to 9% among non-management employees; German Federal Statistical Office, Statistisches Bundesamt 2021).

Anyone who demands good people management and leadership must ensure that every line manager also has the time resources available to accomplish this. In reality, many line managers spend only a fraction of their working time on people management activities (Penning 2012; Sprenger 2012, p. 28 f.; Hoffmann and Jäckel 2011, p. 33). It is not uncommon for line managers to work full time at the customer's facility or on projects, etc., and tend to their employees only secondarily:

"I don't have time to lead and manage, I need to work." (An unnamed U.S. manager, quoted in Sprenger 2012, p. 29; own translation)

There are two main reasons for this shortcoming. On the one hand, the functional-technical (= non-people) tasks, both those that are indispensable and additional, are usually more clearly defined and often given higher priority by top managers than people management tasks so that there is a general tendency to place a greater weight on the former. Secondly, line managers who have been promoted to management positions on the basis of outstanding professional performance tend to dedicate more time to non-personnel business tasks:

"Our research shows: Line managers in companies spend the majority of their time on management tasks that are urgent at the moment—and see themselves as everyday heroes who bravely throw themselves into every battle. But in doing so, they forget about their six to twelve direct reports—their team." (Jenewein and Halder 2018, p. 82)

This way, people management degenerates into a hobby. So, on the one hand, organizations must ensure that people management activities are clearly defined and given high priority. On the other hand, they must ensure that line managers have enough time to conduct these activities by relieving them of unnecessary activities (Fig. 3.1).

The fourth and final resource is competence, because management and leadership naturally require specific qualifications. Again, the main problem lies in the lack of structures: As long as there is no clear definition of what constitutes good management, it is difficult to carry out effective needs analyses and qualification measures. First of all, therefore, there must be a corporate management model that defines, among other things, management activities, tasks, and instruments. From this, the necessary behavioral competencies (e.g., the ability to conduct employee dialogs) and the elementary competencies required for this (e.g., the ability to communicate or make decisions) can be derived and translated into qualification and development measures. As management competence is particularly important, a separate section is devoted to it below in the context of manager development (Section 3.4.3).

3.2   Counterpart to Management Structures: Dilemmas, Power Safeguarding, and Micropolitics

In Sect. 1.7.6, corporate models of leadership and management were referred to by the "mold" metaphor, a term used in casting technology to describe the negative matrix from which the positive relief to be cast is derived. The model and its rules automatically result in regulatory freedom. Of course, only the actual lived reality is important, i.e., that part of the management model and the management infrastructure which is actually implemented by the actors. The management structures, therefore, determine at which points line managers have to adhere to fixed guidelines and which aspects are left to the free play of forces. Just as a mold that is deformed cannot shape a functionally designed object, a management model that regulates the wrong aspects of behavior will not bring about good people management and leadership. And the attempt to regulate all aspects of management action would be as useless as a completely flat matrix since this never, ever results in authentic and situationally appropriate behavior. The freedoms contained in a corporate management model are therefore just as relevant for the behavior of line managers as are its regulations. In fact, latitude is the key because the goal of norm-setting does not, of course, lie in a maximum degree of regulation, but instead in allowing a maximum scope of action and degree of freedom while at the same time guaranteeing the system's ability to function. Only so is there room for a arange of personalities and ways of acting and for situational flexibility. From the line manager's perspective, this relates to the day-to-day application of the management model and the associated dilemmas, as well as to the issues of securing power and micropolitics.

3.2.1 Dilemmas and Blurs: Inevitable Realities of Everyday Life and no Excuse for Lack of Structures

Line managers do not operate in the field of unambiguous "right" or "wrong," but rather have to constantly make difficult decisions when choosing between equivalent alternatives or alternatives whose consequences cannot be fully assessed. In the literature, such dilemmas are readily presented as conceptual pairs, with some particularly relevant ones being picked out more or less arbitrarily from the multitude of possible examples (see Blessin and Wick 2014a, p. 461 ff.). Line managers therefore constantly find themselves faced with dilemmas, which are unavoidable realities of management work. In reality though, these are no different from those of all other management actors (and many other professionals), who are also confronted with contradictions, complexity, and ambiguity. Consequently, the argument that dilemmas are one of the most important reasons why line managers exist at all (Blessin and Wick 2014a, p. 470) is flawed. Instead, the raison d'être of line managers lies rather in their compensatory work (see Sect. 3.1.3). In fact, dilemmas actually affect all management actors even though the literature mostly relates them to line managers.

At any rate, managerial work is usually characterized by some confusion and a lot of fuzziness. Reality often does not reflect the clichés that are propagated about it at all:

> "Have a look at the popular images of managing [. . .]: well ordered, seemingly carefully controlled. Watch some managers at work and you will likely find something far different: a hectic pace, lots of interruptions, more responding than initiating." (Mintzberg 2009, p. 17)

The fact that dilemmas and ambiguities are an unavoidable part of managerial work should not, of course, lead to their glorification and the abandonment of necessary structures. Leadership and management is not, as Neuberger (2002, p. 47) assumes, merely the influencing of those led in poorly structured situations, but takes place within organizational structures and consists, to a significant degree, of the design and implementation of such structures—or at least it should. It is not very practical and not at all necessary for every line manager in an organization to develop his or her own ideas about the functions, tasks, and actors of people management and, on this basis, to devise management routines, instruments, structure, and resources for themselves. In fact, many line managers find that they are supposed to lead and manage employees but do not quite know how and to what end. They find that they have difficulty combining desirable self-management of the employees and necessary intervention in a meaningful way or that they see management needs but cannot or do not want to find the time to actually take action, etc. However, none of this is inevitable but rather an expression of corporate failure with regard to management structures (see also Sect. 1.7.6).

3.2.2 Power Safeguarding and Micropolitics: Self-Management Needs and Organizational Needs

Securing power and micropolitics are inseparable from any management position and take up not an inconsiderable amount of a line manager's time and energy. For a long time, they were quasi-secret topics, later the subject of heated debate (see Neuberger and Gebert 1996). Nowadays, people take a more sober view of this, and most line managers deal with it outright. Professional literature and the business press also take up corresponding topics as a natural part of management and leadership (see Neuberger 2002, p. 689 ff.; Bruch et al. 2012; Scheidt and Wiedenbrüg 2012; Barsoux and Bouquet 2013; Scholl 2014; Oltmanns 2014a, b; Blessin and Wick 2014a, p. 443 ff.).

Micropolitics can aptly be defined as using other people to pursue one's own interests in organizational zones of uncertainty (Neuberger 2006, p. 18; for alternative definitions, see supplementary material to Blessin and Wick 2014a, p. 442). It definitely has negative sides for the organization, but is by no means bad per se; rather, it fulfills an important dynamizing and flexibilizing function (Neuberger 2002, p. 689 ff.; Blessin and Wick 2014a, p. 443 ff.). Table. 3.3 provides an overview of examples of micropolitical influence tactics and illustrates the breadth of the corresponding spectrum.

At this point, this book will not delve deeper into specific micropolitical strategies, e.g., in dealing with one's own bosses (e.g., Welch and Welch 2005, p. 322; Happich 2012; Rettig 2013; Domsch and Ostermann 2014) or examine foundational works, from Sun Tzu (1971) to Carnegie and Kotter (1987) to Greene

Table. 3.3 Micropolitical influence tactics (modified from Neuberger 2002, p. 714, and Blessin und Wick 2014a, p. 444; own translation; tabular compilation: © Boris Kaehler 2019. All rights reserved)

General precautions	Self-promotion and image cultivation
	Networking and relationship management measures
	Systematically recognizing attacks
Communication tactics	Factual/rational argumentation/information in one-on-one conversations or team meetings
	Covert communication before/after official meetings
	Friendliness/flattery or determined/demanding appearance
	Manipulation and persuasion
	Invoking rights, traditions, duties, and regulations
	Appeal to higher values or idealism, charismatic inspiration
Transactions	Creating a fait accompli, acting in a hands-on manner
	Bartering, promising, or procuring benefits in exchange for concessions
	Pressuring, threatening with sanctions
Involvement of third parties	Forming alliances and coalitions based on purpose
	Seeking advice (from colleagues/friends, mentors, or external parties)
	Engaging higher-level entities (e.g., supervisors, stakeholders, and courts)

(1998). Instead, it will briefly illustrate how the topic can be accommodated in the theoretical model of Complementary Management.

Micropolitics was defined above as the pursuit of one's own interests in organizational zones of uncertainty by utilizing other people (Neuberger 2006, p. 18). This already makes it clear that the fewer certainties there are, i.e., the fewer organizational regulations, the more necessary power politics becomes. The micropolitical activities of those involved multiply when there is no clear assignment of tasks, when processes are poorly defined or have unnecessary interfaces, or when there are no explicit rules of conduct and escalation paths for conflicts. If the senior manager then has a laissez-faire attitude and does not ensure that energies are focused on common goals and that unfair micropolitical games are stopped, power struggles fill the vacuum. Sooner or later, subordinate line managers then spend most of their time guarding against attacks, neutralizing potential adversaries or, for their part, deliberately encroaching on other people's territory. Without rules and referees, every playing field degenerates into a battlefield. A residual need for micropolitics exists, even when there is optimal organization.

In the triad of the task fields of functional-technical management, people management, and self-management (Sect. 3.1.4), micropolitics first relates to self-management and, in this respect, the management of collaboration (relationships and conflicts). As a self-manager, the line manager must ensure that he or she has viable networks, resilient relationships, and suitable conflict resolution strategies, both in the interest of his or her own career development and in the interest of the substantive issues needing to be resolved. Management takes place not only in the direction of subordinate employees, but "in all directions" (see Malik 2007, p. 95 ff.). This requires, among other things, political approaches, and so here, exceptionally (see the delimitation of the two areas made in Sect. 1.3), there is an overlap between organizational and political management and leadership. No one stays in a management position for long if he or she does not know how to cultivate relationships, build negotiating power, and persuade opponents. The special significance of micropolitics for line managers thus arises primarily from their own involvement in the context of self-management. But of course, the management of relationships and conflicts is also a task of employee management in the sense that the superordinate bodies must compensate for deficits in the field of relationships and conflict.

3.3 What Is Management Performance?

The performance of the line manager naturally results from the underlying definition of management and leadership. However, it also depends on its assumed target functionality. Classically, the three starting points of company ("performance"), line manager ("career success"), and employee ("satisfaction") are chosen (Blessin and Wick 2014b, p. 56 f.), but many other criteria for leadership success are also used in academia and practice (Rosenstiel 2014, p. 5, claims to have counted more than 1000). For example, appraisal systems can only be as good as the underlying implicit or explicit corporate model of leadership and management. The more unclear and vague the concept, the more arbitrary and often psychologizing are the assessment and feedback. Useful feedback is possible primarily on the basis of task- and behavior-oriented management models, which must of course also be translated into behavior-oriented management assessments. The corporate example of Google illustrates this:

> "In the surveys, employees don't assess their managers' motivations, values, or beliefs; rather, they evaluate the extent to which their managers demonstrate each behavior. Either the manager has acted in the ways recommended consistently and credibly—or she has not." (Garvin 2013, p. 82)

It can therefore be stated that management performance is what an explicit or implicit management model defines as management performance.

One of the major advantages of the Complementary Management Model is that it provides a clear structure for conducting people management and makes it measurable. In this context, the general concept of work performance can simply be applied to management performance. It makes good sense that performance appraisals should cover not only work *results*, but also work *input* and work *behavior* (Kaehler 2014b). When this is so, it is difficult to hold anything else to be true for management work. In addition to management results, therefore, management input and management behavior are quite essential elements of management performance. In this context, the basic principle that, under German labor law, employees do not owe the work result, but only their work input (the work, and not the result; Bundesarbeitegericht 11.12.2003; 2 AZR 667/02), also applies to the work of line managers. The employee's work success is certainly relevant because it is, after all, the reason and purpose of employment. Strictly speaking, however, it should only serve as anchor information for assessing commitment and behavior. This fundamental value decision under German labor law puts into perspective the widespread fixation on results that makes many appraisal systems seem so counterproductive and unfair in practice. The results of work are not the sole responsibility of the jobholder. In fact, while he or she is responsible for striving to achieve work results, the employer must organize and direct the work in such a way that the results are actually achieved. Managing employees is ultimately just a specific form of work activity and therefore follows the same principles. This means that if the line manager does not achieve management success, it could indicate a lack of commitment and dysfunctional behavior; but it could also be an indication of inadequate management structures, which would put the line manager's performance in a significantly different light.

The bottom line is: management performance is measured in terms of management *input*, management *behavior*, and management *results*. Which concrete contributions are required in these three areas cannot be answered in general terms, but depend on the specific circumstances and strategic requirements of the respective organization or organizational unit. In any case, the people-related management performance and the functional-technical (= non-people) management performance of the line manager must be assessed separately.

3.3.1 Management Input

So what exactly do these three components of management performance consist of? As far as the first aspect of performance (people management *input*) is concerned, it is proposed here that it be regarded as the conducting of management routines. Unlike management tasks, which describe what has to be achieved in terms of personnel, these are real activities, i.e., actions that can be evaluated in terms of time and content. Firstly, it is a question of whether the line manager actually carries out the defined routines at the scheduled intervals (e.g., weekly task meetings and annual reviews). In practice, it is often incumbent upon HR departments to demand appropriate reports, and many find they are powerless when line managers, especially those with good standing in the organization, simply sit this out and refuse to do the appropriate activities. This is a design flaw in the management structures because, in these cases, people management activities are apparently not defined clearly enough as a component of the management job (see Sect. 3.1.4) and/or are not sanctioned consistently enough in the course of the assessment. The situation is actually clear: line managers are not only paid for functional-technical business management, but also—and in particular—for people management. Those who do not show commitment here and refuse to perform the activities defined by the company—their contractually owed work!—are neglecting an important part of their management job and, if all goes well, must expect a warning and later a dismissal. Secondly, it is a question of the content-related quality of the input. This does not yet refer to the fulfillment of management tasks (Section 3.1.2), even if the boundary may be blurred. Rather, it is a question of whether the routines, i.e., conversations and meetings are approached with commitment and care, or listlessly and clumsily. This can be easily queried in the context of management feedback and is usually also revealed to senior managers and HR advisors quite quickly when they sporadically participate in management routines. A line manager who carries out his or her people management routines is the equivalent of a salesperson who makes and keeps customer appointments—a necessary prerequisite for success.

3.3.2 Management Behavior

The second aspect, management *behavior*, relates to the line manager's working and social behavior, i.e., his or her dealings with the other management actors, as well as his or her handling of the formalized personnel instruments (compliance with/ implementation of the instrument-related specifications). The way in which a line manager deals with other management stakeholders is deliberately not standardized by the Complementary Management Model because good management and leadership leaves room for a wide variety of personalities and communication styles. However, this only affects the corporate management model, i.e., the formal management structures. Precisely because line managers are supposed to live out their individual idiosyncrasies and patterns of action in day-to-day operational management, they need ongoing feedback in order to be able to effectively align their behavior to the situation. Also, as members of the organization, line managers must, of course, comply with the minimum standards of respectful and professional communication, which are to be defined as part of the general rules of conduct. This, too, can be queried as part of management feedback and hardly goes unnoticed by senior managers and HR advisors when they participate in management routines from time to time. The extent to which HR tools are used is usually known anyway to the HR specialists involved in the process. Massive problem behavior such as discrimination, bullying, sexual harassment, or bribery/fraud naturally fall under the general rules of conduct anyways. In such cases, line managers are not to be treated differently from any other organizational member. A line manager who demonstrates good management behavior is the equivalent of a salesperson who deals respectfully with customers and colleagues and abides by the rules.

3.3.3 Constitutive, Strategic, and Operational Management Outcomes as an Intermediate Result

One result of the line manager's personnel work is the accomplishment of the management tasks. Here it is a question of whether, as a result of the sum of conducted management routines (= activities), a fulfillment of all 24 personnel management tasks was actually achieved. For example, it must be determined whether there are actually clear work assignments, effective incentives, the necessary qualification, etc. for every employee in the organizational unit. Rosenstiel (2014, p. 8) calls this "human" management success as opposed to "economic" success. In the case of the constitutive and strategic tasks (Sect. 2.3.3), the completeness and quality of the created norms must be considered. The line manager is indeed responsible for the fulfillment of these tasks. However, since several actors— first and foremost the employee as a self-manager—accomplish them, the line manager is to be regarded here as a compensatory entity (Sect. 3.1.3). It is therefore not a question of whether the line manager him/herself has set goals and incentives, has initiated qualification measures, or mediated conflicts, etc. Rather, it is a matter of assessing whether corresponding deficits have been identified and compensated for. The question surrounding these management outcomes is therefore: Does the line manager know whether the employees are practicing comprehensive self-management (i.e., whether they are taking on all defined management tasks themselves, e.g., looking for the right work and knowing their performance level) and, if necessary, has the line manager intervened in a compensatory manner? If, for example, it turns out that employees do not know what to do or how to assess their past performance, the line manager has neglected these people management tasks. In accordance with the logic of the task element, namely the premise that precisely these influences are required to generate sustainable human work performance, these are not yet the actual results of people management and leadership, but "only" those that are to be fulfilled in relation to the employees. A line manager who ensures the fulfillment of people management tasks is like the salesperson who ensures that the customer shows up for the sales meeting and has all the documents needed for placing an order—an intermediate result to be achieved, but not yet a success.

3.3.4 Business Results as the Ultimate Management Outcome

The third aspect concerns management *results*. These are logically derived from the objective of people management and leadership as a whole, i.e., its overriding purpose. If they are achieved, this means management success. Rosenstiel (2014, p. 8) calls this "economic" management success as opposed to "human" success. Thus, we are concerned here with the contributions to success made by people management and leadership. As explained in Sect. 1.6.4, three dimensions are relevant here: firstly employees' short- and long-term work performance, secondly short- and long-term personnel costs, and thirdly the fulfillment of other requirements, in particular with regard to the legal situation and stakeholder interests. True management success is only achieved if the constitutive and strategic requirements of the organization's business are optimally met in all three respects. Of course, there is no general standard for this; rather, the constitutive and strategic objectives defined for the respective company or business unit are decisive (Sect. 1.6). A line manager who generates the required work output at reasonable personnel costs and fulfills other predefined objectives achieves management success. This corresponds to the salesperson who actually generates sales while keeping costs under control and meeting certain other targets.

3.4 Manager Development

Manager development (or leader development)—as an umbrella term for all measures used to qualify and develop line managers—is such an essential building block of HR management that it has rightly been called the "HR crown jewel" (Werle 2014, p. 108). Almost every organization practices it, and in most cases an enormous amount of effort is rightly put into it. Naturally, academia has also studied manager and leader development in depth (see the overview by Day et al. 2014). The terms management development and leadership development are more commonly used in this context; however, if the construct really is about line managers rather than about corporate concepts of leadership and management, "leader development" or "manager development" appear more fitting. In any case, the literature repeatedly emphasizes the importance of strategically anchoring and aligning it with the overarching purpose of the organization (Ochmann and Schuh 2011; Armbrüster and Hehn 2011; CIPD 2021). However, that is only possible if, in addition to this corporate purpose, the constructs of management and people management are also defined sharply enough. Section 1.6.2 explained the relationship between the two. It became clear that both the corporate management model and the personnel strategy serve to relate personnel work to the corporate purpose and the actual business. This makes it possible to translate period-related business strategies into needs-based development measures and to incorporate findings from previous development activities into the overall strategy. The management model and people strategy are therefore the links between business objectives and manager/leader development. To forego this and derive manager development measures directly from the business mission or business strategy is generally stretching their mission and possibilities.

3.4.1 Knowledge of the Management Model as the First Step to Management Competence

The effectiveness of manager development stands and falls with a corporation's management model and a uniform understanding of management and leadership among the members of the organization. All too often it suffers from the fact that those involved are not guided by common principles, but in fact, each bring with them their own understanding. Therefore, the corporate leadership structures must, first and foremost, be presented and communicated in such a way that they are understood not only by the line managers but also by the other management actors and the development experts involved. In the course of introducing a new corporate management model, it has proven useful to create standardized presentation graphics, brochures, and guides that explain the management model in a comprehensible way (see Sect. 2.6.2). The development and dissemination of these materials can certainly already be seen as part of manager development. If a holistic management model exists and is understood by all those involved, much has already been achieved.

3.4.2 Management Diagnostics and the Need for Alternative Career Options

It was suggested above that people management and leadership should be regarded as a professional activity. Like with any other occupation, requirements can be identified for management work which are to be assessed within the framework of professional personnel selection. Management diagnostics, i.e., management- and leadership-related aptitude diagnostics, naturally start with the respective competence model (see Jochmann 2012). Before a systematic selection of line managers can take place, therefore, the conceptual issues discussed above must be clarified; in particular, organization-specific definitions of leadership and management competence must be established. A glance at any of the standard works (e.g., Sarges 2013) is sufficient to establish that the current practice of management diagnostics does indeed reflect a wide variety of management models and approaches, and, just like these, breaks down into diverse facets, many of which are incompatible with one another. Organizations that opt for a behavior- or task-based management model (see Sect. 2.3.1) generally have little problem in compiling the corresponding requirements and testing them in a systematic process of aptitude diagnostics. In addition, the aspect of self-selection must be taken into account. It should be kept in mind that people on their self-chosen path toward line management positions always already have the will to manage/lead under the given framework conditions. The general conditions (e.g., clearly defined management tasks) can then also influence the self-selection of candidates. In this sense, a good and transparent corporate management model is the foundation of an effective selection of executives. On the other hand, those who describe leadership and management in fuzzy terms and semi-esoteric cause–effect relationships will have difficulty deriving clear requirements and generating functional self-selection effects.

Many organizations use management audits (also: "management reviews", "executive assessments", "management appraisals") to check management suitability (see Stulle and Weinert 2012; Stoffmehl 2014). For the reason mentioned above, of course, they are only justified if they refer to a meaningful management model in the respective organization. Worryingly, however, they seem to be used in many places instead as non-transparent instruments of domination. Today, it is quite common for seasoned line managers to have to prove again every few years on the occasion of a restructuring, etc. that they are still suitable for the job and that they meet the requirements of the newly acquired and often completely non-transparent/ dysfunctional competency model (see, e.g., Losmann 2011). This has little to do with serious aptitude diagnostics. The equally undesirable opposite pole is formed by organizations that do not test people management and leadership aptitude at all, but allow functional-technical business aptitude and micropolitical ruthlessness alone to facilitate promotion to line management positions (Demmer 2014, p. 60).

The root problem in selecting line managers is usually not aptitude diagnostics, but the lack of alternatives to a management career (see Sauer and Cisik 2013, 2014, p. 15; Weilbacher 2012, p. 24). Due to the fact that, in most companies, high salaries, extended scope for action, and special status privileges can only be achieved through a line management career, employees who aspire to such a career are pushed into people responsibility regardless of their inclinations. Many of them—thanks to valid aptitude diagnostics that weed out the fundamentally unsuitable—are perfectly capable of performing personnel management tasks, but ultimately do not do so because they feel no inclination and because their organization does not consistently encourage them to do so. This can hardly be remedied by extended requirements in the context of personnel selection, even if the personal predisposition and inclination to lead and manage employees can certainly be tested, at least theoretically. It is simpler and more effective to create equivalent alternatives to management careers in the form of different career paths, e.g., project and expert careers (see, e.g., Kokoschka 2009; Ladwig and Domsch 2013; Astheimer 2013; Trost 2014; Hergert 2014). At the same time, every holder of a management position must be consistently required to fulfill specifically defined people management tasks, which automatically results in those who do not feel the corresponding inclinations looking elsewhere.

3.4.3 Management Competencies and Management Training

The term management competence (or leadership competence) is used in very different ways in literature and in practice, whereby there is naturally a close connection with the respective understanding of management and leadership. At any rate, where management tasks serve as the conceptual starting point, management competence is usually simply understood as the ability to successfully perform the necessary activities. This corresponds to the general concept of professional action competence, which encompasses all professional knowledge, skills, and abilities that function as a prerequisite for the successful performance of professional activities (Holling and Liepmann 2007, p. 345). Since the Complementary Management Model differentiates between management tasks, routines, and tools, the action competencies are related to the routines. This results in the following definition:

> Management competence is the ability to successfully perform management activities (= management routines) which means that the relevant management tasks are achieved within them and existing management instruments are applied in a meaningful way.

It has been pointed out on various occasions that management routines are made up of elementary activities. Management routines are therefore nothing more than framework activities within which the many elementary activities take place that are needed to fulfill the management tasks and their elementary tasks. For example, the management task "to round off the incentive field" includes, for example, the elementary task "praise", which is fulfilled by the elementary activity "communicate" within the routine "work dialog". Accordingly, the skills required to successfully perform the elementary activities are elementary competencies. Table. 3.4 clarifies this distinction, although the definition of the individual "elements" is ultimately arbitrary and could just as well be further differentiated (e.g., "communicate" consists of "speak" and "listen"). It is crucial to note that neither elementary activities, nor elementary competencies or elementary tasks are specific to personnel management. While they are also and especially relevant to managing employees, they are equally relevant to many other jobs, such as those of salespeople, teachers, secretaries, doctors, railroad conductors, hairdressers, and lifeguards. Those who

Table. 3.4 Elementary tasks, elementary activities, and elementary competencies (modified from Kaehler 2017, p. 432; © Boris Kaehler 2019. All rights reserved)

Elementary tasks	Define action goals, praise/reprimand, allocate resources, etc.
Elementary activities	Communicate, decide, reflect, plan, control, etc.
Elementary competencies	Communication competence, decision-making competence, planning/controlling competence, etc.

Table. 3.5 Essential elementary competencies of management (modified from Kaehler 2014a, p. 71, 2017, p. 433; © Boris Kaehler 2019. All rights reserved)

Communication and negotiation skills
Functional and technical competence
Judgement and decision-making competence
Mindfulness competence (see, e.g., Beard 2014)
Learning competence
Reflective competence (DGFP 2015)
Planning and structuring competence
Creative and conceptual competence
Time management and work methodology
Resilience and regeneration competence

have to deal with people must accomplish certain tasks (e.g., define goals for action or praise them) by performing certain activities (e.g., deciding or communicating) that require certain competencies (e.g., decision-making or communication skills). The mix and prioritization of elements vary across occupations and results in specific occupational tasks, routines and competencies (e.g., praise is more important for teachers and doctors than for train conductors). In this respect, only personnel management tasks (e.g., defining work assignments), personnel management routines (e.g., conducting employee dialogs), and personnel management competencies (e.g., the ability to successfully conduct such dialogs) are specific to personnel management, but not their elements.

Elementary competencies (the most important ones are listed in Table 3.5) are therefore not specific to management and leadership. Although they are also and especially relevant for the performance of management tasks, they are equally relevant for many other activities. For example, contrary to what many scientific and practical management models postulate, the ability to communicate effectively with other people is not a management or leadership competence, but merely one of its elementary building blocks. The same applies to the ability to make meaningful decisions (see the popular success of Dobelli's 2011 bestseller on errors of judgement). Every salesperson needs it, every train conductor, every teacher—and every line manager. This differentiation is very important for manager development. When elementary competencies are regarded as management competencies, line managers are usually trained too one-sidedly and employees receive too little training in them.

Excursus: Functional-Technical Competence
The importance of functional-technical (= non-managerial) competence for people management and leadership is often underestimated. The prerequisite for an effective steering influence on an organization or an organizational unit is a fundamental understanding of all the tasks that arise in the manager's area of responsibility. This can be understood as elementary competence:

(continued)

"Not only dispositional but also functional-technical requirements are placed on the managers [. . .], because they only have authority if they have such a mastery of the work process that they are able to give technical and functional instructions. Thus, they must be required to be able to convince their subordinates of the correctness of their decisions." (Gutenberg 1979, p. 255; own translation)

Those who have to make decisions about the work of others do not have to be able to perform this work as well or as quickly as they do, but they should understand the processes, problems, and challenges in detail (Blessin and Wick 2014a, p. 463). Mere management and methodological skills are not enough to properly lead professionals. Hans L. Merkle writes:

"Delegation of a task presupposes that one knows it well oneself. You can't delegate anything with any chance of success—and in view of your own ultimate responsibility, which we were talking about—if you don't have an overview of it yourself." (Merkle 1979, p. 171; own translation)

Especially line managers who are moving into previously unfamiliar territory from other functional areas are faced with the challenge of acquiring good, detailed knowledge of the activities in their own area and keeping this knowledge up to date. Personal experience is irreplaceable here. A great tool for this is internal job shadowing which should be an absolute must for all line managers and all employees in central functions (see Sprenger 2012, p. 168). New line managers should ask for an "internship" of several days before starting work, ideally at a location that will later not report to them. Established line managers or employees in central functions should spend a few days a year observing the essential functions in their own area. Genuine understanding can only be achieved here by doing things oneself, not by looking over the shoulders of others. This can be supplemented, but never entirely replaced, by observing and questioning employees at work, talking to experts (e.g., external consultants), and studying the literature. The fact that many "promoted" specialists are very knowledgeable in functional matters and not very competent in people management should not tempt us to endorse the opposite: lateral entrants who are competent in management and lack functional-technical expertise.

From what has been stated so far, it has already become clear that high-quality management and leadership cannot be achieved primarily through training, but through intelligent management structures, the standardization of concrete responsibilities, and the sensible selection of line managers. Equally clear is the systematic connection between what is regarded as management and leadership competence and the underlying corporate management model. Thus, if it is repeatedly doubted in literature and practice whether management or leadership can be learned at all (e.g., Kellermann 2012, pp. 177, 183 f.; Sauer and Cisik 2013, 2014,

p. 20), this is generally only a symptom of a diffuse understanding that is primarily focussed on personality and relationships. If, on the other hand, we take the path recommended here of defining leadership and management in terms of concrete tasks and routines, there is no doubt that it can be learned (see Malik 2000, p. 31f). Certainly, as in all other professional activities, there are some who are actually unable to acquire the necessary competencies; however, these are exceptions. Anyone who is capable of being a salesperson, teacher, or secretary can usually also acquire people management skills. Whether they feel the inclination to do so and actually want to take up the profession is another matter. In general, however, the following applies: Like any professional activity, people management and leadership can and must be learned.

> **Excursus: Supposedly New Management Competencies**
> Another interesting competence area that deserves additional consideration is that of the supposedly new management competencies. Almost all management tasks involve the need for communication and negotiation. Naturally, these communicative processes change depending on the media used, the participants, and the distance to be bridged. Accordingly, developments such as advancing internationalization and digitization demand new competencies from line managers (Molinsky et al. 2012). However, these are not new management tasks or competencies, but merely new elementary skills that are also required by every salesperson and clerk when they are active in communication. If, for example, it is claimed that management or leadership in virtual structures (i.e., remotely) requires new, very special competencies (see Albrecht and Albrecht-Goepfert 2012; Schäfer 2012; Wilken 2012; Forchhammer 2012; Höhne 2014), then what is ultimately meant are mostly conventional managerial competencies plus new elementary competencies, in particular new types of media competencies. The same applies to leading diverse workforces or leading in an international environment, which by their very nature require special intercultural competencies or the intercultural application of conventional competencies (as was already advocated 30 years ago, see Conger 1993). A line manager who wants to use new video conferencing and collaboration tools to deal with his or her employees will need relevant competencies just as much as a journalist who has no management responsibilities. In other words, this is a completely normal personnel development topic and not one that has any particular theoretical connection to leadership and management.

In order to ensure that all line managers have the necessary action and elementary competencies, the way to go is to select personnel in such a way that only line managers are hired that already have a pronounced competency profile. Even here, however, it is advisable to provide basic training that conveys the organization's specific understanding of management and leadership, identifies deficits in individual competencies, and systematically closes them. Because the required competencies are highly definition-dependent, it cannot be assumed that experience gained in another company automatically guarantees the competencies relevant to management and leadership in another (see Kanning and Fricke 2013). Often, they were understood to mean something quite different elsewhere than what is required in the new position. The same applies when organizations adopt a new corporate management model. Here, too, the introduction should be accompanied by initial training for all line managers.

Initial leadership and management training are absolutely indispensable for all employees who do not have relevant experience and have only yet to be promoted to a management position. As for any other professional activity, people management and leadership requires a wide range of specific action and elementary competencies, which necessitates systematic basic training. It should follow the general principles of qualification and development and draw on the appropriate methods. A sensible format for the initial training of all line managers can be a classroom event lasting several days with a focus on practicing management routines (work dialogs, annual review, etc.), prepared by imparting knowledge via "e-learning" and rounded off by an optional coaching offer (for typical formats of management qualification, see, e.g., Felfe and Franke 2014; Faul and Rehberg 2014; see also the practical examples in DGFP 2015, p. 14 ff.). In addition to line managers, HR supervisors should also undergo initial training in order to be able to fulfill their role as HR co-managers (see Sect. 4.2.3).

Assuming the line manager has good basic qualifications, there is actually little need for ongoing qualification measures in the area of leadership and management. Provided that leadership activities are well structured and supported by HR advisors, they are tantamount to permanent job-integrated learning because new situations always arise and environmental conditions change. In principle, however, it can be assumed that even competent line managers will require occasional retraining. On the one hand, this ensures that management structures are not forgotten over time and that intended standards are not replaced by dysfunctional preferences and habits. On the other hand, many personal and employee-related difficulties only become apparent in day-to-day management. It, therefore, makes sense to offer targeted in-depth training in individual action and elementary competencies that is adapted to actual needs, each of which should also include a refresher course on the corporate management model as a whole. Needs analyses and evaluations are of decisive importance here. In many companies, there are obvious deficits in this regard (see DGFP 2012). Of course, the compensatory principle of Complementary Management applies here as well: Qualification is a management task which the person needing the qualification (in this case the line manager) ideally performs him or herself. If this does not happen—i.e., if the line manager shows no interest in a refresher course despite competence deficits—the senior manager or the HR supervisor must intervene.

3.4.4 Feedback and Appraisal Systems as a Means of Enforcing Good Management

Feedback is an indispensable prerequisite for all management actors and, according to the system represented here, is the subject of the implementation element "management resources" (see Sect. 3.1.7). With regard to the development of line managers, it is of such central importance that it seems justified to deal with it in detail at this point. Formalized feedback instruments are a core component of human resource management and manager development in almost all larger companies (see, e.g., Hauser 2012, p. 35; Steel et al. 2012, p. 201; Scherm 2013; Ernst 2014; Abel 2014). This is usually designed as 270- or 360-degree feedback, i.e., management and leadership performance is assessed from several sides at the same time, sometimes including customers, suppliers, top management, and self-assessments in addition to the line manager, colleagues, and, if applicable, the line manager's own employees. Sometimes, however, line managers are simply encouraged to obtain informal feedback on their own or to deal with it productively according to certain patterns (see, e.g., Kaplan 2012; Fröhlich 2014; Heen and Stone 2014). Management feedback is also a useful component of many development measures, e.g., development centers (Klebl and Nerdinger 2010, p. 57). Online assessments are becoming increasingly common (Doerfler 2014). In the future, special computer programs will, at least theoretically, make it possible to check at any time whether a conversational behavior is promising through real-time evaluations of conversational components, voice pitch, gestures, and physical reactions (Kaiser 2014, p. 12 f.).

Management feedback is nothing other than feedback related to managerial work. It is therefore ultimately a specific form of performance appraisal or performance feedback so that all the general principles pertaining to this issue also apply here. Table. 3.6 provides an overview of the relevant key points in this regard. Probably the most important and at the same time most disregarded systematic aspect is the differentiation between initial data and actual assessment. A holistic assessment of management performance is only possible if a wide variety of personnel indicators and performance assessments from different management stakeholders are included. Although these already contain evaluations and can be understood as feedback, they are systematically only excerpts of initial data that are to be interpreted and evaluated later. Feedback systems that understand management feedback exclusively as feedback from employees, for example, shorten the assessment of management performance to a single stakeholder perspective and thus set massive impulses of mis-steerage. Employees' opinions on various aspects of management performance are highly relevant, but they must not be the only assessment of these aspects, nor the final one.

All these points are derived from general principles of performance appraisal. In addition, the content-related aspects of management performance described in detail in Sect. 3.3 must be taken into account. By their very nature, these always reflect the underlying understanding of management and leadership, i.e., they usefully must refer to the respective corporate model.

Table. 3.6 Performance appraisal and performance feedback with regard to management perfor-mance (modified from Kaehler 2017, p. 437; © Boris Kaehler 2019. All rights reserved)

Objectives of the appraisal	Steerage and motivation
	Administration: Information basis for the derivation of other personnel measures (e.g., those relating to management selection, advanced training, or performance-related remuneration)
Appraisal occasions and periods	Cumulative for the past fiscal or calendar year
	Ongoing as part of regular task discussions with the line manager
	Ad hoc assessments of management processes that are currently underway
Holistic concept of performance (see Sect. 3.3)	Management results: (1) employees' short- and long-term work performance, (2) short- and long-term personnel costs, (3) fulfillment of other requirements, in particular with regard to the legal situation and stakeholder interests
	Management input: degree and quality of fulfillment of management routines and management tasks
	Social management behavior: Social interaction with other management actors
	Instrument-related management behavior: Adherence to/implementation of specifications for management instruments
Conversion into appraisal criteria and operationalization	Specification of all performance facets through precise assessment criteria
	Operationalization of the criteria in the form of ratios and evaluations of the stakeholders involved (360°)
Generation of initial data	Collection of initial data per performance criterion by analyzing reporting systems and interviewing work participants
Actual appraisal	Evaluation of the initial data in terms of their significance: comparison of the performance data (actual values) with the evaluation criteria (target values) and interpretation of the deviations.
	Additionally, if necessary: condensing into an overall evaluation
Feedback dialog and use of results	Not applicable in the case of self-assessment; in the case of assessment by compensatory entities (senior manager or HR), care must be taken to ensure that communication is self-value preserving
	Tips for dealing with feedback are helpful
	Consideration of the information content and the methodical quality of the assessment results for further use

Feedback from those involved in management thus contributes to the assessment as one of several data sources; the actual performance feedback is provided on the basis of a summary assessment. In this context, the question arises as to who is to conduct the assessment and provide the summary performance feedback. The general compensatory mechanism of the Complementary Management Model (see Sect. 2.4.5) applies here, since it is applicable to all management tasks and thus also to the performance appraisal. According to this, line managers should ideally assess their management performance themselves, i.e., obtain the performance-relevant information (ratios, assessments of stakeholders) themselves and evaluate it themselves. If this does not happen, and only then, does the line manager and/or the HR advisor intervene in a compensatory manner. To do this, they must be constantly aware of the state of affairs, i.e., keep themselves informed. All of this takes place within the framework of management routines, i.e., among other things, in the regular work dialogs between the line manager and his or her senior manager as well as in the annual reviews. Formalized assessment tools can guide and support the process (Kaehler 2014b).

This approach is not exactly conventional. Peter F. Drucker recommended using feedback information only for the manager's self-control and not for control from above (Drucker 1954, p. 131). Even today, many companies practice a strictly confidential feedback system in which the initial data, in the form of feedback from individual participants, is only brought to the attention of the line manager. This apparently achieves quite good results in terms of behavioral changes (see Garvin 2013). Others even make the all-round feedback voluntary and leave it up to the respective line manager to decide whether he or she wants to receive any formalized feedback from those involved in management (see, e.g., Ernst 2014, p. 453). Systematically, this corresponds to the approach of unconditional self-management, which initially appears to make sense and actually works in many cases. As with all other management tasks, however, it must be assumed that, by no means, are all line managers always willing and able to constructively manage themselves. It is often those with weak leadership skills and behavioral problems who refuse to take or accept performance feedback. In this respect, the ability of the senior manager and the HR advisor to intervene in a compensatory manner is also especially important with regard to management feedback.

As is generally the case, the art of the compensatory actor is to supervise and intervene when necessary, but not to violate the primacy of self-steerage. In the long term, each line manager must be able to obtain performance-relevant initial data in the form of key figures and feedback, to assess this data him or herself, and to adjust his or her behavior accordingly. The compensatory entities then only take note of this and encourage the line manager to do so. If formal summarized annual appraisals are carried out—which makes perfect sense—the final assessment is generally given to the line manager. Although this means a limitation of self-control, it is acceptable as long as it only supplements the situational-compensatory dynamics of ongoing performance appraisals and leaves room for the line manager's self-assessment.

3.4.5 Individual Career Accompaniment and HR Co-management as On-demand Support

No matter how carefully line managers are selected and trained, manager development remains piecemeal without ongoing guidance and support. Firstly, this applies to the line manager's professional development. New tasks bring with them different requirements, individual career steps can fail, additional private or professional burdens lead to increased psychological pressure at times, micropolitical maneuvers by other managers or unusual business events require special circumspection at times. None of this can be planned for in the long term. Leaving line managers on their own here exposes them unnecessarily to the risk of failure and thus accepts not only human hardship but also the devaluation of previous development investments. Secondly, career accompaniment relates to the practical implementation of the management standards set by the management structures and imparted in management training. The focus here is on the dilemmas and implementation problems addressed in Sect. 3.2, which are of an individual and situational nature. Here, too, low-threshold career accompaniment in everyday management practice is advisable.

The instruments of such career accompaniment are well known and also widely used. For example, the coaching method for line managers can now be considered firmly established in most organizations (see Meifert 2012; Martens 2012; Winkler et al. 2013). The same applies to the related methods of mentoring (Graf and Edelkraut 2014; critically: Biemann and Weckmüller 2014) and supervision. Cross-organizational mentoring, so-called cross-mentoring, may be an option, especially for companies that cannot get together a sufficient number of mentors and mentees (see Liebhart 2012). "Collegial case consulting" or "peer mentoring" is also becoming increasingly common (see Meifert 2010, p. 210; Ochmann and Schuh 2011, p. 57; Smolak 2014). The assumption of new positions should always be accompanied by a systematic induction process (see Naporra 2012; Osterchrist and Mundet 2014). Even in the event of failure in a particular position (derailment), accompanying offers can help to ensure a successful new start (Sander and Birkner 2012; Marks et al. 2014).

As a general rule, supportive consulting should always be available when needed—i.e., especially in phases of particular professional or private stress and in the event of current challenges—and should actually be called upon. Simply offering support measures is generally not enough since line managers in need of support do not always actually register their needs and, at least in larger organizations, approval processes, etc. usually have to be gone through. This is where the role of HR advisors (HR co-management, Sect. 4.2.3) and senior managers envisaged in the Complementary Management Model proves fruitful. According to it, in the course of the normal management routines, management successes are acknowledged, management problems are discussed and possible approaches are weighed up. On the one hand, this enables compensatory intervention by the senior manager and the HR advisors in the event that the line manager does not recognize and address his or her own need for support (see Sect. 2.4.5). On the other hand, it already includes ongoing informal management support, which often makes recourse to formalized measures unnecessary.

3.5 Summary

This chapter describes the role of line managers in the theoretical context of the Complementary Management Model. Their people management activities can be structured on the basis of the theory's seven elements. On the one hand, line managers help employees to take up and sustainably achieve their work performance (support function); on the other hand, line managers maintain order by ensuring that rules and requirements of the corporate community are enforced (disciplinary function). This principle of management as a dual service is concretized in each of the 24 management tasks that describe the prerequisites of human performance. Ideally, they should be performed by the employee him or herself. The line manager only intervenes as a compensatory entity when self-steerage fails. Since by no means are all employees always willing and able to engage in comprehensive self-management in the interest of the company, this compensatory entity is absolutely necessary. It is only for this reason that line managers need to exist at all. Intervention can be corrective, joint, delegative, or substitutive. If the line manager neglects his or her responsibility, the senior manager or HR advisors intervene as higher-level authorities. This multiple compensatory mechanism ensures that all employee-related management tasks are actually performed, even when the line manager is inactive. It also prevents abuse of power.

In order to practically implement management tasks, which are ultimately only abstract goals in the sense of performance prerequisites, management routines, i.e., concrete activities such as dialogs and meetings are required. Within the framework of these management routines, the line manager ensures that the management tasks are implemented and applies the existing management instruments (i.e., the formalized tools and systems). From the line manager's point of view, the management routines are thus the focal point of the entire management process and constitute his or her people management work. Which management routines are defined and which parts of them are the responsibility of the line manager is a matter for the respective corporate or individual management model. A distinction must be made between routines for the management of functional-technical matters, routines for people management, and routines for self-management. Senior managers manage the subordinate line managers that report directly to them and also practice higher-level management of the employees that these line managers manage. The design of management positions is a classic organizational issue that relates, in particular, to the definition of the work content. Position power is definitely required. The span of control must be designed in such a way that it is neither too large (= no longer manageable) nor too small (= unnecessary management interfaces), which is why the buzzword "flat hierarchy" is misleading. Since management structures cannot and should not regulate all aspects of day-to-day management, dilemma situations and micropolitics are unavoidable realities of management work. This should not, of course, lead to their glorification; rather, functional organizational structures are needed to limit contradictions and power-political maneuvering to a meaningful, flexibilizing level. To manage effectively, line managers must have the appropriate management resources—directional/situational information, management feedback, working time, and management competence. This relates, among other things, to the field of manager development, which has been discussed in detail here.

References

Abel, Roland (2014): Die richtigen Fragen und Weichen stellen; Personalführung 9/2014; pp. 36–41.

Albrecht, Arnd/Albrecht-Goepfert, Evelyn (2012): Vertrauen, Verantwortung, Motivation und Kommunikation–Was Führung in virtuellen Strukturen von klassischer Teamarbeit unterscheidet; Personalführung 6/2012; pp. 44–50.

Armbrüster, Thomas/Hehn, Roland (2011): Kein Platz für humanistische Ideale; Human Resources Manager Juni/Juli 2011; pp. 78–79.

Astheimer, Sven (2013): Häuptling ohne Indianer; Frankfurter Allgemeine Sonntagszeitung 26./27.1.2013; p. C1.

Barsoux, Jean-Louis/Bouquet, Cyril (2013): How to Overcome a Power Deficit; MIT Sloan Management Review Summer 2013; pp. 45–53.

Beard, Ellen Jane (2014): Das Leben besteht aus Augenblicken (Interview with Ellen Langer); Harvard Business Manager 4/2014; pp. 34–42.

Biemann, Torsten/Weckmüller, Heiko (2014): Mentoring: Wann nützt es und wem nützt es?; Personal Quarterly 2/2014; pp. 46–49.

Blessin, Bernd/Wick, Alexander (2014a): Führen und Führen lassen; 7th Edition UVK/Lucius/UTB 2014a.

Blessin, Bernd/Wick, Alexander (2014b): Erfolg ist, was ich dafür halte!; Personalwirtschaft 5/2014b; pp. 56–58.

Bruch, Heike/Böhm, Stephan A./Dwertmann, David J. G. (2012): Führen mit Emotionen; io management März/April 2012; pp. 11–15.

CIPD–Chartered Institute of Personnel and Development (2021): Factsheet Management development; http://www.cipd.co.uk/hr-resources/factsheets/management-development.aspx (Accessed 01/05, 2022).

Claßen, Martin/Sattelberger, Thomas (2011): Vor dem Platzen der ‚Leadership Bubble‘; Organisationsentwicklung 2/2011; pp. 58–65.

Conger, Jay A. (1993): The Brave New Word of Leadership Training; Organizational Dynamics Winter 1993; pp. 46–58.

Day, David V./Fleenor, John W./Atwater, Leanne E./Sturm, Rachel E./McKee, Rob A. (2014): Advances in leader and leadership development: A review of 25 years of research and theory; The Leadership Quarterly 2014 (25); pp. 63–82.

Dellekönig, Christian (1995): Der Teilzeit-Manager–Argumente und erprobte Modelle für innovative Arbeitszeitregelungen; Campus 1995.

Demmer, Christine (2014): The Show must go on; Personalwirtschaft Jubiläumsheft 1/2014; pp. 58–60.

DGFP Deutsche Gesellschaft für Personalführung e. V. (2012): DGFP-Kurzumfrage Führungskräfteentwicklung; https://www.dgfp.de/mediathek/publikationen/ (Accessed 01/05, 2022).

DGFP Deutsche Gesellschaft für Personalführung e. V. (2015): Schlüsselkompetenz Reflexionsfähigkeit–Führungskräfteentwicklung der Zukunft; https://www.dgfp.de/mediathek/publikationen/ (Accessed 01/05, 2022).

Dobelli, Rolf (2011): Die Kunst des klaren Denkens–52 Denkfehler, die Sie besser anderen überlassen; Carl Hanser Verlag 2011.

Doerfler, Wolfgang (2014): Eigenverantwortlich lernen; Personalmagazin 8/2014; pp. 24–26.

Domsch, Michel E./Ostermann, Ariane (2014): Führung von unten: Der Einfluss des Mitarbeiters auf den Vorgesetzten; in von Rosenstiel, Lutz/Regnet, Erika/Domsch, Michel E. (eds.): Führung von Mitarbeitern–Handbuch für erfolgreiches Personalmanagement; Schäffer-Poeschel 2014; pp. 260–270.

Drucker, Peter F. (1954): The Practice of Management; new edition HarperCollins 2006 (first edition 1954).

Drucker, Peter F. (1973): Management–Tasks, Responsibilities, Practices; new edition Harper Business 1993 (first edition 1973).

Ernst, Christian (2014): Führungs-Feedback; in Sauer, Joachim/Cisik, Alexander (eds.): In Deutschland führen die Falschen–Wie sich Unternehmen ändern müssen; Bundesverband der Personalmanager e. V. 2014; pp. 447–468.

Faul, Joachim/Rehberg, Jürgen (2014): Führungskräfte grenzenlos qualifizieren; Personalwirtschaft 8/2014; pp. 51–53.

Felfe, Jörg/Franke, Franziska (2014): Führungskräftetrainings; Hogrefe 2014.

Ferrari, Bernard T (2012): The executive's guide to better listening; McKinsey Quarterly 2/2012; pp. 50–65.

Fockenbrock, Dieter (2014): Das Geheimnis des Wir-Gefühls, Handelsblatt 9./10./11.5.2014; pp. 74–75.

Forchhammer, Lorenz (2012): Der virtuelle Chef; Personalwirtschaft 8/2012; pp. 58–59.

Foss, Nicolai J./Klein, Peter G. (2014): Why Managers Still Matter; MIT Sloan Management Review Fall 2014; pp. 73–80.

Fröhlich, Caspar (2014): Frag dein Umfeld–Wie Führungskräfte direkte Kontakte nutzen, um sich systematisch weiterzuentwickeln; zfo 2/2014; pp. 103–104.

Garvin, David A. (2013): How Google Sold Its Engineers on Management; Harvard Business Review December 2013, pp. 75–82.

Graf, Nele/Edelkraut, Frank (2014): Mentoring–Das Praxisbuch für Personalverantwortliche und Unternehmer; Springer Gabler 2014.

Greene, Robert: The 48 Laws of Power; Penguin 1998.

Greenleaf, Robert K. (1970): The Servant as Leader; new edition The Robert K Greenleaf Center 1991 (first edition 1970).

Groyberg, Boris/Slind, Michael (2012): Leadership Is a Conversation; Harvard Business Review June 2012; pp. 76–84.

Gutenberg, Erich (1979): Grundlagen der Betriebswirtschaftslehre–Erster Band: Die Produktion; 23th edition Springer.

Hammer, Michael/Champy, James (1993): Reengineering the corporation–a manifesto for business revolution; Harper Business 1993 New York.

Happich, Gudrun (2012): Die Brückenbauer–Zweite Führungsebene; Managerseminare 7/2012; pp. 68–72.

Hauser, Frank (2012): Auf einer Wellenlänge; Personalmagazin 7/2012; p. 35.

Heen, Sheila/Stone, Douglas (2014): Aus Feedback lernen; Harvard Business Manager; pp. 20–29.

Hergert, Stefanie (2012): Mitarbeiter brauchen mehr Freiraum (Interview with Richard Straub); Handelsblatt 16./17./18.11.2012; pp. 69.

Hergert, Stefani (2014): Geradeaus statt immer höher; Handelsblatt 8./9./10.8.2014; pp. 52–53.

Hölzl, Hubert (2014): Eine bunte Truppe führen; Personalwirtschaft 5/2014; pp. 45–47.

Hoffmann, Joachim/Jäckel, Ingo (2011): Bewusstsein für exzellente Führung; Personalwirtschaft 11/2011; pp. 33–35.

Höhne, Gudrun (2014): Virtuelle Teams zusammenschweißen; Personalwirtschaft 7/2014; pp. 58–59.

Holling, Heinz/Liepmann, Detlev (2007): Personalentwicklung; in: Schuler, Heinz (ed.): Lehrbuch Organisationspsychologie; 4th edition Verlag Hans Huber 2007.

Jenewein, Wolfgang/Halder, Jonas (2018): Ab auf die Bank; Harvard Business Manager Juli 2018; pp. 81–84.

Jochmann, Walter (2012): Schlüsselpositionen strategisch besetzen; Personalwirtschaft 10/2012; pp. 63–65.

Kaehler, Boris (2014a): Komplementäre Führung–Ein praxiserprobtes Modell der organisationalen Führung; 1st edition Springer Gabler 2014.

Kaehler, Boris (2014b): Leistungsbeurteilungen gestalten–Systematische Zusammenhänge und typische Umsetzungsfehler; Arbeit und Arbeitsrecht 11/2014; pp. 652–655.

Kaehler, Boris (2017): Komplementäre Führung–Ein praxiserprobtes Modell der Personalführung in Organisationen; 2nd edition Springer Gabler 2017.

Kaehler, Boris (2019): Führen als Beruf–Andere erfolgreich machen; 1st edition Tredition 2019.

Kaiser, Stephan (2014): Roboter statt Recruiter?; Personalmagazin 8/2014; pp. 12–15.

Kanning, Uwe Peter/Fricke, Philipp (2013): Führungserfahrung–Wie nützlich ist sie wirklich?; Personalführung 1/2013; pp. 48–53.

Kaplan, Robert S. (2012): Raus aus der Isolationsfalle; Personalmagazin 8/2012; pp. 26–30.

Karlshaus, Anja/Kaehler, Boris (Hrsg.) (2017): Teilzeitführung–Rahmenbedingungen und Gestaltungsmöglichkeiten in Organisationen; Springer Gabler 2017.

Kellerman, Barbara (2012): The End of Leadership; HarperCollins 2012.

Klebl, Ulfried/Nerdinger, Friedemann W. (2010): Kompetenzentwicklung durch Development-Center–Eine quasiexperimentelle Untersuchung im Finanzdienstleistungsbereich; Zeitschrift für Arbeits- und Organisationspsychologie 2/2010 (54); pp. 57–67.

Kokoschka, Sonja (2009): Alternative zur Führungslaufbahn; Personalmagazin 6/2009; pp. 24–25.

Kotter, John P. (1987): Überzeugen und Durchsetzen–Macht und Einfluß in Organisationen; Campus 1987.

Ladwig, Desiree H./Domsch, Michel E. (2013): Karriere der anderen Art; Human Resources Manager Februar/März 2013; pp. 80–83.

Liebhart, Ursula (2012): Cross-Mentoring–Organisationsübergreifende Lernbeziehungen erweisen sich als besonders fruchtbar; zfo 4/2012; pp. 251–258.

Link, Oliver (2015): Ein Mann der Mitte; Brand eins 3/2015; pp. 110–113.

Losman, Carmen (2011) (director): Work Hard Play Hard (German documentary film); filmkinotext 2011.

Malik, Fredmund (2000). Managing performing living: Effective management for a new era (English edition 2006). Frankfurt am Main: Campus (first published in German 2000).

Malik, Fredmund (2007): Management–das A und O des Handwerks; new edition Campus 2007.

Marks, Mitchell Lee/Mirvis, Philip/Ashkenas, Ron (2014): Rebounding from Career Setbacks; Harvard Business Review 10/2014; pp. 105–108.

Martens, Andree (2012): Coaching ist angekommen–Zehn Jahre Marktanalyse (Interview with Jörg Mittendorf); Managerseminare 6/2012; pp. 30–34.

Meifert, Matthias (1999): Systematische Information von Führungskräften; Personal 10/199; pp. 516–519.

Meifert, Matthias (2010) (eds.): Führen–Die erfolgreichsten Instrumente und Techniken; Haufe 2010.

Meifert, Matthias (2012) (eds.): Management-Coaching–Wie Unternehmen Führungskräfte zum Erfolg führen können; Haufe 2012.

Merkle, Hans L. (1979): Dienen und Führen–Anmerkungen zur Abwertung von Begriffen; in Merkle, Hans L.: „Dienen und Führen–Erkenntnisse eines Unternehmers; 2001 Hohenheim Verlag; pp. 159–173.

Merkle, Hans L. (1983): Führung im multinationalen Unternehmen–Über das internationale Geschäft der Bosch-Gruppe; in Merkle, Hans L.: „Dienen und Führen–Erkenntnisse eines Unternehmers; 2001 Hohenheim Verlag; pp. 174–194.

Mintzberg, Henry (1975): The Manager's Job–Folklore and Fact; Harvard Business Review July/August 1975; pp. 49–61.

Mintzberg, Henry (2009): Managing; Berret-Koehler Publishers 2009.

Molinsky, Andrew L./Davenport, Thomas H./Iyer, Bala/Davidson, Cathy (2012): [single contributions to] Skills Every 21st Century Manager Needs; Harvard Business Review January/February 2012; pp. 139–143.

Naporra, Edgar (2012): Ich bin der Neue–Wechsel auf dem Führungsposten; Managerseminare 8/2012; pp. 40–44.

Neuberger, Oswald (2002): Führen und führen lassen; 6th edition UTB Lucius & Lucius 2002.

Neuberger, Oswald (2006): Mikropolitik und Moral in Organisationen; 2nd edition UTB Lucius & Lucius 2006.

Neuberger, Oswald/Gebert (1996): Politikvergessenheit und Politikversessenheit–Zur Allgegenwart und Unvermeidbarkeit von Mikropolitik in Organisationen / Sprachspiele der Mikropolitik–zwischen Aufklärung und Verwirrung; Organisationsentwicklung 3/1996; pp. 66–73 (reader's reaction on it in Organisationsentwicklung 1/1997).

Ochmann, Hans/Schuh, Oliver (2011): Von der Qualifizierung zur Strategieumsetzung; Personalwirtschaft 11/2011; pp. 55–57.

Oltmanns, Torsten (2014a): Prolog–Theoretisch nicht vorhanden; Human Resources Manager Juni/Juli 2014; pp. 22–23.

Oltmanns, Torsten (2014b): Wer ist hier der King?; Personalmagazin 7/2014; pp. 12–14.

Osterchrist, Renate/Mundet, Xavier (2014): Herausforderung Delegation–Transition in eine erste Führungsaufgabe; Personalführung 12/2014; pp. 72–77.

Parker Follett Mary (1930): Some Discrepancies in Leadership Theory and Practice; in Metcalf, Henry C./Urwick, L.: Dynamic administration–The Collected Papers of Mary Parker Follett; Harper & Brothers 1942 (first published 1930); pp. 270–294.

Penning, Stephan (2012): Mehr Macht den Mittelmanagern; Personalwirtschaft 9/2012; pp. 42–45.

Rettig, Daniel (2013): Die Kunst des Cheffings; Wirtschaftswoche 48/2013; pp. 80–85.

Roosevelt, Theodore (1901): Speak softly and carry a big stick; https://en.wikiquote.org/wiki/Theodore_Roosevelt#Speak_softly_and_carry_a_big_stick_(1901) (Accessed 12/20, 2021).

Rosenstiel, Lutz von (2014): Grundlagen der Führung; in Rosenstiel, Lutz von/Regnet, Erika/Domsch, Michel E. (eds.) „Führung von Mitarbeitern–Handbuch für erfolgreiches Personalmanagement; Schäffer-Poeschel 2014; pp. 3–28.

Sander, Damaris/Birkner, Burkhard (2012): Endstation für die Karriere–das Derailment-Phänomen; Personalführung 9/2012; pp. 70–72.

Sanner, Bet/Bunderson, J. Stuart (2018): The Truth About Hierarchy; MIT Sloan Management Review Winter 2018, pp. 49–52.

Sarges, Werner (2013) (ed.): Management-Diagnostik; 4th edition Hogrefe 2013.

Sauer, Joachim/Cisik, Alexander (2013): Führung in der Krise; Human Resources Manager Februar/März 2013; pp. 106–107.

Sauer, Joachim/Cisik, Alexander (2014): Führung in Deutschland–Problemstellungen und Lösungsansätze; in Sauer, Joachim/Cisik, Alexander (eds.): In Deutschland führen die Falschen–Wie sich Unternehmen ändern müssen; Bundesverband der Personalmanager e. V. 2014; pp. 15–27.

Schäfer, Petra (2012): Adieu Flipchart, hallo Live Message; Human Resources Manager Juni/Juli 2012; pp. 49–51.

Scheidt, Stefan/Wiedenbrüg, Ricardo (2012): Plädoyer für einen reflektierten Umgang mit Macht; Personalführung 6/2012; pp. 36–43.

Scherm, Martin (2013): 360-Grad-Beurteilungen in Sarges, Werner (ed.) Management-Diagnostik; 4th edition Hogrefe 2013; pp. 864–872.

Scholl, Wolfgang (2014): Führen und (sich) führen lassen; Personalmagazin 7/2014; pp 22–24.

Sprenger, Reinhard K. (2008): Gut aufgestellt–Fußballstrategien für Manager; Campus 2008.

Sprenger, Reinhard K. (2012): Radikal führen; Campus 2012.

Schrehardt, Nicole (2012): Eine Lehrstunde für HR; Personalmagazin 8/2012; p. 13.

Smolak, Harald (2014): Lernen auf Augenhöhe; Personalwirtschaft 4/2014; pp. 64–65.

Statistisches Bundesamt (2021): Qualität der Arbeit–Überlange Arbeitszeiten in der EU; https://www.destatis.de/Europa/DE/Thema/Bevoelkerung-Arbeit-Soziales/Arbeitsmarkt/Qualitaetder-Arbeit/_dimension-3/04_ueberlange-arbeitszeiten.html;jsessionid=E76CF1 65777DDACD14D3EAF3512EDCB0.live711 (Accessed 12/23, 2021).

Steel, Gary/Lewis, Paul/Brügger, Erika (2012): Firmenspezifische Führungsphilosophie und deren konsequente Umsetzung–Das Beispiel der ABB; in Bruch, Heike/Krummaker, Stefan/Vogel, Berd: Leadership–Best Practices und Trends; 2nd edition Springer Gabler 2012; pp. 193–207.

Steinmann, Horst/Schreyögg, Georg/Koch, Jochen (2013): Management–Grundlagen der Unternehmensführung; 7th edition Springer Gabler 2013.

Stoffmehl, Thomas (2014): Management Audit bei bofrost; in Sauer, Joachim/Cisik, Alexander: "In Deutschland führen die Falschen–Wie sich Unternehmen ändern müssen; Bundesverband der Personalmanager e. V. 2014; pp. 307–318.

Straub, Reiner/Jessl, Randolf (2012): Da wundere ich mich über mich (Interview with Thomas Sattelberger); Personalmagazin 6/2012; pp. 12–14.

Stulle, Klaus P./Weinert, Stephan (2012): Geprüfte Führungsstärke; Personalwirtschaft 10/2012; pp. 36–39.

Sun Tzu (1971): The Art of War; Oxford University Press 1971.

Trost, Armin (2014): "Fachkarrieren auf kleiner Flamme; Personalwirtschaft 1/2014; pp. 38–40.

Weibler, Jürgen (2014): "Führung der Mitarbeiter durch den nächsthöheren Vorgesetzten; in von Rosenstiel, Lutz/Regnet, Erika/Domsch, Michel E. "Führung von Mitarbeitern–Handbuch für erfolgreiches Personalmanagement; Schäffer-Poeschel 2014; pp. 271–283.

Weibler, Jürgen (2016): "Personalführung; 3th edition Vahlen 2016.

Weilbacher, Jan (2012): "Bye, bye, einsame Helden; Human Resources Manager Juni/Juli 2012; pp 23–27.

Weise, Carolin/Selck, Andreas (2007): "Fehlende Orientierung? Führungsinstrumente richtig einsetzen; Arbeit und Arbeitsrecht; pp. 712–717.

Welch, Jack/Welch, Suzy (2005): "Winning–Das ist Management; Campus 2005.

Werle, Klaus (2014): "Die Bonsai-Manager; Manager Magazin 11/2014; pp. 103–109.

Wilken, Bernd A. (2012): "Wie viel Führung verträgt der Mensch? Virtuelle Führung; Managerseminare 3/2012; pp. 18–22.

Winkler, Brigitte/Lotzkat, Gesche/Welpe, Isabell M. (2013): "Wie funktioniert Führungskräfte-Coaching? Orientierungshilfe für ein unübersichtliches Beratungsfeld; Organisationsentwicklung 3/2013; pp. 23–35.

Yukl, Gary (2013): "Leadership in Organizations; 8th edition Pearson 2013.

The Role of the Specialized HR Function in Complementary Management

4

4.1 The HR Function as a Designer of Management Structures

This chapter describes the role of the specialized HR function (synonym: "personnel or HR department", "human resources", "HR") in the theoretical context of the Complementary Management Model as outlined in Chap. 2. It is aimed at those interested in the theoretical aspects of management and leadership, and especially corporate models of management and leadership. The benefit of such models is that they provide orientation for management actors with regard to relevant issues, thereby shaping their behavior. Not only do HR specialists count among these actors, they also play a major role in developing such corporate models.

4.1.1 Strategic Importance: Discussion and Definition

The HR departments of many organizations have been in a phase of self-discovery for quite some time. Around the turn of the millennium, large-scale restructuring was carried out in many places with the aim of streamlining, increasing efficiency, and strengthening strategic alignment. In the majority of cases, this does not seem to have resulted in the hoped-for success so there continues to be a broad discussion in the HR literature and among practitioners about the HR function's lack of strategic importance (see, e.g., Scholz and Müller 2011; Prieß 2013; Jochmann and Faltin 2014; Ritter et al. 2014; Krings 2014; Bilhuber Galli and Müller-Stewens 2014; Lau 2014; Lehnen 2014; Jochmann 2014; Martin and Jacobs 2014; Wehner et al. 2014; Heimann 2014; Werle 2014; Boudreau and Lawler 2014; Scholz 2014c; Demmer 2014b). While this discussion is justified in principle, it also seems somewhat neurotic at times:

> "But the crucial question is: Can HR realistically ever achieve the significance in the company that some would like to see? And I am very skeptical about that. [...] This discussion about HR as a strategic partner is often exaggerated and overly ideologized; it

B. Kaehler, *Complementary Management*, Management for Professionals, https://doi.org/10.1007/978-3-030-98163-1_4

sometimes even has something religious about it." (Joachim Sauer, ex-president of the German Association of Human Resources Managers, quoted from Straub 2015, p. 13)

Specifically, the discussion addresses whether the HR function as a whole intends to work strategically at all (more likely yes), whether it can (more likely no), whether its partners within the company want this (partly), whether this actually takes place in practice (partly) and whether it would be appropriate in terms of content in the interest of the business (predominantly yes). Quite apart from the fact that such questions can actually only be answered meaningfully in relation to a specific company, the discussion suffers from a completely unspecific use of the term strategy, which, depending on how it is interpreted, includes almost all aspects of HR (Kaehler 2016, p. 22). Progress with respect to content presupposes that the various sub-aspects and needs for action are worked out more clearly.

Excursus: What is Personnel Strategy?

The concept of personnel strategy (or HR strategy) is multifaceted. The term can essentially be interpreted in three ways (Kaehler 2015, 2016, p. 22). According to the first interpretation, which is also used here, HR strategy consists of normative specifications relating to HR work in a specific business period in the sense of a plan for achieving objectives, including the definition of these strategic objectives. It is closely related to the overall business strategy for the corresponding period. As a rule, the HR function plays a leading role in the development of the HR strategy and ideally also contributes to the overall business strategy by providing impulses. Whether and in what form this involvement occurs in a given company depends, however, on the respective corporate management and leadership model.

Secondly, the term HR strategy is often also understood to mean the internal positioning of the HR department—this aspect will be discussed in more detail in Sect. 4.3. This positioning becomes all the more important the more unstructured the internal corporate environment of the HR department is and the more the HR function operates according to market principles. The decisive factor here is the realization that no matter how professionally HR positioning issues are addressed, they can never be a substitute for a functional management model and effective strategic people management.

Thirdly, the term "personnel strategy" is often used in the literature and in practice to refer to fundamental definitions of leadership and management in the sense of a meta-management structure or the constitution of personnel work in a specific organization. According to the concept of corporate management advocated here (Sect. 1.5), this is actually systematically not part of strategic management, but rather of constitutive management. It is therefore not a matter of period-related, but of permanent stipulations. In view of the largely very generous use of the term "strategy" and the similarly normative

(continued)

approach, this may not be of any great significance in practice. In any case, the personnel function plays a decisive role in shaping these structures, which is discussed in more detail below.

4.1.2   The Influence of the HR Function on Formal and Informal Management Structures

How people management and leadership is structured in an organization, who is involved in it and what principles it follows depends on the corporate management model. This in turn is part of governance, i.e., the regulatory framework of corporate management. Following the systematics of Complementary Management, they should entail seven elements: the functions, tasks, actors, routines, instruments, structure and resources of people management. According to the basic theoretical assumption, these are precisely the seven elements that are necessary for the effective design of organizational people management and leadership. Even where not all elements are explicitly addressed, they are implicitly present (e.g., leadership and management is inconceivable without actors or tasks).

When only such informal management structures exist, which are not codified in a management model, they are the result of the free interaction of the management actors involved. Changes in the activities and organization of one actor automatically shape people management and leadership as a whole and are reflected in the structures of the other actors. If, for example, a line manager takes on certain people management tasks him or herself, such as training or personnel selection, these tasks are no longer performed by the HR department. If the HR department decides, for example, to downsize or limit its area of responsibility, it withdraws support capacities from the other units. If the management actors do not compensate for the changes made by other actors by making their own structural adjustments, corresponding governance gaps ensue. Conversely, if two actors claim the same fields of action, conflicts are inevitable.

The HR function thus shapes the management structures even if there is no formal management model at all or only a rudimentary one. This influence is exacerbated by the fact that the development and administration of HR tools is almost always the responsibility of the HR function. If, for example, it introduces self-service systems, it shifts HR activities to the user; if it defines a personnel selection process or a company car policy, it regulates the personnel work of the line managers, etc. Especially when all other management elements are only informal in nature, the (by definition formalized) people management and leadership instruments have a strong impact on people management as a whole. But since instrument development is generally not aimed at holistic people management and leadership, but rather at the facilitation of specific HR tasks, it is not surprising that salary or appraisal systems, for example, are so often associated with bureaucracy. For this reason, HR has a special responsibility to consider the concerns of the business and the people affected by its structural decisions. This is of practical importance, but can also be derived from management theory, because HR instruments are constitutive regulations in their own right and thus part of the governance of an organizational unit (Kaehler and Grundei 2018, 2019, p. 39 ff.).

If, in contrast, all of the structures are explicitly laid down in a formalized corporate model of management and leadership and its respective infrastructure (which is advisable), the question arises as to who is to be involved in the development of the content and formal preparation of this model. As a rule, the HR function will take the lead here as project manager by initiating the model and coordinating its development. However, since the design of a management model addresses a very fundamental dimension of constitutive corporate management, it is advisable not to let HR act alone here, but to strive for the involvement of top management and a broad participation of all stakeholders (see Sect. 2.6). It would be only a first step to define the HR function as the architect of HR processes with the right to make proposals, and line managers as the ultimate owners of the processes, as, for example, the US author and consultant Dave Ulrich once proposed (Demmer 2014a, p. 29). Being the unit that usually has the most in-depth HR expertise in the company and which, as a management actor and compensatory body itself, also plays an essential role in the management process, the HR function is definitely a co-owner of the management structures.

4.2   The HR Function in the Context of Management Structures

In order to understand and define the role of the HR function in an organization, a theoretical framework of knowledge is required that maps the entire solution space of HR work. The HR function always assumes the role that the existing de facto management architecture grants it, regardless of who created these structures and whether they are formalized/explicit or informal/implicit. The seven elements of the Complementary Management Model are used below to highlight the main challenges and options for action of the HR function. Regardless of the theoretical basis, however, the following applies: Neither the efficiency nor the effectiveness of HR work can be optimized without precisely locating the HR department in the overall context of people management and leadership—actors, objectives, activities, etc.

4.2.1   Management Functions: HR as a Dual Service Provider

People management and leadership is not an end in itself but an essential part of managing and leading an organization. Apart from in some special cases, organizations do not maintain workforces for their own sake, but as a resource because they need the work performance to achieve certain organizational goals.

Accordingly, personnel management must be aligned with regard to its contributions to the company's purpose and business success. One of the main accusations leveled at the HR function has always been that it fails to relate HR work to the actual business and tends to pursue its own one-sided, inward-looking agenda (e.g., Spilker et al. 2013, pp. 41, 90, 107 ff seq.; Charan 2014; Bilhuber Galli and Müller-Stewens 2014, p. 93). Curiously, it is precisely the implementation of Ulrich's structural concepts that seems to have led to an increased preoccupation of HR departments with themselves (Scholz and Müller 2011, p. 201), even though Dave Ulrich himself is one of the greatest advocates of a resolute business and strategy orientation (see, e.g., Ulrich 1997, pp. 24 f., 37, 2011, 2014; Ulrich and Brockbank 2005, p. 177 ff.; Ulrich et al. 2008, p. 163, 2009, p. 62):

> "I advocate a simple two-word question that moves HR forward: "So that?" (Ulrich 2011, p. 4)

> "HR is not about HR. HR begins and ends with the business." (Ulrich et al. 2017, p. 3)

In the overall interest, therefore, what is needed is contribution-oriented human resource management, which structurally links people management and business and consistently aligns all human resource activities with business benefits (Kaehler 2016, p. 23):

> "There is no HR strategy, only a strategy that supports the business strategy." (Frank Appel, CEO of Deutsche Post; quoted from Werle 2014, p. 103)

This contradicts the widespread division of tasks according to the maxim "HR takes care of human-personal matters and HR instruments, line management takes care of all functional-technical business matters," because this separation is artificial and encourages all conceivable aberrations. Instead, the business relevance must be clearly recognizable in all fields of activity of HR management. All HR measures and instruments—from hiring processes and employee dialogs to separation practices—must be geared not toward whether they bring relief and prestige to the HR function, but toward whether they enhance business success (Kaehler 2016, p. 23).

The systematic relationship between people management and corporate management ("management" for short) was explained in detail in Sect. 1.6 and illustrated there in Fig. 1.3. If one follows this management model, operational people management is identical to operational management of the entire business—all sales, resource, and production work is ultimately performed by people. This operational management serves to fulfill the specifications of strategic management for the respective business period, which in turn serve to fulfill the specifications of constitutive management (in particular mission, regulatory framework, and management system). This triad of constitutive, strategic, and operational management takes place both at the level of the overall organization and at the level of each individual organizational unit. Whatever the explicit and implicit strategies of a particular organization or organizational unit, the function of operational people management and leadership is to implement these strategic directions. Hence, the HR department, as one of its actors, is nothing more than a business supporter. There is no legitimate human resource management beyond general business management.

This functionality of people management and leadership *in relation to the constitutive and strategic management context* must be distinguished from the functionality *in relation to the personnel* who carry out the actual business operations. The Complementary Management Model implements this in the form of the element of management functions. According to this, people management and leadership is a service with two functions, the support function and the disciplinary function (as was explained in detail in Sect. 2.2). On the one hand, Management as a Service is intended to help employees take up and sustainably achieve their work performance; on the other hand, it is intended to have a disciplining effect and to enforce the rules and requirements of the corporate community. This is based on the assumption that sustainable work performance requires both a concern for the employee and his or her integration into the corporate collective context. In this way, the theoretical element of the management functions links people management and leadership to its actual purpose: the sustainable and stakeholder-compatible generation of work performance. The primary management and leadership service provider is the line manager, whereby he or she becomes active as a compensatory entity only when an employee does not self-manage, i.e., does not help and discipline him or herself (which is ideally the case).

In the literature, the fundamental dual function of HR departments is indeed recognized and demanded, at least with regard to HR instruments and guideline sovereignty. In this context, the concept of service usually refers only to the support function. The disciplinary function, on the other hand, is paraphrased as an "order policy dimension" (Rüger 2014), "governance function" (Scholz 2014b, pp. 16, 18), or "steering body" (Scholz 2014b, p. 16) as well as an "entrepreneurial corrective function for the whole", "overview competence", "strategic-normative function", "order role", and "normative steering and corrective function" (Spilker et al. 2013, pp. 44, 47, 107, 111).[1]

4.2.2 Management Tasks: Clear Definition of Personnel Tasks

The complementary management tasks form the second element of the Complementary Management Model (see Sect. 2.3). They are the concrete expression of the two rather abstract service functions. In most cases, both the support function and the disciplinary function are fulfilled in each management task. If, for example, the

---

[1] All in own translations. German originals: "ordnungspolitische Dimension" (Rüger); "Governancefunktion"/"Lenkungsinstanz" (Scholz); "unternehmerische Korrekturfunktion fürs Ganze"/"Überblickskompetenz"/"strategisch-normative Funktion"/"Ordnungsrolle"/"normative Steuerungs- und Korrekturfunktion" (Spilker).

personnel function ensures regular performance feedback, this represents both assistance and regulation. Management tasks are not to be regarded as concrete activities, but as people-related goals which require practical implementation within the framework of management routines, i.e., activities (more on this in Sect. 4.2.5).

Before personnel work can be distributed among the management actors and thus the responsibilities of the HR department can be defined, the overall package of people management tasks must be determined. The task canon of the Complementary Management Model represents an attempt to map the entire spectrum of people-related management tasks in organizations in a normative manner. Behind this is the question of which tasks the management actors have to perform in order to ensure sustainable work performance on the part of the employees. Organizations can, of course, develop their own catalogs and indeed do so. However, the need for most of the 24 tasks of the Complementary Management Model (Sect. 2.3.3) should be immediately obvious, so that a much shorter task catalog makes little sense.

Excursus: Organizing as an Underestimated HR Task
One of the management tasks most underestimated by HR departments is that of organizing. People management and organizing often appear as separate spheres in literature and practice but they are closely connected. Those who want to shape human work must first start with the structures. It is simply ineffective to address employee performance and behavior by means of personnel selection, personnel development, or personnel motivation if organizational deficiencies and dysfunctional structures prevent optimal performance or steer it in the wrong direction (see Kern 2013). The consequences are significant:

> "Inadequate, badly thought-out job design is one of the main sources of demotivation, dissatisfaction, and low productivity of human resources." (Malik 2000, p. 268)

The management—above all the human resource specialists—must therefore discover that organizing is a priority field of action. This organizing can be defined as the design of permanent structures and thus as a subarea of constitutive management. This concerns governance in the sense of regulations for (people and non-people) management. However, it also relates in particular to the broad field of regulations for exercising (non-managerial) behavior, i.e., process organization, organizational structure (i.e., the units and their linkages) and the code of conduct. In reality, though, most HR departments work more to relieve personnel symptoms and make corresponding behavioral interventions than on establishing organizational causes (Kern 2013). They are particularly encouraged in this by large parts of the "systemic" and "agile" HR literature, which is characterized by a latent hostility to organization. However, one of the prerequisites of effective people management and leadership lies in the reduction of complexity through clear organizational structures—units, processes,

(continued)

rules (see Neuberger 2002, pp. 618, 620). According to the understanding represented here, organization—insofar as it concerns the work of people and not, for example, purely technical matters or processes—is one of 24 management tasks and falls under the category of "setting HR norms". In this way, it is an integral part of HR work and, like all management tasks, is the subject of the HR function's management mandate. If a separate department for organization does exist, it can also take on this role; however, for reasons explained in the next section (4.2.3), the HR function must remain involved.

4.2.3 Management Actors: HR as a Co-Manager and Compensatory Entity

The third core element of the model comprises the complementary management actors. In practice, people management and leadership is not the sole responsibility of the HR department or line managers, but of various actors (see Sect. 2.4). For good reason, HR experts such as Dave Ulrich or Christian Scholz have for decades opposed the myth that "HR is HR's job", naming line managers as primarily responsible for HR work and assigning a supporting and safeguarding role to the HR function (see, e.g., Scholz 1996, p. 1084; Ulrich 1997, p. 18; Ulrich and Brockbank 2005, p. 72; Prieß 2013, p. 41 f.). Scholz describes personnel organization as a process based on the division of labor and integrative division of responsibility among the HR department, top managers, line managers and employees (Scholz 2014a, p. 4 f.; see also p. 1081), and pointed out a long time ago that the aspect of the distribution of work between the HR department and line managers was paid too little attention in structural discussions (Scholz 1996, p. 1084). The role of the personnel function can thus be meaningfully discussed only in the context of the entire field of actors of which it is a part. The personnel organization is a subsystem of leadership and management (Prieß 2013, p. 41 f.). While the actors may specialize in certain aspects of management and leadership, they nevertheless interact with (or against) each other in one and the same process. A theoretical-conceptual separation between human resource management and employee leadership is artificial and almost automatically leads to the ineffectiveness of many personnel measures (see Sect. 1.2.2). Effective HR departments—and even downstream units such as HR competence centers or HR service centers—see themselves as holistic management supporters.

In principle, management tasks can certainly be shifted away from the HR department to other actors, especially line managers—this is a worldwide trend (see, e.g., Capelli 2013). Some management experts even deny the HR function its raison d'être per se and suggest dissolving it completely, i.e., shifting HR work to non-HR or external service providers and transferring any remaining HR specialists to the business units (see, e.g., Weilbacher 2012; Scholz and Hansen 2012; Charan 2014; Bilhuber Galli and Müller-Stewens 2014, p. 94; Demmer 2014b, p. 25 f.; The Wall Street Journal Digital Network 2014). In fact, this concept was already discussed in the mid-1990s under the name "virtual HR department" (Scholz 1995, 1996). On this topic, Spilker et al. (2013, p. 10) write:

> "… every company needs good personnel work. But does every company need an HR department? Certainly not - and there will be no guarantee to maintain the HR department."

The question of the actual contribution and value of the HR function and the justification for its involvement in HR processes is therefore becoming increasingly urgent (Kaehler 2016, p. 23). However, it can only be answered by disentangling the strands of argumentation, because on closer examination, the topic of "abolishing the HR department" addresses quite different questions of organizational configuration, which are to be examined in more detail in Sect. 4.2.4. In anticipation of the answer: The HR function is indispensable as an actor. It is possible to virtualize it in terms of organizational design, but mixed forms are generally appropriate and extreme forms rarely make sense.

The compensatory role of the HR function has already been briefly addressed above. Accordingly, it should, within the framework of traditional HR advisory services, not only pursue an HR strategy and provide HR tools, but also actively intervene in the management process as needed. Just as the line manager, following the primacy of self-management, only intervenes in a compensatory manner if the employee does not perform certain management tasks him or herself, the HR function only intervenes if the line manager does not fulfill his or her management responsibility in this regard.

The need for this is obvious: as it is unlikely that all employees will comprehensively manage themselves at all times, it is unlikely that all line managers are willing and able to take compensatory action at all times. This is why it is so important to involve other actors in the management process—namely the senior manager and the HR advisor—who in turn act as higher-level compensatory entities. This interaction of management actors has already been explained in more detail and illustrated in Sect. 2.4.5. On the one hand, the compensatory mechanism ensures that all management tasks relating to an employee are actually performed even if the line manager is inactive, thus ensuring effective people management and leadership. On the other hand, such a multilevel system is suitable for preventing abuse of power by the line manager. In practice, an HR manager usually oversees various organizational units and often finds that most line managers and employees hardly need any impulses, while a few require constant and massive intervention. Of course, it is also true that if a line manager is permanently unwilling or unable to fulfill his or her own compensatory role and thus his or her management responsibility, he or she is thereby overstretching the compensatory resources of the HR function and should be replaced.

The role of the HR advisor as a compensatory entity is to ensure that all management tasks are fulfilled with regard to all those being managed. In doing

Table 4.1 Intervention options of the HR advisor (shown here using the example of the management task "resolving conflicts") (according to Kaehler 2017, p. 463; © Boris Kaehler 2019. All rights reserved)

Indirect corrective intervention	The HR advisor prompts the line manager to step in in a compensatory way, i.e., to intervene (the line manager, of course, also has different intervention options as shown in Table 2.8 in Sect. 2.4.5)
Joint intervention	The HR advisor helps the line manager to intervene in a compensatory way (i.e., to mediate the conflict in a compensatory way or to get the employee to settle the conflict)
Escalating intervention	The HR advisor prompts the senior manager to prompt the line manager to intervene
Immediate corrective intervention	The HR advisor, in place of the line manager, prompts the employee to perform the management tasks (i.e., to settle the conflict him or herself)
Delegative intervention	The HR advisor prompts a colleague of the employee to perform the management tasks (i.e., to mediate the conflict)
Substituting intervention	The HR advisor takes over the management tasks him or herself (and mediates the conflict)

so, he or she must first assess—in relation to each individual management task—the extent to which the line manager ensures that all management tasks are performed and then (only) take compensatory action in the event of deficits. This is done within the framework of the established advisory routines, e.g., dialogs (Sect. 2.4.5). There are several options for the compensatory intervention of the HR advisor in the management process (Table 4.1), which can be used in combination. Intervention takes place with the full authority of classic authoritarian leadership and management and requires appropriate positional power (see Sect. 2.4.5) but should preferably be gentle through informal behavioral reinforcement and implicit communication (see Sect. 1.4.2 and 1.4.3).

This direct intervention of the HR function in the management process, which can be described as "HR co-management" (or "HR co-leadership"), is by no means unusual in organizational practice. However, it is hardly ever explicitly designated as such and, as far as can be seen, is not treated in the literature. However, where leadership and management really do work well throughout a company, HR advisors are practically always involved as compensatory co-managers—whether officially or informally. Without this important regulator, good management and leadership simply cannot, in effect, be realized. Organizations that take away the HR role's capacity to intervene become blind and helpless to the management deficiencies that inevitably occur in any system. In many organizations, people management and leadership only works because HR professionals informally transcend the role actually assigned to them and, in tacit agreement with the units they oversee, fulfill their necessary disciplinary function even without formal positional power (Kaehler 2016, p. 25). When no formal management model constitutes it, HR must struggle for and preserve this important mandate through micropolitical means, which is a great waste of resources. In any case, whether it has a clearly regulated official mandate or a purely informal one, genuine HR co-management is the key to effective people management and leadership across the board.

4.2.4 Management Unit Design: Functional HR Positions and Units

In most larger organizations, the HR function has undergone extensive restructuring over the last 10–20 years. The blueprint for the new management unit design has often been the structural proposals of Dave Ulrich, who has established an astonishingly unique position for himself as an expert in the global HR scene. The popularity of the three-pillar model he inspired (Ulrich et al. 2009, p. 62; Ulrich 2014; see also Ulrich 1997, pp. 83–121) is probably simply due to the fact that it is a self-evident division to which there are no meaningful alternatives. After all, above a certain company size, tasks need to be bundled in centralized, specialized units from an administrative point of view. The tasks that come into question for this can be roughly divided into two groups: simpler, highly automatable and less salary-intensive activities (payroll accounting; administrative tasks of all kinds) and complex, highly qualified and thus salary-intensive activities (design, implementation, and support of personnel instruments). The terms "HR shared service center" and "center of expertise/competence" have become established for this (ultimately arbitrary since service is certainly also a task of competence centers and competence is certainly also a desirable characteristic of service centers). In addition to these two pillars, experience has shown that there is a need for a generalist contact function that ensures constant, personal, and broad contact with internal customers. This is the third pillar of the model, irrespective of whether the corresponding positions are called "HR officer", "HR advisor", or "HR business partner". While a structural division into three large units makes no sense for smaller organizations, it is more or less self-evident for large companies. If the changeover has nevertheless led to major upheavals in many companies and has often still not been satisfactorily completed, there are a number of thoroughly avoidable reasons for this, which are listed in Table 4.2.

While Ulrich's restructurings continue to be hotly debated in the literature, a certain transformation fatigue has been observed in practice for some time (Siemann 2014, p. 5). Quite a few specialists also wonder what the efforts to date have actually achieved:

> "Recently, in familiar company with senior HR consultants, we wondered if anyone knew of a company that had already reached the finish line in business partnering. No role model came to mind. We also wondered if there was a new business model for HR based on the business partner model. But we had to pass on that as well. So let's stick with the unfinished for now and keep tweaking." (Martin Claßen, co-author of the standard work "HR Business Partner"; quoted from Claßen 2017, p. 25)

Therefore, the effort to optimize the structure of the HR function continues. In this context, it seems advisable to ease up on the corresponding optimizations, plan systematically, and implement them with a steady hand in small or at least well-supervised steps. One of the greatest productivity levers is often to refuse the back and forth of changing trends and to concentrate on good HR work and continuous improvement.

Table 4.2 Possible reasons for suboptimal HR restructuring following the "HR Business Partner" model (according to Kaehler 2017, p. 465; © Boris Kaehler 2019. All rights reserved)

Radical full reorganization instead of gradual adaptation	This is indeed in line with Ulrich's paradigm of "HR transformation" (Ulrich et al. 2009). Of course, there are constellations in which the functionality of the HR department can only be ensured by an immediate radical reorganization. In these cases, careful planning and comprehensive change management are of utmost importance. In general, however, it is advisable to view organizational optimization as an ongoing task and to implement it continuously, i.e., in small steps
Focus on self-reflection	Although Ulrich himself is one of the fiercest proponents of a clear business orientation and alignment with value contributions, in many cases the focus is on self-reflection; the business perspective is neglected (see Scholz and Müller 2011, p. 201; Lau 2014, p. 35)
Unfortunate designation "HR business partner"	The term has been assigned changing meanings by Ulrich and is therefore very blurred. However, this may be the very reason for its amazing success (Claßen and Kern 2010, p. 83). The original model saw the entire HR function as a business partner (Ulrich 1997, p. 37); the term is often used for HR positions that provide strategic advice (Claßen and Kern 2010, pp. 86 f., 107; CIPD 2021). Many criticize this as merely a relabeling of traditional profiles (Krings 2012; Berthel and Becker 2013, p. 631; Zisgen 2014, p. 31). Moreover, the term "partner" implies a separateness from the business, when HR should actually be an integral part (Ulrich et al. 2008, p. 163)
Strategic ambition and dysfunctional design of the advisory function	In many instances, the HR support function, renamed "HR Business Partner", was to take on more strategic tasks, which raised problems (see, e.g., Fischer 2013). The corresponding lines of argumentation have already been outlined in Sect. 4.1.1. Ultimately, the idea that all HR advisors must free themselves of the ballast of administrative and operational work so that they only provide strategic advice is probably simply unrealistic (see Spilker et al. 2013, p. 108 f.) and certainly not intended by Ulrich (Ulrich in Crabb 2008). HR strategy is important, but it is not everything
Excessive cost orientation	In many cases, the actual drivers of restructuring were cost considerations (see Sattelberger and Weckmüller 2008, p. 26; Siemann 2012, p. 5, 2014, p. 6; Fischer 2012, p. 60). Restructuring has often been used as a pretext to specifically outsource legacy employees. There was and is a potential for savings in many cases, and the idea of a lean HR function as such is certainly not wrong (see Wolff and Breitling 2013). However, the HR setup must follow a clear functional model and be given the necessary capacities to do so

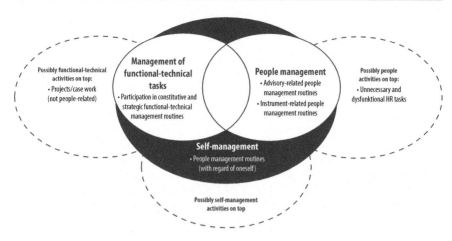

Fig. 4.1   Areas of activity of the personnel function (modified from Kaehler 2017, p. 466; © Boris Kaehler 2019. All rights reserved)

Before decisions can be made on detailed questions of HR organization, the rough fields of activity must be defined for individual positions and for entire HR organizational units. These can be represented graphically as fields (Fig. 4.1, analogous to those of the line managers in Fig. 3.1), whereby the consideration refers to the management routines (= activities).

The main advantage of this visualization is obvious: It depicts people management and leadership as a core activity and clarifies how to deal with limited capacities. HR managers who are also responsible for purely functional-technical work and projects—something which is perfectly sensible and common in small companies as well as at board level—can devote less attention to people management and leadership. Self-management, understood as the assumption of management tasks or activities by the person or unit itself, is no less significant for the HR function than for employees and line managers. HR professionals must also manage themselves, and that takes time. As far as the core area of people management is concerned, this is structured somewhat differently than for line managers (Fig. 3.1). Whereas involvement in the design of personnel instruments has been presented as an additional task of people management for those, in the case of the HR function these are integral components of the core activity. Mind you, this applies to the function as a whole and does not preclude individual HR positions from being exclusively involved with specific management routines or management instruments. In any case, the presentation is only an illustration; the exact breakdown and thus the decisive question as to where the focus of the activity should lie can only be answered in specific, individual cases.

Insofar as the detailed questions of organizational structure are concerned, the HR function should, in principle, be organized in the same way as any other function in the company. Decisions have to be made in particular about specialization vs. generalization, in-house performance vs. outsourcing, local/hierarchical centralization vs. decentralization. Even though, in this context, there are often intense disputes and micropolitical maneuvering between the divisions involved, every possible decision has its specific advantages and disadvantages, each of which is perfectly acceptable to live with. No specific configuration is the cause of or solution to the problems that so often characterize HR work. These are more likely due to the quantitative overloading of positions with tasks, the qualitative bundling of inappropriate tasks, the omission of a genuine "HR co-management" or simply changes in strategies and structures that are too frequent or abrupt.

Excursus: The Virtual HR Department: A Sensible Design Option?

As mentioned above, the virtualization of the HR function is a concept that has been under discussion since the mid-1990s and essentially consists of shifting HR work to non-staff or external service providers and transferring any remaining full-time staff to the line managers (see Scholz 1995, 1996; Weilbacher 2012; Scholz and Hansen 2012; Charan 2014; Bilhuber Galli and Müller-Stewens 2014, p. 94; Demmer 2014b, p. 25 f.; The Wall Street Journal Digital Network 2014). Buzzwords such as "virtual HR department" or "kill HR" address and mix up very different aspects of HR organization. Table 4.3 answers the main questions relevant in this context. Accordingly, mixed forms are generally indicated from a business economics point of view; extreme organizational virtualization makes sense in the rarest of cases.

4.2.5   Management Routines: Concrete HR Activities

The practical implementation of management tasks, which are actually just goals, requires concrete management activities such as dialogs and meetings. They can be aptly described as "management routines" because they are, at least potentially, recurring, represent an intended action, and should be tested and practiced. Section 2.5.3 goes into more detail on the derivation of the concept. Management routines are nothing more than framework activities within which the many elementary activities necessary to perform management tasks and their respective elementary tasks take place. For example, the management task "rounding off the incentive field" consists of, among other things, the elementary task "praise", which is fulfilled by the elementary activity "communicate" within the routine "work dialog." Organizations should not leave it up to the management actors to decide which management routines they consider useful, because experience has shown that there are very different and unfortunately often dysfunctional ideas in this regard. Instead, it is advisable to clearly define the routines as part of the management structures and to back them up with detailed implementation recommendations. It has proven useful to categorize them into continuous routines, annual routines, and on-demand routines.

The main people management routines were described in detail in Sect. 2.5.3. This actor-independent form of presentation was chosen because several management actors are always involved in the routines. A work dialog, for example, is by no

Table 4.3 Aspects and options of virtualizing the HR function (modified from Kaehler 2016, p. 24; © Boris Kaehler 2019. All rights reserved)

Streamlining the HR function by shifting HR tasks to line managers and employees	This is even unavoidable. No HR department can take over all of the personnel management work, nor would that be desirable. HR management tasks can and should primarily be taken on by the employees as self-managers, e.g., scheduling their own work, maintaining their own data via a self-entry system, or resolving their own conflicts. The line manager supports this and can also theoretically take over the vast majority of HR tasks in a compensatory manner. In practice, however, classic line management positions are usually so overloaded with functional-technical and personnel tasks that their proper completion cannot be guaranteed; moreover, they usually lack in-depth HR know-how. Obviously, achieving a "lean" HR headcount ratio by overburdening and overstraining line managers is purely a window dressing. Against this backdrop, the HR function is predestined to act as a central service provider, taking over tasks from line managers and achieving economies of scale and qualification advantages in the process. In principle, however, it is possible to shift large parts of HR work to line managers.
Justification for the existence of HR specialists who support and control the personnel work of the line managers	HR specialists are necessary even when as much work as possible is assigned to line managers. Without them, an important actor in people management and leadership would be missing—one who takes an overarching overall perspective and acts as a regulator to counteract undesirable developments both large and small (see Spilker et al. 2013, p. 46; Scholz 2014b, p. 18). The complete absence of this actor leads to an overstretching of the roles of the other actors. It is true that it is repeatedly suggested that the HR function be excluded from certain processes altogether (e.g., from recruitment, see Lytle 2013, p. 64). In practice, though, this rarely proves successful and is almost always withdrawn after some time.
In-house and external HR specialists	In principle, all parts of personnel work can also be outsourced. Some companies even outsource strategic and advisory activities to external service providers and HR consultants. However, because of the transaction costs involved, such configurations often make little economic sense. Those who are able to structure processes so clearly and leanly that they function across company boundaries can

(continued)

Table 4.3 (continued)

	generally also efficiently provide the services internally, which is then often less expensive. Internal organizational integration also enables a closer relationship with the overseen business units. Nevertheless, there are certainly many cases in which HR outsourcing represents a sensible solution.
Disciplinary assignment of in-house HR specialists to a single "HR" organizational unit and representation of this unit by an HR department at board/management level	In principle, HR specialists can also report as staff units or mini-central departments to line managers at different levels. However, experience shows that the subordinate relationship that arises in this way is not compatible with the effective exercise of the disciplinary function (see Sect. 4.2.1). In order to ensure this, each line manager should be assigned a personnel position of equal hierarchical rank and micropolitical strength. At the executive board and management level, this means: The HR department must have the full backing of the chairman or chairwoman or be located right there. Whether HR is a full or partial position at this level depends on the corporate and personnel circumstances and cannot be answered in a generalized way.
Local siting of the company's internal HR specialists	HR specialists in the HR department can work in a centralized location or maintain decentralized offices in the business units and travel around. The advantages and disadvantages of these two variants are likely to balance each other out.
Filling personnel positions with lateral entrants from the line (instead of with trained HR staff)	Filling HR positions with lateral entrants from the line is conducive to business proximity and very much to be welcomed. There are, of course, qualification requirements (see Sect. 4.2.7).

means the sole responsibility of the line manager; it is at least as much shaped by the employee and possibly by other management actors. Exactly which parts of the routines are assigned to the HR department varies. Corporate models of leadership and management can produce different definitions in this respect. In principle, however, an actor's part in the different routines results in the entirety of his or her personnel management activity, here, for example, the activity of the HR function. Once determined, the parts of the actor-specific routine cannot be delegated meaningfully. The management actors must therefore participate in their respective routines. However, they do not necessarily have to be in charge of organizing and chairing the routines themselves. For example, the HR advisor can take over the lead in critique dialogs and job interviews, etc. This is of practical importance because it offers the possibility of shifting work volumes between the actors.

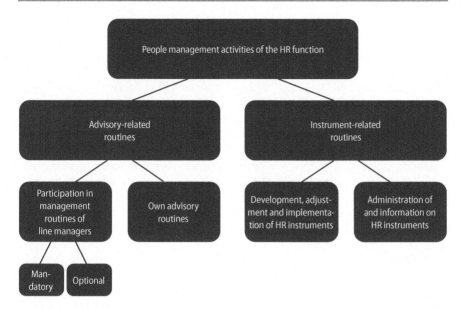

Fig. 4.2   Personnel management routines of the HR function (modified from Kaehler 2017, p. 470;

HR is generally responsible for two types of management routines: advisory-related routines, which deal with advising line managers and employees, and instrument-related routines, which serve to develop and administer personnel instruments (Fig. 4.2). As already mentioned above, this almost automatically results in an organizational specialization in the form of advisory, conceptual and administrative HR positions or units—at least in larger companies. In smaller companies, which employ only a few HR staff, they usually take on both types of routines as generalists in a personal union.

In the advisory-related routines, the principle of "HR co-management" (or "HR co-leadership") takes on a concrete form. These, in turn, are divided into two categories. Firstly, HR advisors participate in the line manager's actor-specific management routines, i.e., the parts of the general routines assigned to line managers in a given company. This can be on a mandatory basis (as is often the case, for example, with job interviews and dismissal dialogs) or on an optional basis (as is often the case, for example, with conflict and critique dialogs). The respective continuous, annual, and on-demand routines were described in Sect. 2.5.3 and need not be repeated here. Secondly, the HR function should have its own advisory routines, including, at minimum, regular dialogs with all line managers in the overseen business unit and consultation hours for employees. Informal dialogs in the workplace are also part of the HR advisor's tried-and-tested routines. These own advisory routines therefore have a cross-hierarchical character. They serve, at least in part, to support senior managers in hierarchy-spanning management (see Sect. 3.1.3).

Like the latter, HR advisors also need the resulting broad database; without it, they would not be able to fulfill their role in management.

In effect of the advisory-related routines, HR advisors take over parts of the management tasks. This compensatory mechanism has already been explained in detail in Sect. 2.4.5 and will only be briefly recounted here. Against the backdrop of the primacy of self-management and the line manager having first responsibility, it is merely a higher-level role. Just as the line manager should only intervene if employees do not fulfil management tasks through self-management, the HR advisor only intervenes if the line managers do not fulfill their responsibility (because they cannot or will not). This intervention is, therefore, also of a purely compensatory nature. The HR advisor does not take over the entire people management, but only compensates for deficits. On the one hand, this multilevel compensatory mechanism ensures that all management tasks are actually performed even if the line manager is unable to do so, thus ensuring effective people management and leadership. On the other hand, it is suitable for preventing the abuse of power.

The second type of routines, those that are instrument-related (i.e., the development and administration of formalized HR tools), also involves a wealth of activities. Very different expertise is required depending on whether, for example, salary systems or HR information systems are involved. In principle, it makes sense to bundle the majority of these activities into the HR function. Although other management actors also have their own instrument-related activities to perform, this is usually done as part of the application of the instruments within their "normal" management routines. For example, a team manager may create a checklist for him or herself or fill out an HR form and make suggestions for improvement in this regard. In the case of the HR function (and to some extent senior managers), however, this is such a focus of activity that it seems useful to systematically distinguish instrument-related routines from advisory-related ones. Which instrument-related routines are assigned to the HR function and its subunits is again a question of the configuration of the corporate model of leadership and management in the specific organization. It particularly depends on which instruments the structures provide for in the first place. In terms of content, the work to be performed results from the respective instrument, so that at this point it may be enough to refer to the detailed presentation of the essential personnel instruments in Sect. 2.5.4. Systematically, they can be divided into four categories (see Table 4.4).

In larger companies, these activities will generally be broken down organizationally into at least conceptual and administrative units, while in smaller companies

Table 4.4 Instrument-related management activities (modified from Kaehler 2017, p. 471; © Boris Kaehler 2019. All rights reserved)

Conceptual development of a new instrument
Evaluation and conceptual adaptation of the instrument
Administration of the instrument, especially exchange and processing of data
Assistance with questions concerning the instrument

they will often be outsourced to external service providers. These units are then each assigned their own routines. The concept of management routines also seems appropriate in cases where new personnel instruments are being developed. Even if, for example, there has been no formalized appraisal system to date, and therefore no expertise in this area, there must at least be a well-established procedure as to where this expertise can be obtained.

In general, there is a tendency among many HR practitioners and authors to regard at least the administrative instrument routines as adding little value and to spin them off from the core HR function. However, since many of their internal clients associate the HR function with precisely this administrative expertise, and since support services often are what make it possible to enter into deeper consulting and advisory relationships at all, there are justified warnings against retreating from this area altogether (Spilker et al. 2013, p. 108 f.; Ulrich as cited in Crabb 2008). No matter how instrument-related routines are divided up, it must be ensured that they continue to be experienced as an integral part of the HR department's work in order to prevent reputational damage. To achieve this, efficient HR processes and continuous improvement are just as necessary as the use of modern information technologies and the close dovetailing of instrument routines with advisory-related routines.

4.2.6   Management Instruments: Tools Instead of Bureaucratisms

The term "management instruments" is used here to refer to formalized tools that support management and leadership. These are to be distinguished from the management activities referred to here as "management routines" (e.g., dialogs), which may follow formalized guidelines but are not themselves instruments. The management instruments available in a given company apply to all management actors and are to be used by them as part of their actor-specific management routines. An overview of the main personnel instruments, which include, in particular, rules and regulations, systems, programs and forms, can be found in Sect. 2.5.4.

The differentiation between instruments and routines proposed here, which is by no means common in the literature, can also be maintained with regard to the work of the HR function. However, two—perhaps subtle, but very necessary—concretizations are indicated here. Firstly, management *instruments*, as formalized tools, support the management *activities* of management actors, which include the HR function. Thus, if HR is involved in management routines (e.g., employee dialogs), the tools provided (e.g., interview guidelines) must be used (see Sect. 2.5.4). Secondly, the HR function not only uses instruments, but is usually also primarily responsible for developing and advising on them (e.g., designing and administering compensation or training systems). This is a matter of "doing" in the sense of special, concretizing management activities. Systematically, instrument development and support are therefore actor-specific "management routines" of the HR function (see Sect. 4.2.5). By designing and developing HR instruments, the HR function itself creates part of the management structures within which it operates (see Sect. 4.1.2)—similar to the case of the HR organizational structure.

Few aspects of personnel work are criticized as frequently as personnel instruments. In fact, these tools have, in many instances, developed into bureaucratisms that hinder rather than promote good people management and leadership and degenerate into unproductive busywork. The problem here is not the formalization as such, but the formalization of unsuitable procedures that are not aligned with the actual management tasks and routines. Another problem is the often excessive rigidity of formalization, which does not allow for decision-making leeway and exceptions. Finally, many personnel instruments suffer from a lack of evaluation and adaptation to changing contextual conditions. However, this already identifies the three countermeasures: stringent alignment with management tasks and routines, provision for decision-making leeway and exceptions, and ongoing review and adaptation based on user feedback. This ensures that the people management tools are actually helpful (Kaehler 2016, p. 25).

4.2.7   Management Resources: What HR Needs

Just like line managers, human resources managers require certain management resources: competence, information, time, and feedback. The systematics of this model element of Complementary Management has already been explained in detail in Sect. 2.5.5 and will not be repeated here. The thing to remember is that the four resources are a more or less arbitrary selection from the catalog of performance requirements.

Management and leadership require specific competencies. It is not uncommon to hear the accusation that HR specialists lack key competencies and an understanding of business (e.g., in Faltin et al. 2014; Heimann 2014, p. 33; Jochmann and Faltin 2014; see also Spilker et al. 2013). The renowned German scholar Christian Scholz spoke of "appalling deprofessionalization" (cited in Buchholz and Werle 2011, p. 141). Again, the main problem lies in the lack of structures: as long as there is no clear definition of what constitutes good management and leadership, no effective needs analyses and qualification measures can be carried out. Therefore, there must first be a corporate model that defines, among other things, management activities, tasks, and instruments. From this, the necessary behavioral competencies (e.g., conducting dialogs) and the elementary competencies required for this (e.g., communicating or deciding) can be derived and implemented in qualification and development measures. Sections 2.5.5 and 3.4 go into more detail about the different competence requirements for the management actors.

Functional-technical business competence plays a special role in the discussion about HR qualifications. The prerequisite for effective management is indeed a fundamental understanding of all tasks arising in one's own area of responsibility (see Sect. 3.4.3). Those who have to decide on the work of others do not have to be able to perform this work as well or as quickly as those that are assigned the work, but they do have to have a detailed understanding of the processes, problems and challenges of the work (Blessin and Wick 2014, p. 463). Mere management and methodological skills are not enough to appropriately manage and lead professionals. This is also and especially true for HR, whether in HR advisory services, which after all mean co-management, or in instrument design, which should be nothing else than management support. HR employees must lose their shyness about the actual business and get up close and personal with the business processes of their respective areas of responsibility—like sales, production and administration (Spilker et al. 2013, pp. 90, 107 ff.). Those who have neither an interest in nor detailed knowledge of the work that the staff is doing can never, ever effectively foster its work performance. To ensure this functional-technical business competence, there are repeated calls to fill HR positions with lateral hires from the line (see, e.g., Spilker et al. 2013, p. 114; Charan 2014; Siemann 2014, p. 5; skeptically Ulrich 2014; see also again Skinner 1981, p. 114). This is of course possible and also makes sense from the point of view of business proximity; however, the question then automatically arises as to the HR expertise of these lateral hires. Ultimately, it makes no difference at all whether HR specialists acquire business expertise or line specialists acquire HR expertise. HR professionals need both. The decisive factor is that qualification deficits are identified and systematically eliminated.

Closely linked to functional-technical business competence is the resource of directional and situational information. To do justice to their role, HR managers must be well informed. This applies to the business mission and the selected business strategies, as well as to the existing corporate structures and the current business situation, especially with regard to the market, revenues and costs. By no means are these information needs always met, if only because HR is often not included in the relevant distribution lists. HR advisors usually receive a lot of relevant information from the line managers in the overseen business units, but this usually does not provide a complete picture; also, many HR managers are simply not sufficiently interested in it. What is needed are tools that allow them to continuously supply themselves with relevant information. Knowledge management systems can make a valuable contribution here. It is also advisable to develop an information system tailored to the needs of the HR department, which can include newsletters, morning briefings, press reviews, and events in addition to the aspects mentioned above (see Meifert 1999). More generally, HR managers should make themselves the seismograph of the company and set all channels to receive information (Runge 2011).

The third resource is time. Anyone who is supposed to work needs the corresponding working time to do so. How much depends first and foremost on what needs to be done. Thus, in the case of management, the management routines and thus the respective management model must be addressed. In the course of the structural changes implemented in recent years, HR headcount ratios have been dramatically reduced in many instances, i.e., fewer employees in HR departments are looking after more employees. Mostly, a ratio of around 1:95 or 1:100 is now considered reasonable (see Jochmann and Faltin 2014, p. 27), although some major German corporations are apparently closer to 1:50 (see Siemann 2014, p. 6). This reflects efforts to automate, centralize, and optimize processes, but the change is also due to a large-scale shift of HR activities to line managers. Unfortunately, many HR managers bask in the supposed success of this "streamlining" and forget that ultimately the principle of "robbing Peter to pay Paul" is being practiced here. Anyone who shifts HR tasks must also provide line managers with corresponding time resources (which requires relieving them of functional-technical tasks) or live with them being overloaded (see Claßen and Kern 2010, p. 64). Unfortunately, the latter is often the case so that the streamlining of HR departments is, in effect, paid for with a decline in management and leadership quality. In particular, the active advisory function of HR co-management propagated in Sect. 4.2.3 cannot be slimmed down at will.

Management feedback from employees and other management actors is also indispensable for HR departments. Just as employees need feedback on their work performance, HR professionals need feedback on their management performance. This requires a dialog with the performance recipients, i.e., the internal customers of the HR department. Written surveys are a useful, but not sufficient, tool. They need to be supplemented by regular face-to-face dialogs (Spilker et al. 2013, p. 107): What are the expectations? What has gone well? Where do we need to do better? The fact that these feedback loops are, in effect, hardly established and used in most companies may be one of the reasons for the "agility" hysteria of recent years. Absurdly, though, the experiments with "agile" methods that have been conducted in many instances rarely improve anything because, generally, it is not the imposed formal methods that are lacking, but genuine structural and communicative work.

4.3   In-house Positioning of the HR Function

Like all management actors, the HR function must engage in micropolitical activity, act in a contribution-oriented manner, and position itself correctly in order to be able to make substantive contributions. In the triad of task areas presented above—functional-technical management, people management, and self-management—this relates to self-management. As a self-manager, HR must ensure that it positions itself correctly within the company and has viable networks, resilient relationships, and suitable conflict resolution strategies—both in the interest of its own positioning and in the interest of the business issues needing to be resolved.

4.3.1   Micropolitical Positioning

Micropolitics can be aptly defined as using other people to pursue one's own interests in organizational zones of uncertainty (Neuberger 2006, p. 18; for alternative definitions, see supplementary material to Blessin and Wick 2014, p. 442). This means that power-political action becomes all the more necessary the fewer certainties there are i.e., the fewer organizational and social structures. The micropolitical activities of the management actors multiply when there are no clear assignments of tasks, when processes are poorly defined or provided with unnecessary interfaces, or when there are no explicit rules of conduct and no escalation paths for conflicts. To prevent too much energy from flowing into ultimately unproductive micropolitical maneuvers, clear and transparent management structures are required.

HR needs certain policy powers, budgetary responsibility, process-related veto rights, self-advocacy rights, and process characteristics (Scholz and Müller 2011, p. 202 f.) to ensure good management and leadership. Far too often, these powers must be painstakingly fought for and defended using subtle micropolitical strategies, which usually succeed because the HR function typically has privileged access to key people and resources. A more efficient and effective alternative is to negotiate and stipulate them in the course of establishing a holistic corporate management model. A residual need for micropolitics always exists, but functional structures limit it to a reasonable level.

4.3.2 Focus on Contributions

One not entirely unjustified accusation leveled at many HR departments is that they fail to relate their HR work strategically to the business and tend to pursue their own, one-sided, inward-looking agenda (see, e.g., Scholz and Müller 2011, p. 201; Spilker et al. 2013, pp. 41, 90, 107 ff.; Charan 2014; Bilhuber Galli and Müller-Stewens 2014, p. 93). Strangely enough, the great HR reorganization wave of the last two decades, which was strongly inspired by the strategy-oriented concepts of Dave Ulrich, seems to have led to navel-gazing and a distancing from the internal customer in many cases (Lau 2014, p. 35; Kaehler 2016, p. 23). Table 4.5 outlines starting points for improvement, in which the "focus on contributions" (Peter F. Drucker 1967, p. 52 ff.) is likely to be the decisive principle.

4.3.3 Plan Versus Market Economy for HR

Organizations, including and especially companies in the free market economy, act as planned economies (in a nutshell: Häring 2012). In this context, planning is not synonymous with rigid, long-term determination, even if this is by no means unusual. Rather, it is advisable to provide for flexibilizing elements (such as change options or resource buffers) and to follow the principle of negotiation-based reconciliation of interests. In this way, it is generally possible to ensure that resources are allocated in line with requirements within higher-level planning.

The decision to align certain fields within such planned economies according to the opposing market principles is one of the most serious organizational issues. It may make sense where a multitude of different needs of individual participants makes cascading planning and control difficult or impossible, so that the allocative function of the market provides a remedy. In the vast majority of areas, however, this is definitely not the case. Internal markets are not indicated then because market mechanisms cause corresponding transaction costs that generally do not justify their

Table 4.5 Starting points for a strong positioning of the personnel function in companies (Kaehler 2017, S. 477; © Boris Kaehler 2019. All rights reserved)

Anchoring in a transparent management model	The role of HR must not be driven by the changing balance of power in the company but must result from a well-founded model of management and leadership. "A strong and credible positioning of the HR function ... at eye level presupposes ... a clear impact model..." (Jochmann 2014, p. 23; own translation)
Argumentation with business aspects	Micropolitically skilled HR professionals first emphasize the actor-independent necessity of (strategic) personnel work and advocate for a convincing, clearly structured model of management and leadership. Following on from this, the suitability of the HR function to take on certain work can then be propagated with good prospects of success (Kaehler 2015, p. 73, 2016, p. 22)
Contribution-oriented HR management	Peter F. Drucker's principle of "focusing on contribution" (1967, p. 52 ff.) suits all management actors well and represents an essential key to effectiveness, success, and productive cooperation. Those who are able to shift the focus from their own person, position, and rewards to their external actions and see themselves as supporters of people, projects, and goals will thereby achieve more—not only for the organization but also for themselves (Kaehler 2016, p. 23)
Holistic HR metrics	Those who condense personnel work to a few quantitative key figures need not be surprised if their contribution does not become clear. What is needed, therefore, is a holistic system of HR metrics that paints a comprehensive picture of the costs and performance.
Competence in human resources and in functional-technical business matters	Everything essential was said about this in Sect. 4.2.7. "Competence ensures acceptance." (Prieß 2013, p. 41)

benefits (see Sprenger 2012, pp. 105 ff., 128). Moreover, the disciplinary function of management and leadership is undermined (see Sect. 4.2.1). It is therefore doubtful whether it makes sense for HR departments to market their training activities or consulting services internally because firstly, a lot of the HR specialist's time and energy then flows into internal positioning and advertising (in some cases even into real brand work, see Uhlig et al. 2014, or pseudo-business models, see Gärtner 2013). Second, it is generally no longer the objectively necessary work that is provided but that which customers ask for from their often quite limited perspective. (Spilker et al. 2013, pp. 43, 47, consider this to be the very core problem of personnel management.) An internal labor market, on the other hand, is highly useful and hardly ever dispensable.

All the same, even where, for good reason, there is no genuine internal market, orientation toward the service concept is advisable. For example, it is certainly advisable to systematically analyze the needs and experiences of "internal customers" with HR processes and tools and to act in accordance with their needs (see Völkl and Menzel-Black 2014). This analogy to market activity is albeit a mere metaphor; only the principle of supply and demand turns the internal market into a market—and HR work into a bazaar.

4.4 Summary

In recent decades there has been a broad discussion in HR literature and among practitioners about the lack of strategic importance of the HR function (personnel department). New insights can only be expected if its multifaceted role is worked out more clearly than is commonly done. The first issue to be addressed is the design of management structures or the corporate management model. As the unit that usually has the most in-depth HR expertise in the company and also plays an essential role in the management and leadership process, the personnel department usually takes the lead here by initiating the model and coordinating its development as project leader. The role of the HR function needs to be illuminated in the context of these very structures. The Complementary Management Model conceives of people management and leadership as a collective process involving various management actors. One of these actors is the HR function. Their personnel management activities can be structured in a meaningful way using the model's seven elements. This ensures that it is functionally aligned with the company's purpose and the actual business.

Like all management actors, the HR department fulfills the two complementary management functions of discipline and support. On the one hand, it helps those being managed to take up and sustainably achieve their work performance; on the other hand, it acts as an entity of order for them and ensures that the rules and requirements of the corporate community are enforced. This principle of Management as a Service is expressed in concrete terms in each of the 24 management tasks. Ideally, they should be performed by the employees themselves. Only when this does not happen does the line manager intervene in a compensatory manner. Analogous to the senior manager, the HR advisor, in turn, acts as a higher-level compensatory entity, i.e., he or she intervenes (only) if the line manager fails to fulfill his or her management responsibility toward the employee. This intervention takes place within the framework of management routines, i.e., the activities through which tasks are implemented, and can be corrective, joint, escalative, delegative, or substitutive. This compensatory "HR co-management," which is practiced in many organizations but hardly ever disclosed, is generally the key to effective people management and leadership. At the same time, it is precisely why the HR function is indispensable in the corporate management structure. In addition, the HR department is usually also the entity that provides and administers formalized HR instruments (salary system, continuing education program, personnel files, guidelines, forms, etc.). Accordingly, the advisory- and instrument-related management routines of the HR function need to be distinguished.

In most larger organizations, the HR function has undergone extensive restructuring in recent years. There are a number of entirely avoidable reasons why these new organizational structures are rarely perceived as optimal. The key is the realization that the abovementioned activities and responsibilities must be defined before the structure of the HR department can be reasonably discussed. Aligning HR work according to market principles is rarely appropriate. A partial virtualization of the HR department is possible, but it must follow sensible structural principles. Just like all other management actors, the HR department must have four management resources—directional and situational information, management feedback, working time, and management competence—in order to fulfill its role in the management process. And like them, HR must also engage in micropolitical activity in order to make substantive contributions. This becomes all the more important the more unstructured the in-house environment is and the more vaguely the management model describes the role of the HR function. There are a number of concrete starting points for a strong positioning of the HR function in the company. It is essential to focus on the company's purpose and to concentrate on clearly defined contributions.

References

Berthel, Jürgen/Becker, Fred G. (2013): Personal-Management – Grundzüge für Konzeptionen betrieblicher Personalarbeit"; 10th edition Schäffer-Poeschel 2013.

Bilhuber Galli, Eva/Müller-Stewens, Günter (2014): Personaler ohne Mehrwert?; Harvard Business Manager 12/2014; pp. 93–97.

Blessin, Bernd/Wick, Alexander (2014): Führen und Führen lassen; 7th edition UVK/Lucius/ UTB 2014.

Boudreau, John/Lawler, Edward E. III (2014): Stubborn Traditionalism in HRM: Causes and Consequences; Human Resource Management Review 2014 (24); pp. 232–244.

Buchholz, Eva/Werle, Klaus (2011): Die Frust AG; Managermagazin 12/2011; pp. 138–144.

Capelli, Peter (2013): HR for Neophytes; Harvard Business Review 10/2013; pp. 25–27.

Charan, Ram (2014): It's Time to Spit HR; Harvard Business Review July–August 2014; p. 34.

CIPD – Chartered Institute of Personnel and Development (2021): Business Partnering; http:// www.cipd.co.uk/hr-resources/factsheets/hr-business-partnering.aspx (Accessed 01/05, 2022).

Claßen, Martin/Kern, Dieter (2010): HR Business Partner – Die Spielmacher des Personalmanagements; Luchterhand 2010.

Claßen, Martin (2017): HR steckt in langwierigen Transformationsprozessen – HR-Strategie und HR-Business Partnering; Personalführung 2/2017; pp. 20–26.

Crabb, Steve (2008): Don't drop transactional role, Ulrich warns HR; People Management April 2008; p. 10.

Demmer, Christine (2014a): Der kritische Faktor wird sein, einen Sinn in der Arbeit zu finden und zu vermitteln (Interview with Dave Ulrich); Personalwirtschaft 4/2014; pp. 28–29.

Demmer, Christine (2014b): Zwischen Utopia und Untergang; Personalwirtschaft 4/2014; pp. 22–27.

Drucker, Peter F. (1967): The Effective Executive; 5th edition Harper Business 2006 (first published 1967).

Faltin, Thomas/Bergstein, Jens/Stolz, Martin (2014): HR hat ein Personalproblem; Personalmagazin 2/2014; pp. 40–44.

Fischer, Stefan (2012): Quartalsdenken ist der natürliche Feind der Nachhaltigkeit; Personalwirtschaft 8/2012; pp. 60–61.

Fischer, Ingo (2013): Am Feinschliff wird noch gearbeitet; Personalführung 1/2013; p. 74.

Gärtner, Christian (2013): Personalarbeit als Geschäftsmodell; zfo 3/2013; pp. 187–192.

Häring, Norbert (2012): Stimmt es, dass … die Funktion von Unternehmen darin besteht, den Markt zu umgehen?; Handelsblatt 19.04.2012; p. 14.

Heimann, Klaus (2014): Nicht im Alltagsgeschäft stecken bleiben – Wie HR Strategien für Arbeit und Organisation entwickeln kann (Interview with Klaus-Peter Buss und Martin Kuhlmann); Personalführung 8/2014; pp. 28–33.

Jochmann, Walter (2014): Steuerungseinheit auf Augenhöhe; Personalwirtschaft 6/2014; pp. 22–25.

Jochmann, Walter/Faltin, Thomas (2014): Strategische Akzeptanz von HR – Spürbarer ‚Skill-Upgrade‘ ist gefordert; Personalführung 8/2014; pp. 21–27.

Kaehler, Boris (2015): HR-Management der langen Linien – Personalstrategie als Erfolgsfaktor; Arbeit und Arbeitsrecht 2/2015; pp. 72–74.

Kaehler, Boris (2016): Die Rolle der Personalfunktion im Unternehmen: Grundsatzfragen und aktuelle Herausforderungen –Wege aus der ewigen Strategiediskussion; Zeitschrift Personalführung 2/2016; pp. 20–26.

Kaehler, Boris (2017): Komplementäre Führung – Ein praxiserprobtes Modell der Personalführung in Organisationen; 2nd edition Springer Gabler 2017.

Kaehler, Boris/Grundei, Jens (2018): HR-Governance im Führungs-Kontext: Der normative Rahmen des Personalmanagements; ZCG Zeitschrift für Corporate Governance 5/2018, pp. 205–210.

Kaehler, Boris/Grundei, Jens (2019): HR Governance – A Theoretical Introduction; Springer 2019.

Kern, Dieter (2013): Mehr Organisation wagen; Human Resources Manager April/Mai 2013; pp. 12–13.

Krings, Thorsten (2012): Der HR Business Partner: Ein Missverständnis?; Personalwirtschaft 7/2012; pp. 35–37.

Krings, Thorsten (2014): Noch Verbesserungsbedarf; Personalwirtschaft 3/2014; pp. 45–47.

Lau, Viktor (2014): Unverständlich und intransparent; Personalwirtschaft 2/2014; pp. 34–35.

Lehnen, Cliff (2014): Die Administranten; Personalwirtschaft Jubiläumsausgabe 1/2014; pp. 68–70.

Lytle, Tamara (2013): Streamline Hiring; HR Magazine 4/2013; pp. 63–65.

Malik, Fredmund (2000). Managing performing living: Effective management for a new era (English edition 2006). Frankfurt am Main: Campus (first published in German 2000).

Martin, Jean/Jacobs, Volker (2014): HR Business Partner: Ein neues Kompetenzmodell ist nur die halbe Miete; Human Resources Manager Dezember 2014/Januar 2015; pp. 102–103.

Meifert, Matthias (1999): Systematische Information von Führungskräften; Personal 10/1999; pp. 517–519.

Neuberger, Oswald (2002): Führen und führen lassen; 6th edition UTB Lucius & Lucius 2002.

Neuberger, Oswald (2006): Mikropolitik und Moral in Organisationen; 2nd edition UTB Lucius & Lucius 2006.

Prieß, Arne (2013): Kompetenz sorgt für Akzeptanz; Personalmagazin 11/2013; pp. 41–43.

Ritter, Jörg K./Sadowski, René/Seidenglanz, René (2014): HR hat ein Autoritätsproblem; Human Resources Manager August/September 2014; pp. 74–75.

Rüger, Uwe (2014): Individuell und spezifisch – was eine gute HR-Strategie auszeichnet; Personalführung 6/2014; p. 61.

Runge, Wolfgang (2011): Seien Sie Seismograf des Unternehmens; Personalmagazin 11/2011; p. 90.

Sattelberger, Thomas/Weckmüller, Heiko (2008): Es geht auch einfacher; Personalwirtschaft 5/2008; pp. 24–26.

Scholz, Christian (1995): Ein Denkmodell für das Jahr 2000? Die virtuelle Personalabteilung; Personalführung 5/1995; pp. 398–403.

Scholz, Christian (1996): Die virtuelle Personalabteilung – Ein Jahr später; Personalführung 12/1996; pp. 1080–1086.

Scholz, Christian (2014a): Personalmanagement – Informationsorientierte und verhaltenstheoretische Grundlagen; 6th edition Vahlen 2014.

Scholz, Christian (2014b): Schwarzes Loch oder Roter Riese; Personalmagazin 7/2014; pp. 16–18.

Scholz, Christian (2014c): Strategielosigkeit als zukünftige Strategie?; Personalwirtschaft 8/2014; pp. 33–35.

Scholz, Christian/Müller, Stefanie (2011): Rollenfindung der Personalabteilung; Arbeit und Arbeitsrecht 4/2011; pp. 200–204.

Scholz, Christian/Hansen, Malte (2012): Ende der HR-Abteilung – Pro/Contra; Human Resources Manager Oktober/November 2012; pp. 14–15.

Siemann, Christiane (2012): Auf gutem Weg; Personalwirtschaft Sonderheft 12/2012; pp. 4–9.

Siemann, Christiane (2014): Selbstbewusste Kurskorrekturen (Round Table-Bericht); Personalwirtschaft Sonderheft 12/2014; pp. 4–9.

Skinner, Wickham (1981): Big Hat, No Cattle: Managing Human Resources; Harvard Business Review September-October 1981; pp. 106–114.

Spilker, Martin/Roehl, Heiko/Hollmann, Detlef (2013): Die Akte Personal – Warum sich die Personalwirtschaft jetzt neu erfinden sollte; Verlag Bertelsmann Stiftung 2013.

Sprenger, Reinhard K. (2012): Radikal führen; Campus 2012.

Straub, Reiner (2015): Entscheidend ist das Image (Interview mit Joachim Sauer); Personalmagazin 5/2015; pp. 12–13.

The Wall Street Journal Digital Network (2014): What Happens When There's No HR Department? (Video); http://www.wsj.com/video/what-happens-when-theres-no-hr-department/D991C72E-CBCF-4C23-83CE-6EE52CB616F5.html (Accessed 01/05, 2022).

Uhlig, Christian/Toll, Alexander/Meenzen, Marco (2014): HR darf auch anecken; Personalmagazin 10/2014; pp. 50–53.

Ulrich, Dave (1997): Human Resource Champions – The next agenda for adding Value and Delivering Results; Harvard Business School Press 1997.

Ulrich, Dave (2011): Celebrating 50 years: an anniversary reflection; Human Resource Management, January-February 2011 (50); pp. 3–7.

Ulrich, Dave (2014): Do Not Split HR – At Least Not Ram Charan's Way; https://hbr.org/2014/07/do-not-split-hr-at-least-not-ram-charans-way (Accessed 01/05, 2022).

Ulrich, Dave/Brockbank, Wayne (2005): The HR Value Proposition; Harvard Business School Press 2005.

Ulrich, Dave/Brockbank, Wayne/Johnson, Dani/Sandholtz, Kurt/Younger, Jon (2008): HR Competencies – Mastery at the Intersection between People and Business; Society for Human Resource Management 2008.

Ulrich, Dave/Allen, Justin/Brockbank, Wayne/Younger, Jon/Nyman, Mark (2009): HR Transformation; McGraw-Hill 2009.

Ulrich, Dave/Kryscynski, David/Ulrich, Mike/Brockbank, Wayne (2017): Victory Through Organization – Why The War Fort Talent Is Failing Your Company and What You Can Do About It; McGraw Hill Education 2017.

Völkl, Christian/Menzel-Black, Christin (2014): Nach Bedarf designt; Personalmagazin 6/2014; pp. 35–37.

Wehner, Marius/Kabst, Rüdiger/Meifert, Matthias (2014): Strategischer Partner: Human Resources fehlt die institutionelle Verankerung; Personal Quarterly 3/2014; pp. 42–45.

Weilbacher, Jan (2012): Der Sohn will die Revolution; Human Resources Manager Juni/Juli 2012; pp. 44–47.

Werle, Klaus (2014): Die Bonsai-Manager; Manager Magazin 11/2014; pp. 103–109.

Wolff, Martin/Breitling, Franziska (2013): Der steinige Weg zu einer schlanken HR-Funktion, Personalwirtschaft Sonderheft 12/2013; pp. 22–24.

Zisgen, Armin (2014): Business Partner – Mode oder Zukunftsmodell?; Personalwirtschaft 4/2014; pp. 30–33.

Printed in Great Britain
by Amazon

45488436R00126